FIRST EDITION

Grammar Fundamentals for Teaching English as a Foreign Language: A Teacher's Reference

International TEFL Academy Press

ISBN 978-0-359-25530-6

Printed in the United States of America
Published by International TEFL Academy Press

First Edition 2019

International TEFL Academy Press
916 West Diversey Parkway
Chicago, Illinois 60614

www.ITAPress.com

CONTENTS

Preface

The purpose of *Grammar Fundamentals for Teaching English as a Foreign/Second Language: A Teacher's Reference* is to improve your confidence and knowledge of English grammar terminology, form, meaning, and use. This reference book addresses the needs of EFL/ESL teachers in training or as a review for more experienced EFL/ESL teachers.

The book is structured in the following format: The first unit (Words) starts by defining and discussing the various parts of speech of English. This is followed by the second unit (Sentences) that demonstrates how larger units of meaning are constructed, including clauses, sentence formation, and question formation. The third unit (Tenses) explores the tense and aspect system of English, and the fourth and final unit (Additional Grammar Points) looks at a few areas of English grammar that don't quite fit into the other units (e.g., passive voice) or that we felt deserved their own chapter (e.g., modal verbs).
We believe in providing the highest training possible to equip our TEFL course graduates with the best mixture of theoretical and practical training to be a confident and competent English language instructor. This grammar reference was designed to do just that.

The Curriculum Team

We have created this curriculum to accompany our TEFL certification course and coursebook, *The Fundamentals of Teaching English as a Foreign Language*. This book was developed by International TEFL Academy instructors, a curriculum development committee, writing committee, review committee and had final oversight by an accreditation board.

We chose to involve a wide variety of our staff and professors in the creation of this book to offer viewpoints from many academic disciplines of TEFL & TESOL training along with the practical and cultural experiences of teaching English on every continent worldwide.
We are sure you will find materials and training through International TEFL Academy at the highest level to support your goals and dreams of teaching English around the world. We wish you many great adventures in the classroom and abroad.

Special Thanks

A special thanks to the co-founders of International TEFL Academy - John Bentley, Kristin Catral, Karen Crone and Ian Davis who each had a vision and dedication to create a school to encourage and empower people to follow their dreams to teach English around the world.

About the Author: International TEFL Academy

International TEFL Academy trains over 5,000 new teachers a year and was founded on the premise that language education offers English speakers from all backgrounds the opportunity of a lifetime to experience other cultures and build relationships abroad while providing a worthy service to others. Combining a wealth of expertise and a commitment to excellence, we provide the finest training and personal guidance to enable students from all walks of life to live their dreams of exploring the world while teaching English. We are committed to complete transparency and integrity in representing who we are, what we do, and what we stand for.

We Believe

- All students have a fundamental right to receive instruction from a trained professional teacher.
- All teachers have a responsibility to their students to provide them with the best possible educational experience, which requires professional-level training.
- English language education enables millions of global citizens to enhance their lives by learning English and promoting tolerance and mutual understanding through cultural exchange.
- Teaching English as a Foreign Language provides English speakers from all walks of life with one of the greatest vehicles and most realistic opportunities to live an extraordinary life abroad.

Our Commitment

To provide our students with the training and guidance that will enable them to travel the world while teaching English and providing a quality educational experience abroad as a trained English teacher.

International TEFL Academy Team

The staff at International TEFL Academy work together as a team to achieve one goal: to ensure that our students realize their dreams of going abroad to teach, travel, and explore. All of our staff members have lived, traveled, and/or taught internationally. Now, we seek to empower our students to share in the experience of discovering new cultures, exploring the world, and becoming true global citizens while teaching English abroad.

The Textbook Team

Primary author
Wayne Walker, MA TEFL/TESL

Wayne received his Bachelor of Arts degree in mathematics and philosophy from Vanderbilt University and his master's degree in TEFL/TESL from Colorado State University. He has taught English in both Prague, Czech Republic and Linares, Spain. An online TEFL Instructor with International TEFL Academy, Wayne has been teaching for ITA since June 2014 and has also worked extensively on edits and improvements to International TEFL Academy's curriculum and videos.

Primary author
Karen Duncan, MA Teaching English as a Foreign Language

Karen received her Master of Arts degree in TESL/TEFL from Colorado State University and a Bachelor of Science degree in Elementary Education from Kansas State University. She was an assistant language teacher (ALT) with the Jet Programme in Sendai, Japan for three years and also volunteered for a summer with the Fundaciòn Cultural de Yucatan in Izamàl, Mexico. Karen has been an online TEFL Instructor with International TEFL Academy since January of 2016 and has also worked extensively on edits and improvements to International TEFL Academy's curriculum and videos.

Contributing author
Jesica Nkouaga, MA ESOL Education

Jesica received her Master of Arts degree in ESOL Studies and her Bachelor of Arts degree in Global Studies. She has taught English to speakers of other languages both locally and abroad. Jesica spent time teaching English to children and adults in Thailand, Jordan, Honduras, and Uganda. An online TEFL course instructor, Jesica has been teaching with International TEFL Academy since March of 2013.

Contributing author
Quinn Cruz, MA TESOL and Intercultural Studies

Quinn received both her Bachelor of Arts degree in English & Spanish and her Master of Arts degree in TESOL & Intercultural Studies from Wheaton College. She has also earned a certificate in translation studies from University of Chicago. Quinn has worked as an English teacher in both Costa Rica and Ecuador. An online TEFL Instructor with International TEFL Academy, Quinn has been teaching for ITA since March 2015.

Contributing editor

Betsy Divine, MA Teaching English as a Second Language

Betsy received her Masters of TESL degree from Northern Arizona University and a Bachelor of Science degree in Political Science from the University of Nebraska. She taught English in China, South Korea, France, Honduras, Costa Rica, and Nicaragua. Betsy started out with ITA as an online TEFL Instructor and then taught the 4-week in-person class in Chicago, Illinois for over one year. She currently resides in Nicaragua where she is employed as International TEFL Academy's Director of Studies.

Special Thanks

A special thanks to Jessica Allison, International TEFL Academy's Chicago TEFL course instructor, for all of her hard work and assistance with the formatting of the grammar module located on Moodle.

Front Page Photo

International TEFL Academy alumna and former ITA Ambassador Laura Nalin teaching English in Vietnam.

International TEFL Academy Textbook Series

In addition to teaching grammar, there are a multitude of skill sets that can be developed within the field of TEFL. To that end, this section introduces additional teacher-training textbooks that are part of the International TEFL Academy textbook series.

The Fundamentals of Teaching English as a Foreign Language

This book is an introductory text for use in the training of EFL instructors. This book is designed to prepare teachers to enter the classroom with a solid repertory of pedagogical theory and practical classroom activities. Anyone who wants to start teaching EFL - or who wants to improve on their present practice - can benefit from the content within.

Teaching English Online

An increasing number of language schools and students are using online tools and platforms to replace face-to-face language instruction. If you are interested in learning more about teaching English to adults or children in an online environment, see International TEFL Academy's *Teaching English Online* coursebook.

Teaching English to Young Learners

For a more in-depth look at the pedagogical differences involved in teaching English as a second or foreign language to younger learners, and to learn more about activities and plans geared for the young-learner classroom, see International TEFL Academy's *Teaching English to Young Learners* coursebook.

Teaching Business English

For an exploration of English instruction that is specifically designed for business professionals – either in a tutoring or classroom setting – see International TEFL Academy's *Teaching Business English* coursebook. This book introduces some key differences between general EFL and Business English courses and provides pedagogical theory as well as practical classroom activities and plans for teachers of Business English.

For textbook purchasing information, visit the following webpage:

https://www.internationalteflacademy.com/textbook-orders

INTRODUCTION

Hello and welcome to *Grammar Fundamentals for Teaching English as a Foreign/Second Language: A Teacher's Reference*. We hope to get you started on the right foot toward a better understanding of English grammar, specifically for the purposes of teaching English as a foreign/second language. Let us begin with a general introduction to the goals and layout of the book.

Content of the Teacher's Reference

This reference book aims to improve your confidence and knowledge of the English language, including basic grammar terminology, form, and meaning. We will start in Unit 1, "Words," by defining and discussing the various parts of speech of English. This is followed by Unit 2, "Sentences," which demonstrates how larger units of meaning are constructed, including clauses, sentence formation, and question formation. Unit 3, "Tenses," explores the tense and aspect system of English. The fourth and final unit, "Additional Grammar Points," looks at a few areas of English grammar that don't quite fit into the other units (e.g., passive voice) or that we felt deserved their own sections (e.g., modal verbs).

How to Use This Reference Book

The content is designed to serve as a self-study grammar reference. The content herein is likely most useful for the novice learner of the explicit rules of English grammar, but it can also serve as a review or to provide samples for more advanced grammarians. Section readings and corresponding quizzes should be completed at your own pace. You are encouraged to revisit sections and retake quizzes as needed.

The units are not structured according to their difficulty, nor are they structured by proficiency levels. Rather, the grammar points are provided in a manner intended to facilitate comprehension and retention for a native speaker of English (or someone with near-native proficiency). You can learn more about how grammar points are organized and presented for different EFL/ESL language levels in International TEFL Academy's coursebook *The Fundamentals of Teaching English as a Foreign Language.*

Important Note to Teachers

The content of this grammar book is intended for use by teachers of English, not students of English as a second/foreign language. There is much terminology and meta-language (language about language) within the book that, although important for teachers to be familiar with, should not be used within an EFL/ESL classroom. The content here is designed to make you a more knowledgeable teacher, one with a more exhaustive explicit language knowledge and who is better prepared to answer student questions about the English language. It is not intended to be used as a sole basis for your future lesson plans. The teaching of grammar and lexis (vocabulary), as well as the classroom application of the language concepts in this book, is the primary focus of Chapter 6 in International TEFL Academy's coursebook, *The Fundamentals of Teaching English as a Foreign Language*.

UNIT 1 WORDS

Introduction to Words

In this first unit, we begin with some of the more basic building blocks of English: words. We will introduce the concept of parts of speech in the English language and demonstrate those parts of speech with each of their subcategories, as well as numerous subsets and distinctions within those subsets.

Organization of Unit

We will start by looking at a text about TEFL that contains examples of each part of speech and most of their subcategories. Each section will then give some quick definitions of those examples. After that, you will find expanded sections about each part of speech, which provide further examples, explanations of subcategories, and more in-depth information.

The sections of Unit 1 are organized as follows:

1. Nouns and pronouns
2. Verbs
3. Adjectives, articles, and adverbs
4. Prepositions and conjunctions

NOTE 1.1: The content in this unit, as with the content for the entirety of this book, is intended for use by teachers of English, not students of English as a second/foreign language. For example, the first section in the unit is entitled "Nouns and Pronouns" because it is useful to package these together in this context. However, it would be extremely rare for a TEFL/TESL teacher to focus an entire unit or lesson on the topic of nouns and/or pronouns in a vacuum (i.e., unrelated to larger, sentence-level grammatical structures and communicative aims based in the skills of reading, writing, listening, and speaking). In short, the content here is designed to make you a better teacher, one with a more exhaustive explicit language knowledge and who is better prepared to answer student questions about the English language. It is not intended to be used as a sole basis for your future lesson plans. The teaching of grammar and lexis (vocabulary), as well as the classroom application of the language concepts in this module, is the primary focus of Chapter 6 in International TEFL Academy's coursebook *The Fundamentals of Teaching English as a Foreign Language.*

1.1 Nouns and Pronouns

Introduction

This first section in "Words" focuses on ***nouns*** and ***pronouns***. Before we begin discussing these important parts of speech and all of their subcategories, we will start by first identifying some simple examples.

Read the following sentences:

The English language has many words. We can teach them to people!

Most native speakers of English can immediately identify that the above sentences are grammatically correct. However, it is more difficult to correctly identify all of the parts of speech within. Are you able to find the nouns and pronouns?

The nouns are *English, language, words, people*. The pronouns are *We, them.*

Beyond the categories of noun and pronoun, we can further separate these words into various subcategories. For instance, did you know that *English* is a proper noun, but *children* is a common noun? Did you know that both *English* and *language* are nouns, and that together they can be called a compound noun? Did you know that *words* is both a countable noun and a regular plural noun? The word *English* is uncountable, and *people* is an irregular plural.

In terms of pronouns, do you know the difference between *we* and *them,* which is that *we* is a subject pronoun and *them* is an *object pronoun*?

Let's dive in and explore these parts of speech. We will start with nouns by looking at a text about TEFL that contains examples of all of the parts of speech and most of their subcategories. And you will see some quick definitions of the examples of our target part of speech. After that, you will find expanded sections about each part of speech, which provide further examples, explanations of subcategories, and more in-depth information.

Objectives

Identify and differentiate various noun forms, including the following:

- Proper and common nouns
- Compound nouns
- Countable and uncountable nouns
- Regular and irregular plural nouns

Identify and differentiate pronouns in all their various forms, including the following:

- Object pronouns
- Subject pronouns
- Possessive pronouns
- Possessive adjective pronouns
- Reflexive pronouns

Nouns in Context: A Text about TEFL

Read the following text about teaching English as a foreign language. It uses all of the different parts of speech of the English language, and we will use it to contextualize some examples in every section of Unit 1.

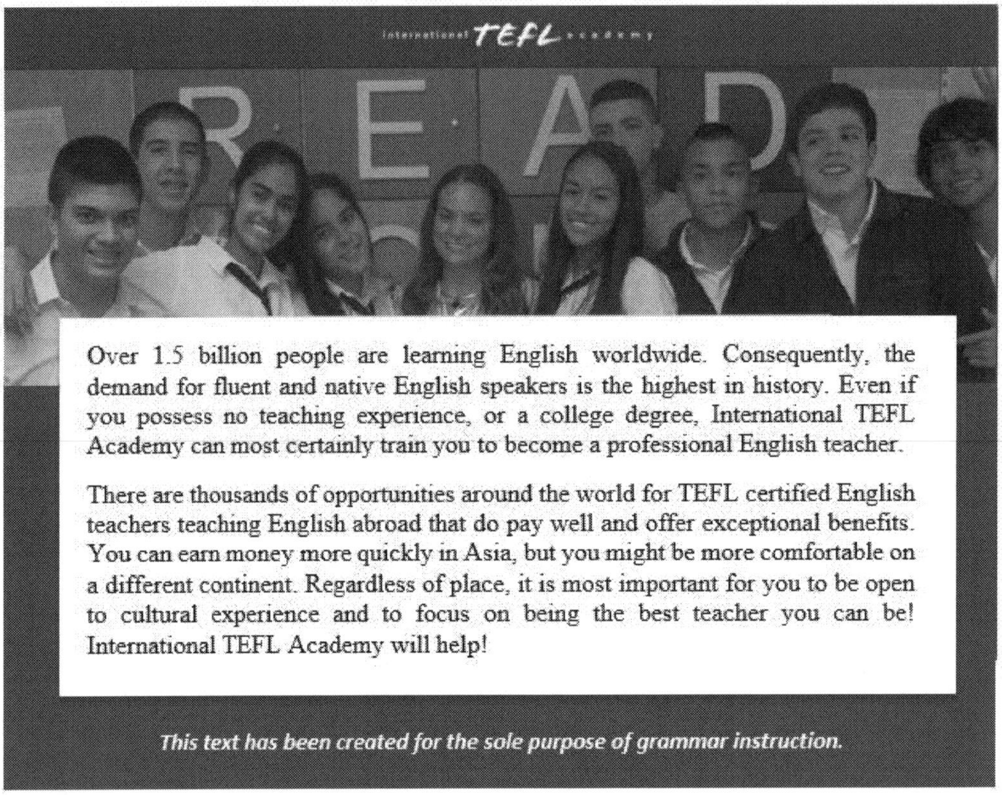

Now that you have read the above passage, are you able to identify which of the words within are nouns? We count 26[1.2] of them. Can you find them all? The answer is on the next page.

NOTE 1.2: Technically, there are 29 nouns in the text. The word *being* ("focus on *being* the best teacher") is the gerund form of the verb *to be,* and gerunds are technically nouns. We will explain gerunds in the next section on verbs. Furthermore—and depending on how you interpret nouns, adjectives, and compound nouns—there could be as few as 22 nouns in the text. See the section on compound nouns for more on this distinction.

Identification of Nouns in Context

Let's examine our first part of speech by looking at all of the examples of nouns in our text about TEFL. Here is that text again, with all 26[1.2] of the nouns in **bold.**

How many were you able to identify?

Now let's use some of these examples to delineate the various subcategories of nouns that we wish to focus upon.

As you may recall from grammar school, a noun is a person, place, or thing. We can further categorize nouns into subcategories of proper/common, compound, countable/uncountable, and regular/irregular.

Let's look at some of these subcategories with examples from our text.

A proper noun refers to the name of a particular person, place, or thing, and it is capitalized.

English (noun – proper)

A common noun is not capitalized and refers to an object in general.

teacher (noun – common)

A compound noun contains multiple words that combine to make a single noun.

English teacher (noun – compound)

A countable noun is a noun that can be singular or plural, and the plural form can be counted numerically.

speakers (noun – countable)

An uncountable noun is a noun that cannot be divided into separate elements and therefore cannot be counted numerically.

money (noun – uncountable)

A regular plural noun is one to which we add *–s*.

benefits (noun – regular plural)

An irregular plural noun takes a plural ending other than *–s*.

people (noun – irregular plural of the noun person)

Now that we have looked at these particular examples from our text, we are ready to consider these subcategories of nouns in greater depth and with numerous other examples.

Nouns

Nouns denote a person, a place, or a thing, and we can further expand the last one of these three to include a quality, an animal, or an idea. Nouns act as subjects of complete sentences in English; they also act as the objects of verbs (pronouns can play the same role). Nouns are also commonly preceded by articles and adjectives to create noun phrases, as in the following example:

a	**happy**	**student** (noun phrase)
(article)	(adjective)	(noun)

Nouns can be divided into the subcategories mentioned previously. Let's consider proper/common nouns, compound nouns, countable/uncountable nouns, and regular/irregular plural nouns in greater detail and depth.

Proper/Common Nouns

Proper Nouns

Nouns can be divided into ***proper nouns*** that refer to particular individuals, places, and things. These are usually official names, and they are always capitalized.

Willis Tower (noun – proper)

Chicago (noun – proper)

International TEFL Academy (noun – proper)
Dr. Noam Chomsky (noun – proper)

Days of the week, months of the year, and names of countries, languages, and religions are all proper nouns and are capitalized in English.

Common Nouns

Nouns that are not proper are called ***common nouns***, which are not capitalized and refer to objects in general.

tower (noun – common)
city (noun – common)
academy (noun – common)
doctor (noun – common)

This is just one way to categorize nouns, and it is fairly straightforward. Another category of nouns is called compound nouns, which is a bit more ambiguous. Let's consider them next.

Compound Nouns

Sometimes we combine two or more words together to create ***compound nouns***. the most common type of compound nouns can be called ***closed*** (or ***fixed***) ***compounds.*** These usually consist of two nouns that have been combined into a single word.

headphones (noun – compound)
doorknob (noun – compound)
backpack (noun – compound)

Sometimes, compound nouns become fixed but retain their status as multiple words.

fruit fly (noun – compound)

In this example, *fruit fly* is a compound noun because it clearly consists of a combination of two nouns, *fruit* and *fly*, that are put together to create a new noun. This is not to be mistaken for a phrase like *fruity wine*, which clearly consists of an adjective and a noun (and is therefore a noun phrase, not a compound noun).

As with so many facets of English (and of language in general), there is not always a single way to interpret these chunks of language. To further consider this point, let's look at an example from our text about TEFL.

a	**professional**	**English**	**teacher** (noun phrase)
(article)	(adjective)	(?)	(noun)

In this noun phrase, we have what is clearly an adjective, *professional*, and a noun, *teacher*, but the word between them, *English*, could be considered an adjective, in which case there is no compound noun.

a	professional	English	teacher (noun phrase)
(article)	(adjective)	(adjective)	(noun)

However, for our purposes, we choose to view *English* as a noun that is acting like an adjective. In this case, *English teacher* can be viewed as two nouns or as a single compound noun within the larger noun phrase.

a	professional	English teacher (noun phrase)
(article)	(adjective)	(noun) (noun)
		(compound noun)

We will touch upon this adjective/noun distinction in the "Adjectives" section as well, but for now, let's move on to another distinction, that of countable and uncountable nouns.

Countable/Uncountable Nouns

Nouns can also be divided into countable and uncountable (or ***noncount nouns*** or ***mass nouns***). ***Countable nouns*** can be singular or plural (e.g., *animal/animals, cat/cats, man/men, child/children*), whereas uncountable nouns cannot be divided into separate elements (e.g., *money, furniture, coffee, love*).

ESL/EFL students need to memorize which words are countable and which ones are uncountable. Some nouns can be both, depending on their meaning. For example: *Our house has four rooms* contains a countable version of *room*. However, *Is there any room for me?* uses an uncountable version of *room*.

Table 1.1 further illustrates the main differences between countable and uncountable nouns.

Table 1.1 Differences between Countable and Uncountable Nouns

Countable Nouns	Uncountable Nouns (Noncount Nouns)
May be preceded by indefinite article *a/an:* *a banknote*	May not be preceded by indefinite article *a/an:* *a money* ("some money" is used)
Take final *–s/–es* in the plural: *2 banknotes*	Have no plural form; do not take a final *–s/–es:* *money*

May be followed by a verb in singular or plural form: *This banknote is green.* *These banknotes are green.*	Always followed by a verb in singular form: *Money is important.*
Use the following expressions, *many, a few/few*: *How many banknotes do you have?* *I have a few banknotes.* *I have few banknotes left.*	Use the following expressions, *much, a little/little*: *How much money do you have?* *I have a little money.* *I have little money left.*

Uncountable nouns are not used in the plural form, of course. Countable nouns, on the other hand, are, which leads us to the next subcategories of nouns: regular and irregular plurals.

Regular/Irregular Plural Nouns

All countable nouns have singular and plural forms. To make a plural form, we usually need to add –*s*. For example, one *apple* becomes two *apples*; however, some nouns have irregular plurals, like the noun *man* that becomes *men* in the plural form.

Table 1.2 will help you better understand regular and irregular plural forms. These are just some examples of irregular plural nouns. For a more complete list, see Appendix 1.

Table 1.2. Regular and Irregular Plural Nouns

Regular Plural Nouns	Irregular Plural Nouns
–s *songs, books, pencils*	man –> men woman –> women child –> children person –> people mouse –> mice foot –> feet tooth –> teeth goose –> geese deer –> deer fish –> fish sheep –> sheep
–es (words ending in *–s, –sh, –ch, –x, –z*) *messes, brushes, churches, boxes*	
–es (some words ending in *–o*) *potatoes, tomatoes, heroes*	
–ies (most words ending in *–y* preceded by a consonant) *baby –> babies, sky –> skies* Note: We *do not* add *–ies* to words that end in *–y* preceded by a vowel: e.g., *toy* becomes *toys*; *key* becomes *keys*.	
–ves (some words ending in *–f* or *–fe*) *knife –> knives, half –> halves*	

This concludes our consideration of nouns. Hopefully, you are feeling more confident in your understanding of this crucial part of speech. Let's move on to our next part of speech, pronouns.

Pronouns in Context: A Text about TEFL

We are now ready to explore our second part of speech. Here again is our text about teaching English as a foreign language. Read through it again, and see if you are able to identify all of the pronouns within (hint: there are eight of them).

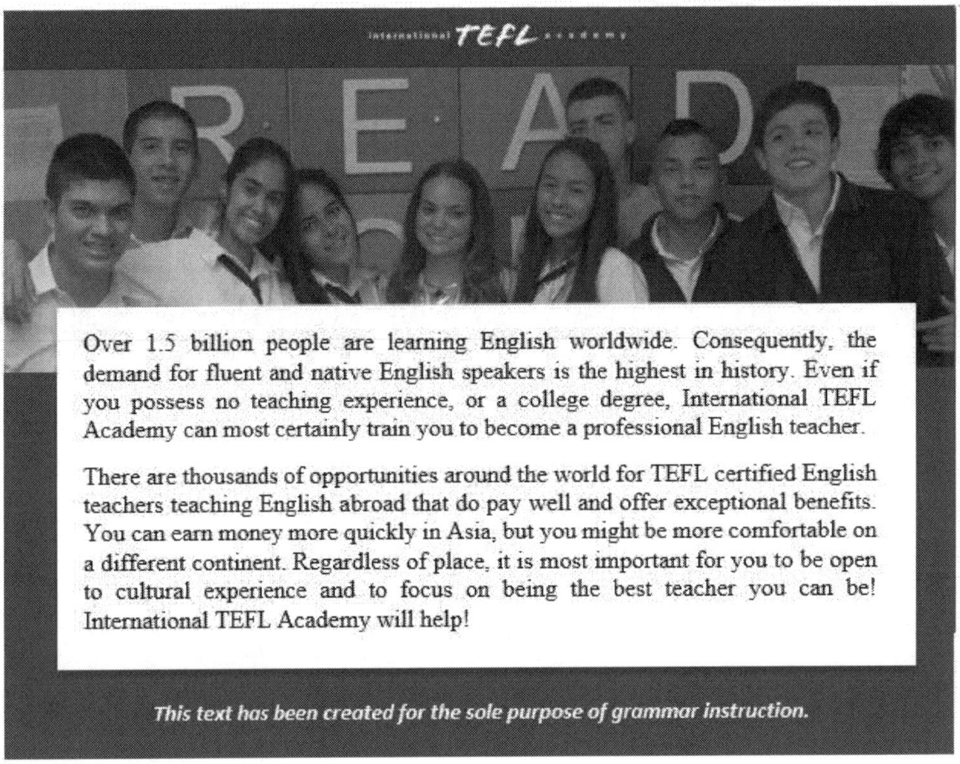

Were you able to identify any of the eight pronouns? The answer is on the next page.

Identification of Pronouns in Context

Here is the text again, with all eight of the pronouns in **bold**.

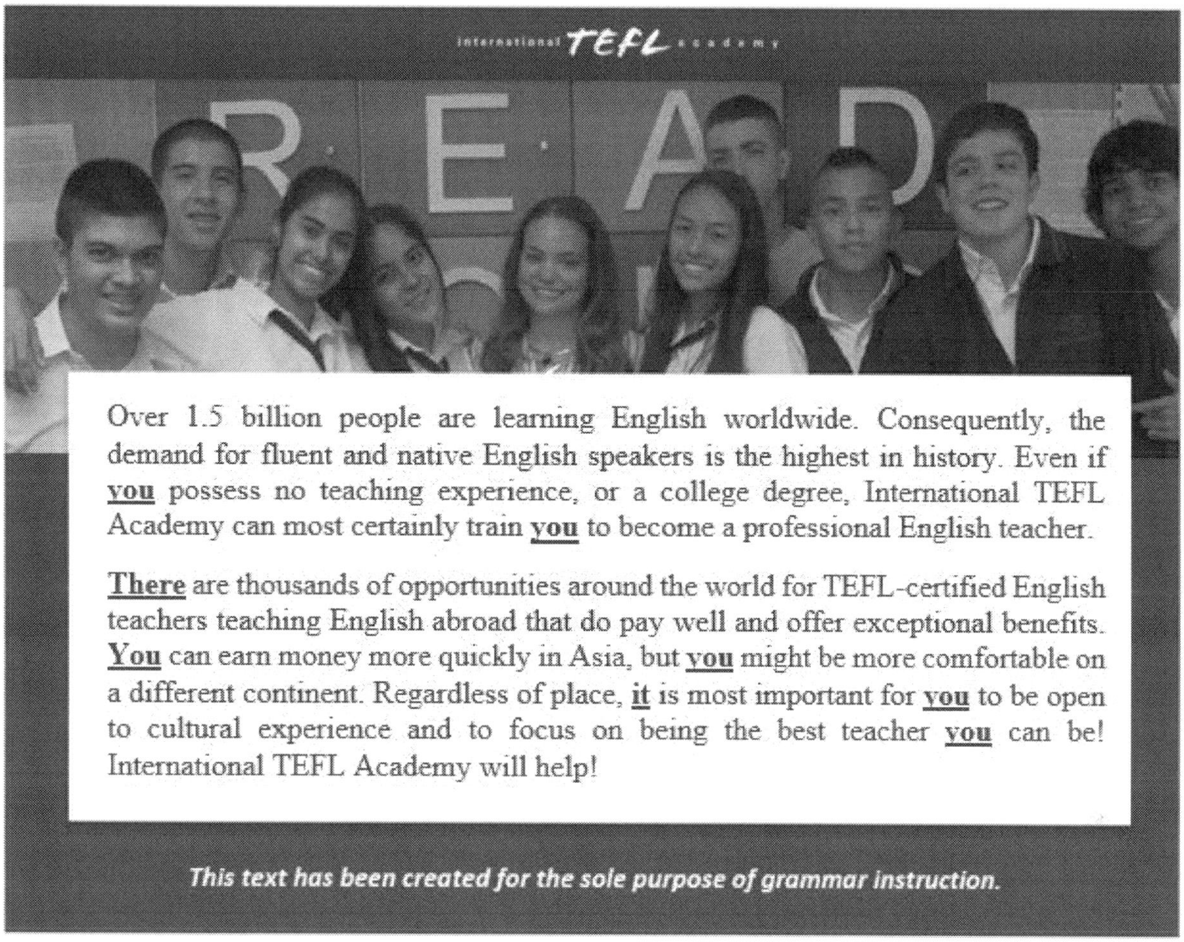

How many were you able to identify?

Now let's use some of these examples to consider pronouns and their various forms.

A pronoun replaces a noun to avoid repetition. Like nouns, they are commonly used as subjects or objects of verbs.

You can earn money. (subject pronoun)
International TEFL Academy can train you. (object pronoun)

In these two examples, we see the same pronoun, *you*, but the first one is the subject of the sentence, and the second one is the object of the verb. The form of the pronouns does not change in this instance, but with many other pronouns, we must change the form if we change positions in a sentence. Let's take a closer look at subject and object pronouns.

Pronouns

Pronouns are words used to replace nouns that have been previously stated or are already understood. We use them to avoid repetition, as in these sentences below:

This book covers a lot of grammar. <u>It</u> should be helpful. (pronoun)

In the second sentence, *It* is a pronoun that replaces the noun phrase *This book*, which was already stated. The authors did not want to repeat the noun, so they used a pronoun, and the proximity and context makes it very clear what *It* is referring to.

Pronouns take several different forms and can perform various functions on top of their duties as noun replacement. The most basic forms of pronouns are subject and object pronouns, so let's explore those first.

Subject and Object Pronouns

Subject Pronouns

In the sentence below, *she* is a pronoun that replaces the proper noun *Lizzy*. It is the subject of the sentence, and we use it so we do not have to repeat the name.

Lizzy is a happy girl. <u>She</u> smiles all the time. (subject pronoun)

Sometimes, the noun being replaced hasn't been previously mentioned, but it is clear from the context, as in this example:

<u>I</u> like movies. (subject pronoun)

In this example, we know that the pronoun *I* refers to whoever wrote or said the sentence, so no previous noun needed to be replaced. We also commonly use the pronoun *it* to describe weather or general conditions.

<u>It</u> is raining hard today! (subject pronoun)

Table 1.3 contains personal subject pronouns (pronouns that we use as the subject of a sentence).

Table 1.3 English Subject Pronouns

Person	Singular	Plural
First	I	We
Second	you	you
Third	She/he/it	they

There is one additional pronoun that we commonly use as a subject but which has not been included in the previous chart: *there*. When used before the verb *to be*, the pronoun *there* is what can be called ***a dummy subject*** or ***the existential there***. Here are some examples:

<u>There</u> is one additional pronoun. (pronoun – existential)
<u>There</u> are four sections in this unit. (pronoun – existential)

Whether *there* is actually a pronoun in these sentences is controversial, as some grammarians argue that *there* is a noun when used as the subject of a sentence. It does not appear to do what other pronouns do (it is not replacing another noun), but it is very common in use, so we have included it here with the other subject pronouns.

Object Pronouns

Subject pronouns are one type of pronoun, and personal pronouns can take various different forms, depending on their use and placement within a sentence. For example, we often use pronouns as the object of a verb, and sometimes the form of the pronoun changes when we do.

Lizzy is a happy girl. Mom gave <u>her</u> a present. (object pronoun)

Thus, if we wish to replace *Lizzy* before the verb (as a subject), we use *she*. But if we wish to replace it after a verb (as an object), we use *her*.

Table 1.4 contains personal object pronouns.

Table 1.4 English Personal Object Pronouns		
Person	**Singular**	**Plural**
First	me	us
Second	you	you
Third	Him/her/it	them

Other Pronouns

Here are explanations and examples of the other various pronouns that we use in English.
The ***possessive adjective pronoun*** designates ownership of a noun that the pronoun is modifying.

<u>My</u> book bag is very heavy. (possessive adjective pronoun)

The ***possessive pronoun*** designates ownership of a noun that has previously been referenced.

This book bag is <u>yours</u>. <u>Mine</u> is in the hall. (possessive pronoun)

The ***reflexive pronoun*** is the form the object pronoun takes when the object of a verb or preposition refers back to the subject of the sentence.

The teacher helped himself. (reflexive pronoun as object of the verb *help*)

Table 1.5 shows all of these types of pronouns in their various forms.

Table 1.5 Types of English Pronouns

Person	Subject Pronoun	Possessive Adjective	Possessive Pronoun	Object Pronoun	Reflexive Pronoun
First person singular	I	my	mine	me	myself
Second person singular	you	your	yours	you	yourself
Third person singular (male)	he	his	his	him	himself
Third person singular (female)	she	her	hers	her	herself
Third person singular (object)	it	its	its	it	itself
First person plural	we	our	ours	us	ourselves
Second person plural	you	your	yours	you	yourselves
Third person plural	they	their	theirs	them	themselves

These are all of the pronouns of English. Tables like this can be helpful for demonstrating the wide array of pronouns and for teachers who are brushing up on English grammar and rules of syntax. But this is not the ideal way to present these important parts of speech to someone who is learning English for the first time. These pronouns would be introduced incrementally, over time, and presented within complete sentences as part of a larger series of communicative lesson plans.

Conclusion

Now that we know more about these vital parts of speech—nouns and pronouns—we can conclude this first section in our "Words" unit. We hope you have learned something new about nouns and pronouns, and we encourage you to start noticing how these parts of speech (and which of their various forms) are being used in the language that you encounter and create every day. Start becoming your own teacher by paying greater attention to the nouns and pronouns all around you. You should also consider going to the "Quizzes" section to take the quiz on nouns and pronouns.

Of course, nouns and pronouns are only the first two parts of speech in our list of eight, which means there are six more left to explore. The next section in this unit will cover verbs and several subcategories and forms therein.

1.2 Verbs

Introduction

The second section in our unit on words focuses on verbs and their various forms. Verbs are crucial because they connect our subjects and predicates, and without them, sentences cannot be complete. Before we begin discussing verbs and their subcategories, we will identify some examples.

Read the following sentences:

I taught children in Mexico last year, and I loved it.
I am considering going[1.3] to Asia to teach soon.
I like China, so I am applying for jobs there.

Do you know which of the words contained in these example sentences are verbs? We count eight of them in total. The verbs are *taught, loved, am, considering, to teach, like, am, applying.*

NOTE 1.3: In the second sentence, the word *going* is a gerund, and gerunds are nouns, not verbs. However, we decided to address them within this book alongside verbs, which allows us to better differentiate them from present participles.

Under the general label of verb, there are many different subcategories. Here are some of those subcategories and the examples from the sentences above that represent them.

The first sentence is in the past tense, and the first verb, *taught,* is an irregular past tense verb. The second verb, *loved,* is regular. The second sentence contains an infinitive verb, *to teach*, but it also contains a present participle, *considering,* and a gerund, *going*. It also contains an auxiliary verb**,** *am.* The third sentence has the same auxiliary verb**,** *am.* It also includes a stative verb, *like,* and a dynamic verb, *apply*. In contrast to these, the main verb in the second sentence is a mixed verb, *considering.* Finally, we can find an example of a transitive verb, *consider*, as well as an intransitive verb**,** *apply.*

It's OK if you don't understand this terminology yet. This second section of Unit 1 introduces verbs and some important subcategories of them. We will start by looking at our TEFL text again, and we will see some quick definitions of the examples of verbs within. After that, you will find expanded sections about each subcategory of verbs, which provide further examples, explanations, and more in-depth information.

Objectives

Identify and differentiate various verb forms, including the following:

- Transitive and intransitive verbs
- Infinitives and gerunds
- Present and past participles
- Regular and irregular verbs
- Stative and dynamic verbs
- Auxiliary verbs

Verbs in Context: A Text about TEFL

You may recognize the following text about TEFL from our previous section. Here is a bigger challenge for you: Can you identify all 25 verbs and gerunds within? The answer is on the next page.

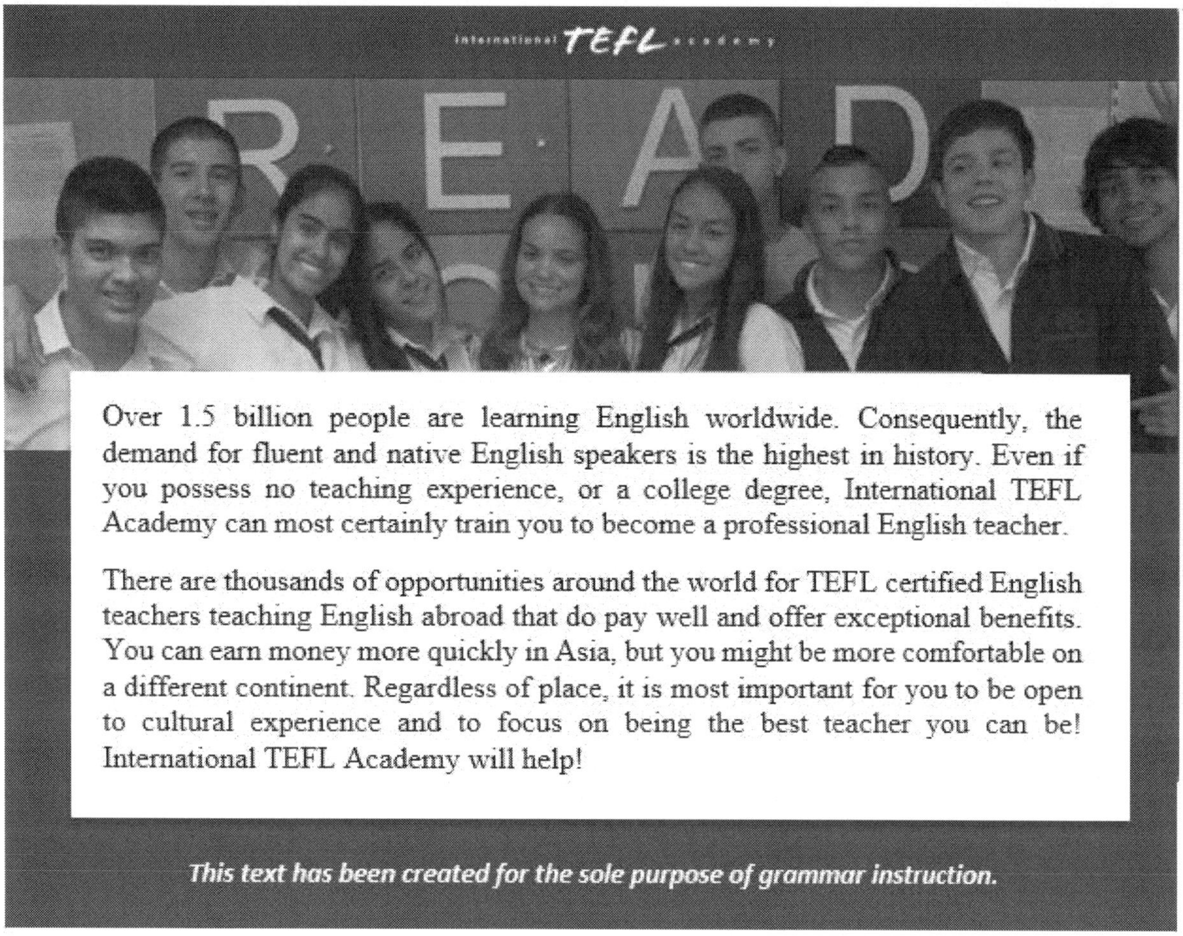

Identification of Verbs in Context

Here you can see all of the verbs in our text in **bold.**

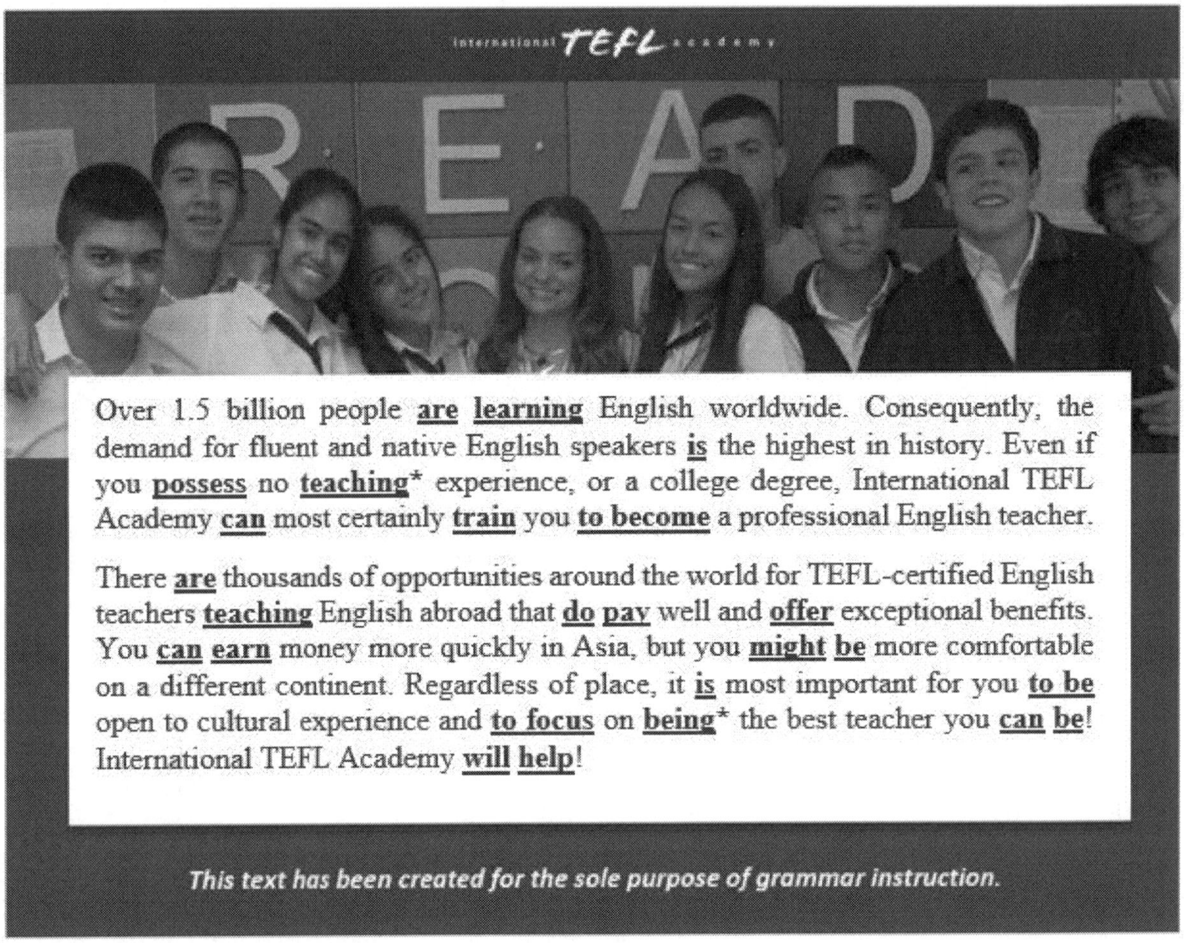

Let's use some of these examples to start exploring some various subcategories of verbs.

Verbs are words that describe actions, states of being, or occurrences. A transitive verb is a verb that is immediately followed by an object; an intransitive verb is a verb that has no object.

Here are examples from the text of the various types and forms of verbs we will discuss in the section.

You can earn money (verb – transitive)
opportunities that pay well (verb – intransitive)

An infinitive verb is the simple form of a verb, usually preceded by the particle *to*.

it is important for you to be open (verb – infinitive)

A gerund is the *–ing* form of a verb that is used as a noun. A present participle is the *–ing* form of a verb that is used to form continuous tenses.

to focus on being the best teacher (noun – gerund)
people are learning English (verb – present participle)

A regular verb is a verb that has a past tense form using *–ed*. An irregular verb is a verb that has past tense and/or past participle forms other than *–ed* (our text does not use past tenses, so here are the past tense forms of two verbs from the text).

helped (verb – regular [past participle form of *help*])
taught (verb – irregular [past participle form of *teach*])

A stative verb is a verb representing a state of being (and is not used in continuous tenses). A dynamic verb represents an action (and can be used in continuous tenses). A verb that can be either is called a ***mixed verb***.

possess (verb – stative)
learn (verb – dynamic)

Finally, an auxiliary verb is a verb that helps other verbs in a sentence.

people are learning (verb – auxiliary)
you can earn money (verb – auxiliary)
ITA will help! (verb – auxiliary)

We are now ready to consider these different verb forms in greater depth and within further examples.

Verbs

Verbs are words that describe actions, states of being, or occurrences. We can view verbs as the fulcrum of English sentences in that they connect the subject and the object and serve as the primary part of a sentence's predicate (concepts that are further discussed in Unit 2 of this book).

People	**learn**	**English**. (sentence)
(noun/subject)	(verb)	(noun/object)

As we have seen, there are several distinct types of verbs, as well as some different forms that verbs can take on within our sentences. The larger subject of how these verbs and forms are used to create meaning within the tense/aspect grammatical system is reserved for Unit 3, "Tenses." For now, and to better prepare us to understand the roles that verbs play in English, let's explore the various types and forms of the verbs themselves, starting with the important transitive/intransitive distinction.

Transitive and Intransitive Verbs

As we said before, verbs serve as the fulcrum for our sentences, separating a subject from a predicate and balancing the subject and object of a sentence. However, we can think of many correct (and meaningful) sentences in which there is no object of the verb, which means the verb is the last word in the sentence. Take the following examples:

Dogs bark. (verb – intransitive)
Birds fly. (verb – intransitive)
Babies eat, poop, and sleep. (verb – intransitive)

In all of these sentences, there is a single subject, and the verbs alone serve as the predicate. None of the verbs has objects, which means that all of the verbs are intransitive. ***Intransitive verbs*** do not require a direct object. Some other common intransitive verbs are a*gree, arrive, live, rain, snow, walk*. Of course, that does not mean that these verbs must be the last word in a sentence.

The baby cried for two hours. (verb – intransitive)

Don't be fooled by the additional information that comes after the verb in this sentence, which is part of the predicate but which is not a direct object of the verb *cry*. We can separate the sentence into two sentences, like so:

The baby cried. (verb – intransitive)
Two hours passed. (verb – intransitive)

We can do that because *cry* is an intransitive verb. So is *pass*, in this example, but *pass* can also be transitive. ***Transitive verbs*** are verbs that must be followed by a direct object for the sentence to be grammatical. Look at these examples:

My friend makes model rockets. (verb – transitive)
She found the treasure! (verb – transitive)
I like scary movies. (verb – transitive)

Hopefully, you can see how these sentences all have direct objects after the verbs because the verbs require as much (try putting a period after any of the verbs—the result is ungrammatical). Some other common transitive verbs are *cut, enjoy, send, use, want*.

Finally, some verbs can be both transitive and intransitive, depending on their use. One example of this is the aforementioned *pass*.

Two hours passed. (verb – intransitive)
Oops, we passed the exit! (verb – transitive)

Interestingly, a third meaning of the verb *pass* belongs to the subset of transitive verbs that can be called ditransitive. ***Ditransitive verbs*** are transitive verbs that require more than one object, a direct and indirect object. (Direct and indirect objects are discussed further in Unit 2.)

> **He <u>passed</u> the ball to me.** (verb – transitive)
> **He <u>passed</u> me the ball.** (verb – ditransitive)

In these examples, *ball* is the direct object because it is the thing that is passed, and *me* is the indirect object. Some other common ditransitive verbs include *give, mail, tell.*

Next, let's explore some different forms that verbs can take, starting with infinitives, gerunds, and present participles.

Infinitives, Gerunds, and Present Participles

You have seen that there are different types of verbs (and we will learn about some other category types later), but there are also different forms that verbs can take when used in sentences. Let's define some of these forms and look at examples of them.

Infinitives

The ***base form*** or ***bare infinitive*** is the form of the verb that you can find in a dictionary (e.g., *walk, study, draw*). Sometimes when teachers write a verb on the board as vocabulary, not as part of a sentence, they will precede it with the particle *to* (*to walk, to study, to draw*) to indicate that it is the infinitive form of the verb.

Gerunds and Present Participles

Other forms of verbs include gerunds and present participles. A ***gerund*** is a verb ending with *–ing* that functions as a noun. A ***present participle*** has the same form, but it functions as a verb within the various continuous/progressive tenses.

gerund = verb + –ing that functions as a noun
present participle = verb + –ing that functions as a verb

> **walk –> walking**
> **read –> reading**
> **swim –> swimming**

Compare:

> **I like <u>reading</u>.** (Here, *like* is a transitive verb, and *reading* is its noun/gerund object.)
> **<u>Reading</u> is my favorite leisure activity.** (Here, *reading* is a noun/gerund and the subject.)
> **I am <u>reading</u> now.** (Here, *reading* functions as an intransitive verb and is a present participle.)
> **I have been <u>reading</u> for three hours.** (Here again, *reading* is a verb/present participle.)

The present participle form of the verb will be covered more extensively in the various continuous/progressive sections of Unit 3. For now, it is important to note that certain verbs in English (when used in their transitive forms) are always followed by infinitives, whereas other verbs are followed by gerunds. Look at the examples in Table 1.6.

Table 1.6 Infinitives versus Gerunds	
Verbs Followed by Infinitives	**Verbs Followed by Gerunds**
want: I *want* to eat.	enjoy: I *enjoy* eating.
decide: He *decided* to dance.	practice: He *practiced* dancing.
choose: I *chose* to go home.	mind: I don't *mind* going home.
agree: She *agreed* to dance with me.	resume: We *resumed* dancing.

Some verbs can be followed by either a gerund or an infinitive, including *like*, *start*, *begin.*

I like to read books. / I like reading books.
We began to study. / We began studying.
It started to rain. / It started raining.

These verb patterns are individual to each verb in question, which means that there are no general "rules" for whether verbs are followed by infinitives or gerunds. Each verb pattern has to be learned individually.

Irregular verb patterns are another form that has to be learned on an individual verb basis, and regular/irregular verbs just happens to be our next subcategory of verbs for exploration.

Regular and Irregular Verbs

Verbs can also be divided into the subcategories of ***regular*** and ***irregular,*** depending on how they form the past tenses. In addition to the infinitive and present participle forms discussed earlier, verbs also have two past tense forms, which we will call the the ***past simple*** (sometimes called ***V2*** or ***verb 2***) and the ***past participle*** (sometimes called ***V3*** or ***verb 3***). The past simple form is used within the past simple verb tense, but the past participle is more versatile, used within the perfect aspect of all tenses, as well as in passive constructions and while using a verb as an adjective.

Both past tenses of regular verbs are formed with an *–ed* ending, whereas each irregular verb follows its own distinct pattern of past simple and past participle forms. It is important to note that many of the most commonly used English verbs are irregular, as can be seen in Table 1.7. It represents only a very small sample; another table with a more comprehensive list of irregular verbs can be found in Appendix 2.

Table 1.7 Examples of Regular and Irregular Verbs			
Type of Verb	**Infinitive**	**Past Simple**	**Past Participle**
Regular verbs	work	worked	worked
	listen	listened	listened
	decide	decided	decided
	study	studied	studied
Irregular verbs	be (am, is, are)	was/were	been
	have	had	had
	do	did	done
	eat	ate	eaten
	break	broke	broken
	put	put	put

The use of these forms will be covered more extensively in Unit 3 of our book, but for now, you only need to know that the past simple form is used to describe finished past actions (e.g., *Yesterday, I worked for an hour after I ate lunch*) and the past participle is primarily used as an adjective (e.g., *the broken chair)* and within the perfect aspects (e.g., *I haven't done my homework yet*).

Another way to categorize verbs is whether they are stative or dynamic (or both), which we will consider next.

Stative, Dynamic, and Mixed Verbs

Stative Verbs

Stative verbs (or ***noncontinuous verbs***) are verbs that cannot be converted to a present participle; you cannot add an *–ing* ending. These verbs are things you cannot see someone doing, such as emotion or abstract verbs (e.g., *like, love, hate, want, need, be*); opinion verbs (e.g., *know, recognize*); possession verbs (e.g., *possess, own, belong*); and sensory verbs (e.g., *taste, smell, see*).

I want some fruit now. (verb – stative)
I am wanting some fruit now. (incorrect)
She needs your help now. (verb – stative)

She is <u>needing</u> your help now. (incorrect)
He <u>owns</u> that car. (verb – stative)
He is <u>owning</u> that car. (incorrect)

Dynamic Verbs

Dynamic verbs (or ***continuous verbs***) are action verbs that can be converted to a present participle and used within the continuous/progressive aspect. These verbs are usually things you can see someone doing (e.g., *run, write, read, drive, listen*).

She is <u>helping</u> me with my homework. (verb – dynamic)
I was <u>driving</u> and <u>listening</u> to music. (verb – dynamic)
She'll be <u>coming</u> 'round the mountain when she <u>comes</u>. (verb – dynamic)

Mixed Verbs

Mixed verbs are verbs that can be either dynamic or stative, depending on their meaning in context (e.g., *have, think*).

I <u>have</u> a car. (Here, *have* means "own" and is stative.)
I am <u>having</u> fun. (Here, *have* means "experiencing" and is dynamic.)
I <u>think</u> that movie is hilarious. (Here, *think* means "have the opinion" and is stative.)
I am <u>thinking</u> about moving to Guam. (Here, *think* means "use mental processes" and is dynamic.)

We have one more major subcategory of verbs to consider: the auxiliary verbs.

Auxiliary Verbs

Auxiliary verbs are helping verbs. They do not carry their own distinct meaning, but they instead "help" the main verb express the meaning of the sentence. Examples of auxiliary verbs include *be, do, have, will*, all of which can be used as main verbs as well.

Examples that use auxiliary verbs:

She <u>is</u> teaching. (The verb *is* is helping the main verb, *teaching,* by forming the progressive[1.4], so *is* is an auxiliary verb.)
I <u>did</u> like the artwork at the museum. (The verb *did* is helping to add emphasis to the main verb, *like*, so *did* is an auxiliary verb.)
I <u>have</u> traveled to 15 different countries. (The verb *have* is providing the perfect aspect[1.4] for the main verb, *traveled*, so *have* is an auxiliary verb.)
He <u>will</u> come to the meeting late. (The verb *will* is adding future temporality[1.4] to the main verb, *come*, so *will* is an auxiliary verb.)

NOTE 1.4: For more in-depth information about these facets of tense and aspect, see Unit 3 of this book.

Examples that use the same verbs as main verbs (and contain no auxiliary verbs):

She is a teacher. (The verb *is* carries semantic meaning, so it is the main verb and not an auxiliary.)
I did the artwork at the museum. (The verb *did* carries semantic meaning on its own, so it is the main verb and not an auxiliary.)
I have souvenirs from 15 different countries. (The verb *have* carries semantic meaning, so it is the main verb and not an auxiliary.)
He willed the meeting to start late. (This somewhat rare usage of the verb *will* carries semantic meaning, so it is the main verb and not an auxiliary.)

There is a special subset of auxiliary verbs called ***modal verbs***, which express modalities, such as ability, obligation, and probability. These include *may, might, can, would, could, have to, must*, and are discussed in their own section in Unit 4, "Additional Grammar Points."

Conclusion

This concludes our section on verbs, the only part in Unit 1 that explores a single part of speech. That choice was a conscious one; verbs play such a crucial role in our construction of sentences and come in so many different forms that we felt they deserved exclusive designation. We hope that you learned something new and useful. Now that you have a better understanding of the various forms and subcategories that verbs can take, we feel you are much better prepared to tackle the other major units, including Unit 2, "Sentences," and Unit 3, "Tenses." You are also prepared to take the quiz on verbs in the "Quizzes" section.

We still have five more parts of speech to explore, starting with our next section, "Adjectives, Articles, and Adverbs."

1.3 Adjectives, Articles, and Adverbs

Introduction

Our third section in the "Words" unit focuses on three different parts of speech, adjectives, articles[1.5], and adverbs. Before we consider each of these in turn, let's identify some examples of each of them. Read the following dialogue between an ESL teacher and her student:

Student: **I am happy about the test! I did good on the test.**

Teacher: **No, you did *well*. An angel does *good*. The Green Lantern does *good*. You did *well* on the test because you are a *good* student.**

The teacher in this dialogue is attempting to correct a common error[1.5] in the usage of adjectives and adverbs (which is one that many native English speakers make as well). Can you identify the mistake? Do you know which of the words in the example dialogue above are adjectives and adverbs? Can you identify any articles in the dialogue?

The adjectives are *happy, good,* but only the last instance, used in the noun phrase a *good student*. For articles, we have *An, a* and three instances of *the*. Finally, both instances of *well* are adverbs.

The student describes his state of emotion by using the adjective *happy*. The teacher then uses the adjective *good* to generally describe what kind of student he is. However, the other uses of the word *good* in the dialogue are nouns (meaning "that which is morally correct," as in the phrase *good and evil*—this is the error[1.5] that the student made; he used a noun/adjective where he should have used an adverb). Adjectives have three forms:

1. The base form
2. Comparatives
3. Superlatives

As mentioned, *good* can be an adjective or a noun, but the adverb that the student should have used is *well*. The student did *well* on the test. Like adjectives, adverbs have three forms:

1. The base form
2. Comparatives
3. Superlatives

NOTE 1.5: The sentence *I did good on the test* may be an error, technically speaking, but it is one that many native English speakers make as well. The questions of how, when, and how much we should correct our EFL students are not easy to answer, but for now, it should be noted that many—if not most—EFL teachers would not correct their student who said "I did good on the test" because the sentence is clear, communicative, and native speaker-like.

Finally, the dialogue contains all of the different forms of English articles: the definite article (*the*), both indefinite articles (*a/an*), and the zero article (*does_good*).

This section, our third in the "Words" unit, introduces our next three parts of speech in the English language: adjectives, articles, and adverbs. We will start by looking again at our text about TEFL that contains examples of all of the parts of speech, and we will see some quick definitions of the examples of our target part of speech. After that, you will find expanded sections about each part of speech, which provide further examples, explanations of subcategories, and more in-depth information.

Objectives

- Identify and differentiate various adjective forms, including comparatives and superlatives
- Identify and differentiate articles[1.6], including the following:
  - Definite articles
  - Indefinite articles
  - Zero articles
- Identify and differentiate various adverb forms, including comparatives and superlatives

---

NOTE 1.6: Many traditional lists of the parts of speech of English do not list articles as a separate category (they are technically a subcategory of adjectives). These lists commonly include interjections as a category. However, because articles play a large role in English sentence construction—and are typically difficult for learners of EFL/ESL—we list them here as their own category. We recognize that interjections can be categorized as a distinct part of speech, but they are not typically difficult for our EFL/ESL learners and, as such, we are not considering them separately here.

Adjectives in Context: A Text about TEFL

We are now ready to move on to our fourth part of speech: adjectives. Here again is our text about teaching English as a foreign language. Read through it again and see if you are able to identify all of the adjectives within (hint: some of them contain more than one word, and we count 14 of them in total, though that number is debatable).

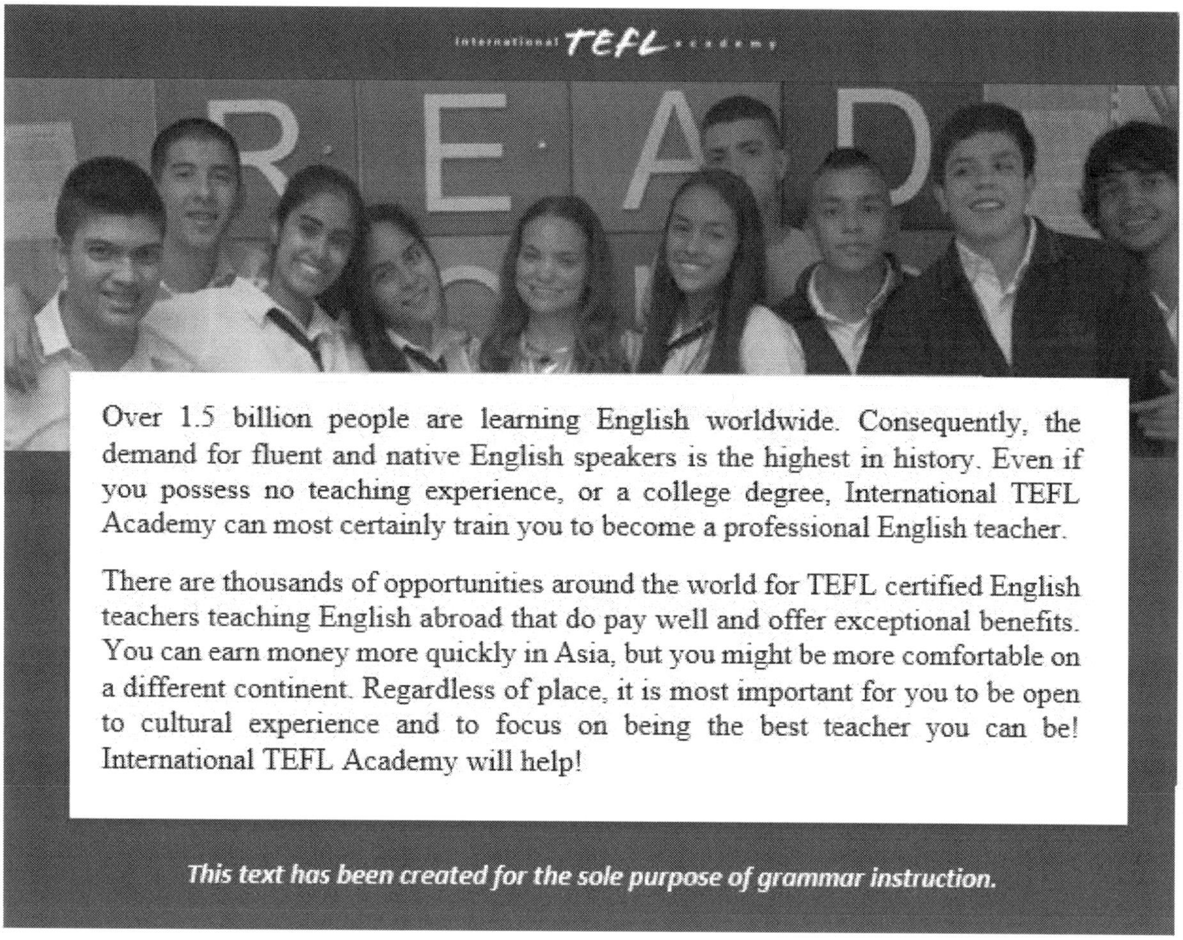

Were you able to identify any of the 14 adjectives? The answer is on the following page.

Identification of Adjectives in Context

Here is the text again, with all 14[1.7] of the adjectives in **bold.**

How many were you able to identify? Now let's use some of these examples to consider adjectives and their various forms.

NOTE 1.7: Some classifications in English are more open to interpretation than others. The section on compound nouns in the "Nouns and Pronouns" section includes a discussion about how some compound nouns contain nouns that act like adjectives. Along those lines, there are several words here that we have classified as nouns but that could also be interpreted as adjectives. Depending on who's counting them, there could be more than 14 adjectives in our text.

Adjectives are descriptive words that modify nouns.

professional English teacher (adjective)
exceptional benefits (adjective)
cultural experience (adjective)

These can take the form of comparative or superlative adjectives.

you might be <u>more comfortable</u> (comparative adjective)
the <u>highest</u> in history (superlative adjective)

Now that we have looked at these particular examples from our text, we are ready to consider adjectives and their subcategories in greater depth and with more examples.

Adjectives

Adjectives are descriptive words that modify nouns; they are used to add detail and specification to those nouns. Adjectives usually precede nouns.

This is a <u>cute</u> baby. (adjective)
That is a <u>beautiful</u> flower. (adjective)
She is wearing a <u>colorful</u> dress. (adjective)

Sometimes adjectives follow a ***describing verb***, or ***copula***, as in the following sentences:

This baby is <u>cute</u>. (adjective)
This flower is <u>beautiful</u>. (adjective)
The dress is <u>colorful</u>. (adjective)

All of the examples above are the base form of adjectives. Let's consider the other forms that adjectives can take.

Comparative Adjectives

Comparative adjectives are used to compare two or more different nouns. To form a comparative of an adjective that is one syllable in length, we add *–er* to the adjective. We use comparatives with the preposition *than*.

My baby is <u>cuter</u> than yours. (adjective – comparative)
I need a <u>faster</u> computer than this one. (adjective – comparative)
My older brother is <u>bigger</u> than I am. (adjective – comparative)

For adjectives that are more than one syllable and end in *–y*, we change the *–y* to *–i* and add *–er*.

I am <u>happier</u> now than I was a year ago. (adjective – comparative)
For me, math is <u>easier</u> than social studies. (adjective – comparative)

For adjectives that are more than one syllable and do not end in *–y,* we leave the adjective unchanged and modify it with the adverb *more*.

My office is <u>more comfortable</u> than my bedroom. (adjective – comparative)
Nothing is <u>more beautiful</u> than a flower. (adjective – comparative)

Finally, some common comparative adjectives are irregular.

You make a <u>better</u> door than a window. (adjective – comparative form of *good*)

I am a <u>worse</u> driver than you are. (adjective – comparative form of *bad*)

Superlative Adjectives

Superlative adjectives are used to compare three or more items. To form a superlative of an adjective that is one syllable in length, we add *–est* to the adjective. We modify comparatives with the definite article *the*.

My baby is the <u>cutest</u> baby in the world. (adjective – superlative)

What's the <u>fastest</u> way to get there? (adjective – superlative)

My <u>oldest</u> brother is the <u>biggest</u> kid in his class. (adjective – superlative)

For adjectives that are more than one syllable and end in *–y*, we change the *–y* to *–i* and add *–est*.

I am the <u>happiest</u> I have ever been. (adjective – superlative)

For me, math is the <u>easiest</u> subject. (adjective – superlative)

For adjectives that are more than one syllable and do not end in *–y*, we leave the adjective unchanged and modify it with the adverb *most*.

My office is the <u>most comfortable</u> room in the house. (adjective – superlative)

Love is the <u>most beautiful</u> thing in the universe. (adjective – superlative)

Finally, some common superlative adjectives are irregular.

Babe Ruth was the <u>best</u> hitter ever. (adjective – superlative form of *good*)

That was the <u>worst</u> movie I've ever seen. (adjective – superlative form of *bad*)

Table 1.8 provides a summary of how to form comparative and superlative adjectives.

Table 1.8 Forming Comparative and Superlative Adjectives

	Base Form of Adjective	Comparative	Superlative
One syllable	small old	smaller older	smallest oldest
Two syllables ending in *–y*	happy pretty	happier prettier	happiest prettiest
Two or more syllables	difficult beautiful	more difficult more beautiful	most difficult most beautiful
Irregular adjectives	good bad	better worse	best worst

Now that you have a better understanding of adjectives and the different forms they can take, we are ready to move on to the next part of speech in this section: articles.

Articles in Context: A Text about TEFL

Here again is our text about teaching English as a foreign language. Read through it again and see if you are able to find all of the articles within (there are seven of them).

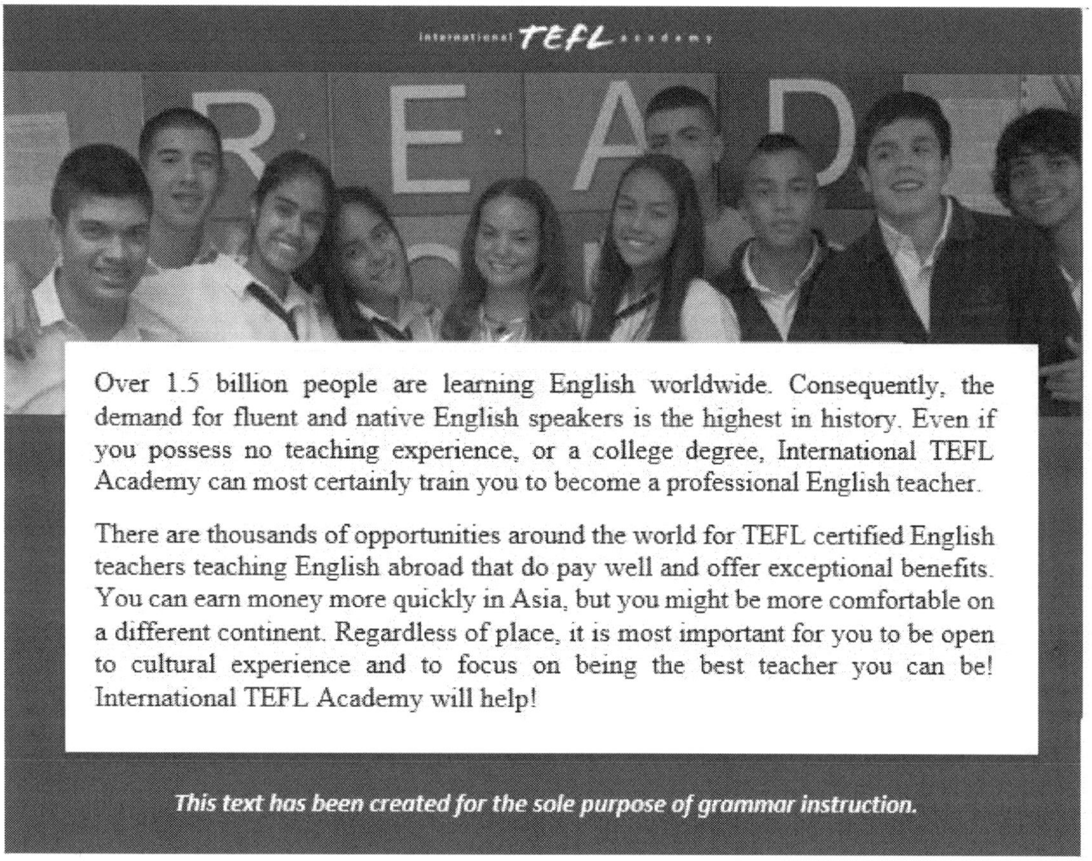

Were you able to find all seven articles? The answer is on the following page.

Identification of Articles in Context

Here is the text again, with all seven of the articles in **bold.**

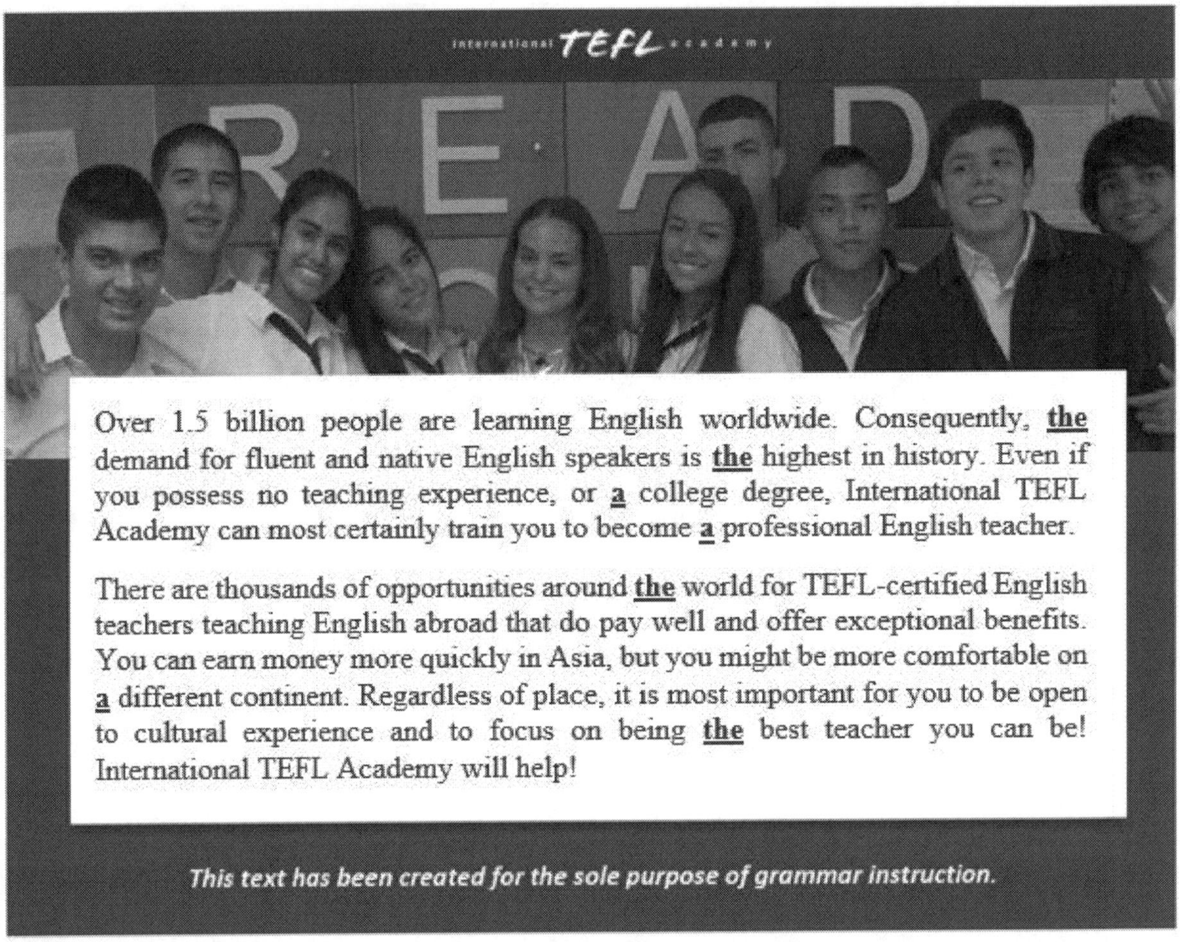

How many were you able to identify? Now let's use some of these examples to consider each of the different articles.

Articles are a subcategory of adjectives that modify and give information about nouns.

Definite articles refer to specific nouns.

the demand (article – definite)
the highest (demand) (article – definite)

Indefinite articles refer to nonspecific nouns.

a college degree (article – indefinite)
a professional English teacher (article – indefinite)
a different continent (article – indefinite)

Zero articles (or lack of article) are used with generalized nouns.

Asia (zero article)

cultural experience (zero article)

Let's take a closer look at these articles and how they are used in different examples.

Articles

Articles (sometimes called ***determiners***) are a subcategory of adjectives that modify and give information about nouns. English has two articles: the definite article, *the,* and the indefinite article, *a/an*. There are also instances in which we use no article with a noun, which is sometimes called a zero article.

As it is easiest to explain these different types of articles in reference to each other, let's jump in and start exploring all three English articles together.

Definite, Indefinite, and Zero Articles

Once again, here are the three types of articles in English:

1. *the* = definite article
2. *a/an* = indefinite article
3. Ø = no article (zero article)

Articles are useful for determining specificity (or lack thereof) of nouns. We use the definite article, *the,* to modify specific or particular nouns; we use the indefinite article, *a/an,* to refer to nonspecific or nonparticular nouns. When referencing nouns in general, we do not commonly use articles (often represented with a Ø symbol).

Let's go to <u>the</u> restaurant. (article – definite)

The above example uses the definite article to refer to a specific restaurant, one that the speaker and listener both know and have already agreed upon. On the other hand, if we want to signify any restaurant, rather than a specific one, we might say:

Let's go to <u>a</u> restaurant. (article – indefinite)

The use of an indefinite article in the above example refers to an unspecified restaurant. It communicates that the choice of restaurant has not yet been established, and any number of restaurants will do. Alternatively, we could also make a general statement about restaurants.

Restaurants are expensive. (zero article)

This last example makes a generalization about restaurants, and no article is used.

There are many more rules governing the use of definite, indefinite, and zero articles. Read Table 1.9 for a general overview of these rules.

Table 1.9 Rules Governing Articles

Indefinite Article: *a/an*	Definite Article: *the*	Zero Article: Ø
Use *a* before a consonant sound: *a pear* *a horse* *a university*	Use *the* before both a vowel and a consonant sound: *the apple* *the pear*	Zero articles (Ø) can be used to reference nouns in general: *Ø Apples are red.* *Ø Horses are mammals.*
Use *an* before a vowel sound: *an apple* *an umbrella* *an hour*		
Use *a/an* with nonspecific objects: *There is a laptop on the table.*	Use *the* when the noun is specific: *There is a laptop on the table.* *The laptop has many colorful stickers on it.*	Zero articles (Ø) can be used to make generalizations: *Ø Fruit is a healthy snack.* *Ø Guns shouldn't be allowed.* *Ø Articles are challenging to learn.*
Use *a/an* with singular countable nouns: *a chair* *a friend*	Use *the* with countable and uncountable nouns: *the chair* *the furniture*	
Other uses: In a group: *a teacher* *an American citizen* Expressions of quantity, with fractions, and with certain numbers: *a number of* *a lot of* *a third* *a couple* *a hundred* Used as part of an exclamatory sentence: *What a great idea!*	Other uses: When the object is unique: *the moon* *the White House* Before superlatives: *the best* *the most talented* Before ordinal numbers that are followed by a noun: *the third day* *the fourth child* With certain geographical and country names: *the Nile* *the South Pole* *the United States*	Uses: With certain proper names: *Ø Obama* *Ø Uncle Mike* With certain geographical and country names: *Ø China* *Ø Asia* *Ø Lake Victoria* With certain prepositional phrases that do not modify nouns: *by Ø car* *on Ø time* *in Ø trouble*

Are you feeling more confident in your knowledge of articles? We hope so! Do not let the short nature of our coverage of articles in this section fool you, however, as they can be very tricky for our learners to acquire and master (and for us as EFL teachers to explain in a clear and concise manner!). In any case, it's time to move on to our next part of speech, the third in this section and our sixth overall: adverbs.

Adverbs in Context: A Text about TEFL

We are now ready to move on to our sixth part of speech: adverbs. Here again is our text about teaching English as a foreign language. Read through it again and see if you are able to identify all of the adverbs within (hint: there are seven of them).

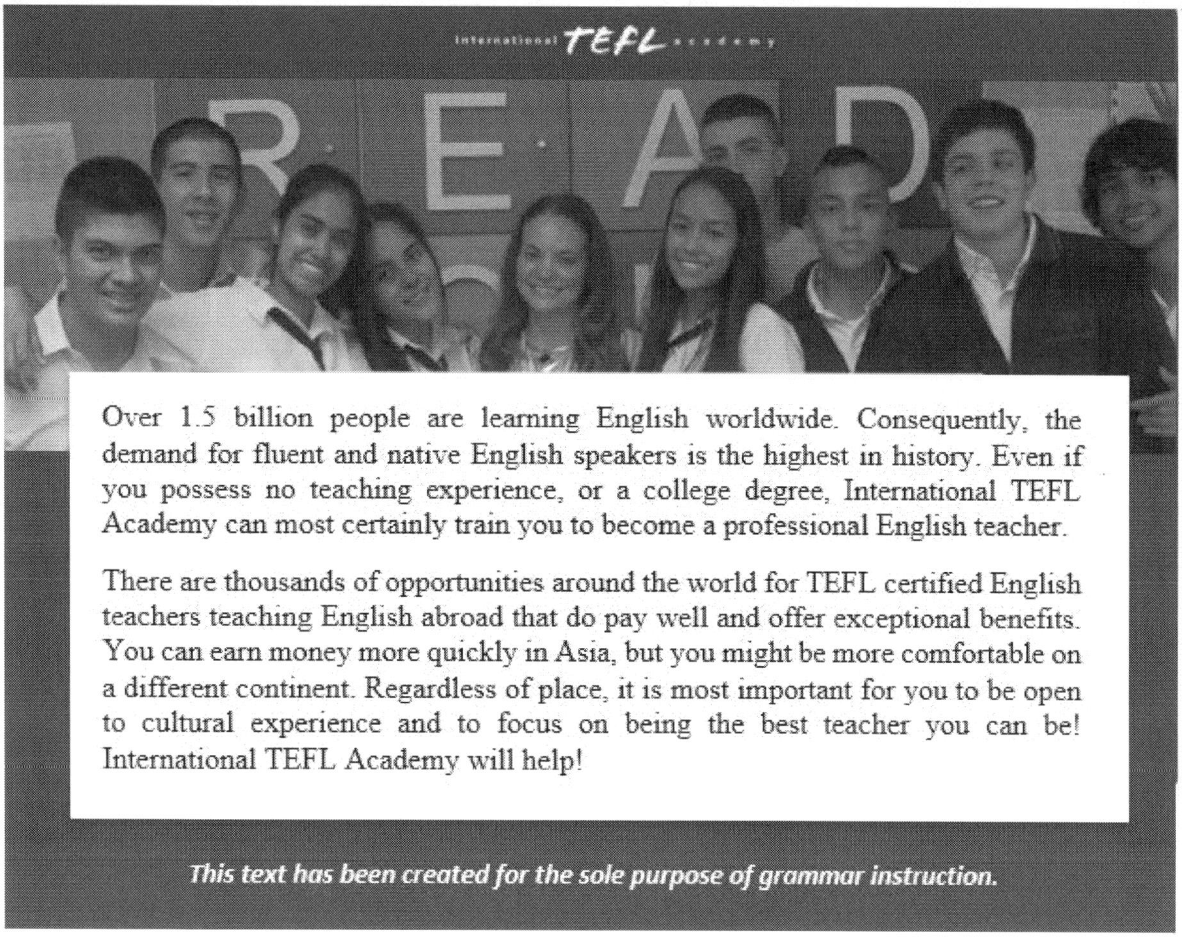

Were you able to identify any of the adverbs? The answer is on the next page.

Identification of Adverbs in Context

Here is the text again, with all seven of the adverbs in **bold**.

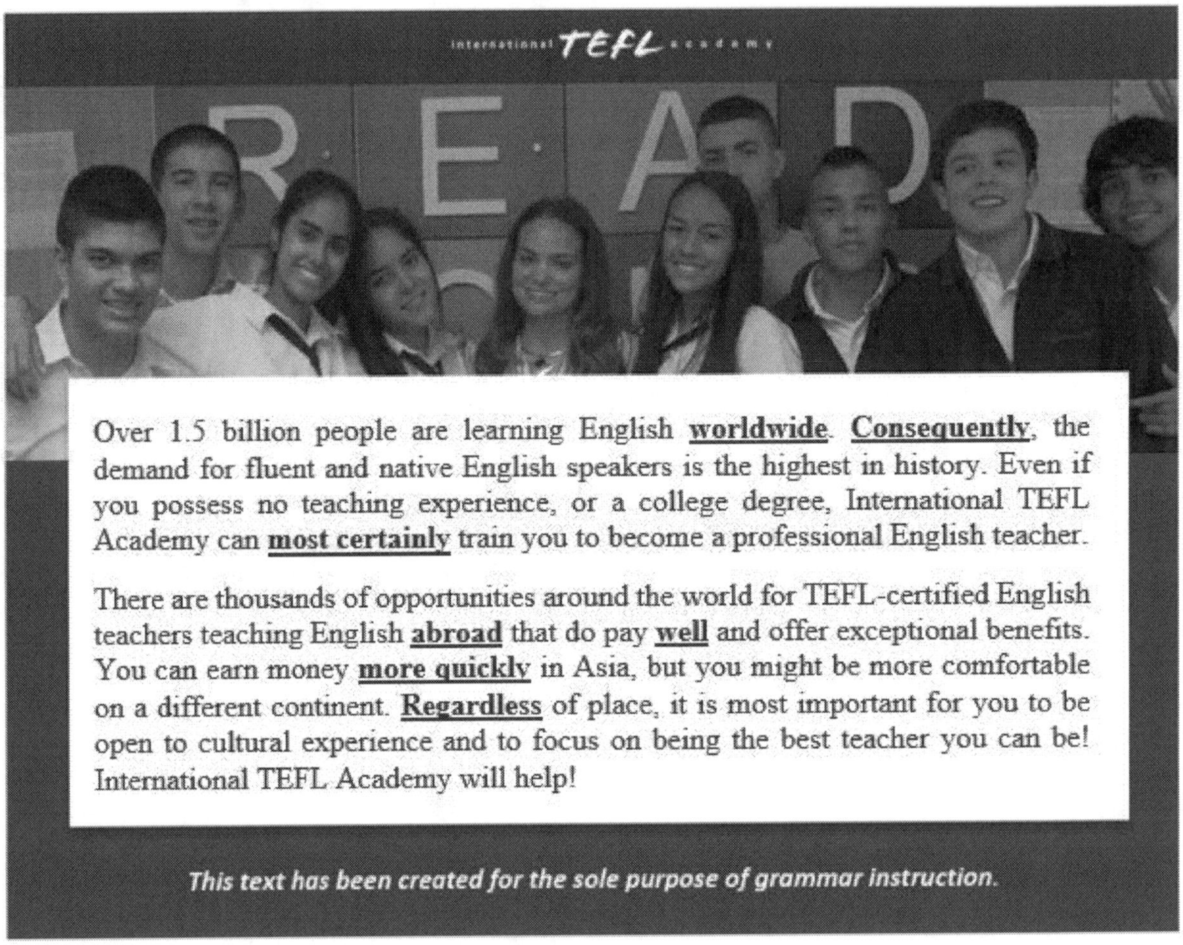

How many were you able to identify? Let's use some of these examples to introduce adverbs and their various forms.

Adverbs are descriptive words that we use to modify other words—verbs, adjectives, or other adverbs—a clause, or the sentence as a whole.

> **consequently, the demand for** (adverb)
>
> **pay well** (adverb)

These can take the form of comparative adverbs.

> **earn money more quickly** (adverb – comparative)

They can also take the form of superlative adverbs.

> **ITA can most certainly train you** (adverb – superlative)

Now that we have looked at these examples from our text, we can more closely consider adverbs and their subcategories via more examples.

Adverbs

Adverbs are descriptive words that we use to modify other words in a sentence. Most adverbs modify verbs, but adverbs may also be used to modify adjectives, other adverbs, a clause, or an entire sentence.

Adverbs that modify verbs are usually formed by adding *–ly* to the end of an adjective. These adverbs can be placed at the beginning of a sentence, the end of a sentence, or immediately before or after the verb they are modifying (which often places the adverb between an auxiliary verb and main verb).

> **I walked quickly toward the door and carefully opened it.** (adverb)
> **Quietly, we were all thinking the same thing.** (adverb)
> **He went down the list slowly and methodically.** (adverb)
> **We had easily won the match.** (adverb)

This also includes adverbs of frequency—like *always, usually, often, sometimes, seldom, rarely, never*—which are typically placed next to the verb they modify (and between an auxiliary and main verb, if applicable).

> **I rarely eat meat.** (adverb)
> **My students are always running late for class.** (adverb)
> **I have never seen *Saving Private Ryan*.** (adverb)

Adverbs like *very* and *quite* can modify adjectives or other adverbs.

> **The very old lady walked quite slowly.** (adverb)

Some adverbs modify an entire clause or sentence.

> **Consequently, she missed the bus.** (adverb)

All of these examples are the base form of adverbs. Let's consider the other forms that adverbs can take.

Comparative Adverbs

Like adjectives, adverbs have three forms. In addition to the ***base form*** that we just considered, a ***comparative adverb*** is used to compare two instances of another word (or words) in a sentence. Comparative adverbs are most often used to modify verbs.

To form most comparative adverbs, we leave the adverb unchanged and modify it with the additional adverb *more.*

I run more slowly than I used to. (adverb – comparative)

I can draw and write more neatly with a good pen. (adverb – comparative)

Some comparative adverbs, however, do not change form from their comparative adjective equivalent. We add *–er* to the base adverb.

I am working harder than ever. (adverb – comparative form of *hard*)

But I need to work faster. (adverb – comparative form of *fast*)

Finally, some common comparative adverbs are irregular and take the same form as their irregular adjective equivalent.

I speak Spanish better than I write it. (adverb – comparative form of *well*)

In addition to the comparative form, adverbs can take on a superlative form, which we will look at next.

Superlative Adverbs

Also, like adjectives, adverbs have a superlative form. A ***superlative adverb*** is used to compare three or more other words in a sentence. Superlative adverbs are most often used to modify verbs. To form most superlative adverbs, we leave the adverb unchanged and modify it with the additional adverb *most.*

I run the most slowly of all my friends. (adverb – superlative)

I can write most neatly with a marker. (adverb – superlative)

Some superlative adverbs, however, are the same as their superlative adjective equivalent. We add –*est* to the base adverb and use the definite article *the.*

This is the hardest I've ever had to work. (adverb – superlative form of *hard*)

My assistant types the fastest. (adverb – superlative form of *fast*)

Finally, some common superlative adverbs are irregular and take the same form as their irregular adjective equivalent.

I work best after my morning coffee. (adverb – superlative form of *well*)

Table 1.10 shows how to form comparative adverbs and superlative adverbs.

Table 1.10 Forming Comparatives and Superlatives

	Base Form of Adjective	Base Form of Adverb	Comparative Adverb	Superlative Adverb
Adverbs formed from adjectives by adding *–ly*	slow beautiful	slowly beautifully	more slowly more beautifully	most slowly most beautifully
Adverbs with the same form as adjectives	hard fast	hard fast	harder faster	hardest fastest
Irregular adverbs	good bad	well badly	better worse	best worst

Conclusion

We have covered a lot of ground in this section, exploring three different parts of speech. You should now feel better about your knowledge of how we use adjectives, articles, and adverbs to modify other words in our sentences (and, in the case of adverbs, entire clauses and sentences). The various forms of these parts of speech take time to master, however, so we encourage you to start paying attention to how you yourself are using them within the sentences you create, and to start noticing the adjectives, articles, and adverbs in the sentences you encounter in your daily life. We also encourage you to go to the "Quizzes" section to take the quiz on adjectives, articles, and adverbs.

Of course, there are two more parts of speech remaining, so let's get to the final section of the unit, which explores those little parts of speech known as prepositions and conjunctions.

1.4 Prepositions and Conjunctions

Introduction

This final section in our unit on words focuses on prepositions and conjunctions, the words that hold our sentences together. Before we begin discussing these parts of speech and their subcategories, we will start by first identifying some simple examples.

Read the following sentence:

> **Because English is used around the world, and people are learning it in every country, if you are interested in teaching it, you can succeed within the field of TEFL.**

That's a long, complicated sentence, and the prepositions and conjunctions are holding it together. Can you find them all?

The prepositions are *around, within, in.* The conjunctions are *Because, and, if.*

Prepositions can demonstrate spatial relationships (e.g., around the world), or act as a complement to other parts of speech, like verbs (succeed within) and adjectives (interested in).

Conjunctions are used to connect clauses in a sentence, and they have two major subcategories. Coordinating conjunctions join two independent words, phrases or clauses (e.g., *world and people*). Subordinating conjunctions join an independent clause with one or more dependent clauses (e.g., *Because English, if you are*).

Let's learn more about these parts of speech. Once more, we will look at the text about TEFL and see some quick definitions of examples within. Then expanded sections about each part of speech will provide more in-depth information.

Objectives

- Identify and differentiate various prepositions
- Identify and differentiate conjunctions, including the following:
    - Coordinating conjunctions
    - Subordinating conjunctions

Prepositions in Context: A Text about TEFL

Once more, take a look at our text about TEFL. We count 12 prepositions within. Are you able to spot any of them?

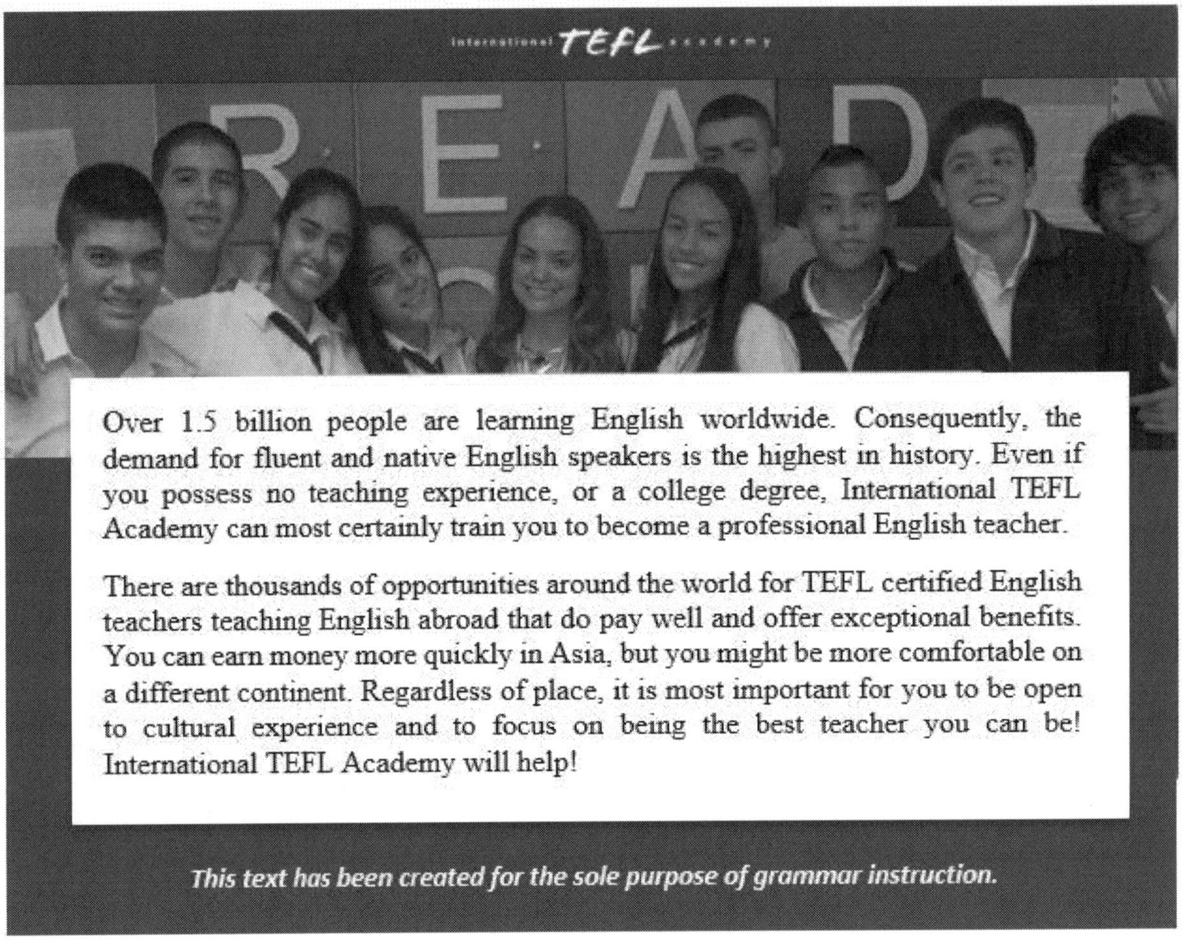

You can find all of the prepositions highlighted on the next page in **bold**.

Identification of Prepositions in Context

Here are the prepositions, highlighted in all of their minute glory.

Let's use some of these examples to explore the roles of prepositions.

Prepositions show a relationship between words in a sentence. Commonly, this relationship is spatial or temporal, placing other parts of a sentence in time and space.

> **around the world** (preposition)
> **in Asia** (preposition)
> **on a different continent** (preposition)

Prepositions can also follow numerous other parts of speech, serving to connect multiple words into various phrases that play a similar role to that part of speech alone.

> **the demand for fluent speakers** (preposition – noun phrase)
> **focus on being** (preposition – verb phrase)
> **most important for you** (preposition – adjective phrase)
> **Regardless of place** (preposition – adverb phrase)

Those are the main roles of prepositions and some examples from our text. Now let's expand upon them and look at some different examples.

Prepositions

Prepositions show a relationship between words in a sentence. They can be relatively easy to implement into lesson plans, but difficulties for students often arise because certain words and phrases are always followed by specific prepositions. These patterns are usually a matter of agreed-upon usage (as opposed to any meaning-based rules). Here are some examples of different types of prepositions.

Prepositions of place—including *on, in, next to, above, below*—describe the spatial relationship between two or more objects.

I got on a bus, but she got in a car.
There is a mistake in the picture on page 12.
He was sitting at the bar among his friends.

Prepositions of time—including *around, at, before, during, on, throughout*—describe various temporal relationships.

I'll see you at 10 a.m. on Monday in 2019.
I had to wake up before 5 a.m. several times throughout the week.

Prepositions like *about, at, of, for, from, with* are also commonly used in combination with specific adjectives and verbs. This type of common combination of words is called ***collocation***. Again, these uses follow individual patterns that differ from adjective to adjective and from verb to verb, and they occasionally differ in connection with the same adjective or verb, depending on the object of the verb or phrase.

Here are some common verb and preposition collocations:

Czech differs from Slovak in several ways.
I plan on abstaining from alcohol while I live abroad.
After we asked for her help, she united with us.
She accused me of everything. (not *for*)
And she blamed me for everything. (not *of*)

Here are some common adjective and preposition collocations:

I'm enthusiastic about becoming proficient in a foreign language.
My son is interested in math.
Nobody is immune from culture shock, but it's nothing to be afraid of.

I'm bad <u>at</u> math. (not *with* math)
And I'm bad <u>with</u> children. (not *at* children)

This concludes our consideration of prepositions. Although it may have seemed relatively short (at least in comparison to some of the other parts of speech), don't let that fool you. Prepositions play important roles in our sentences, and their correct usage can be tricky. It is important for teachers to be aware of this, knowing that because the correct choice of preposition is determined on a case-by-case basis, largely depending on the words around it, these little parts of speech are notoriously difficult for students who are learning a second language (in all languages, not just English).

In any case, let's move on to our eighth and final part of speech: conjunctions.

Conjunctions in Context: A Text about TEFL

We are now ready for our final part of speech: conjunctions. One last time, see if you are able to identify any of the conjunctions within our text about TEFL. There are seven of them (and one of those seven is a combination of two words).

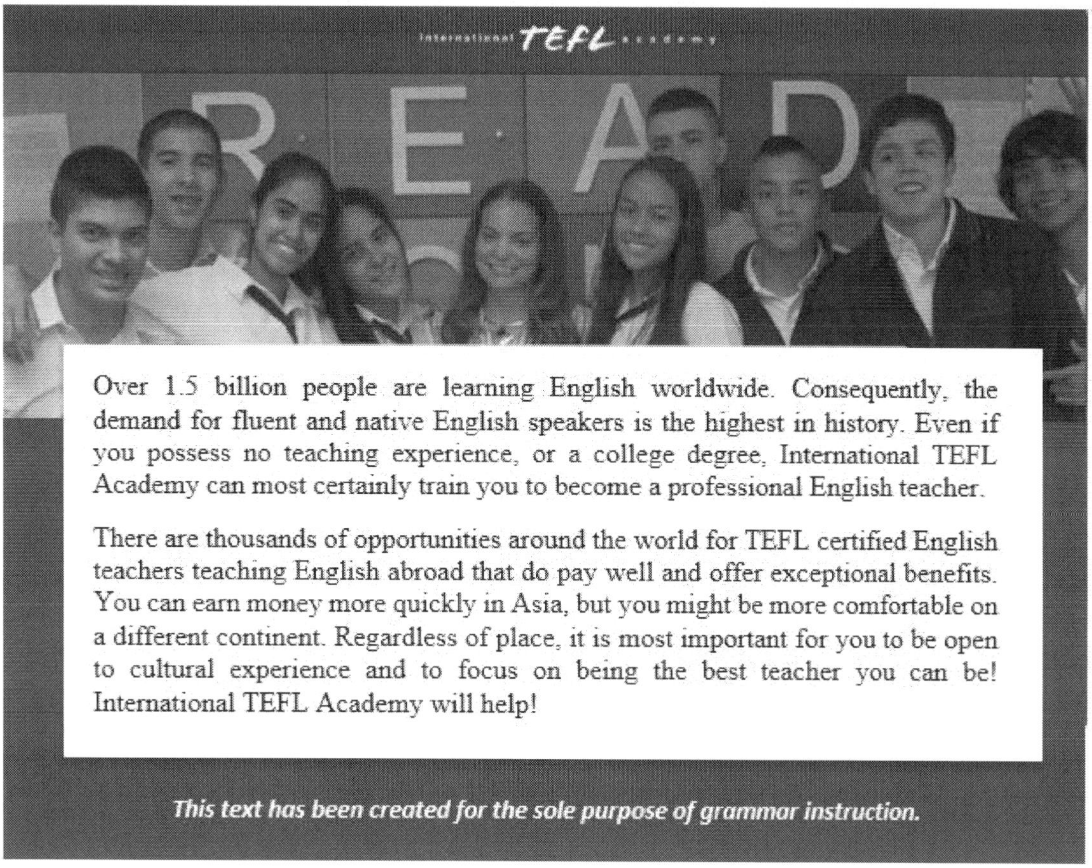

Do you think you have found any of the conjunctions? The answer is on the next page.

Identification of Conjunctions in Context

Here is the text again, with all seven of the conjunctions in **bold**.

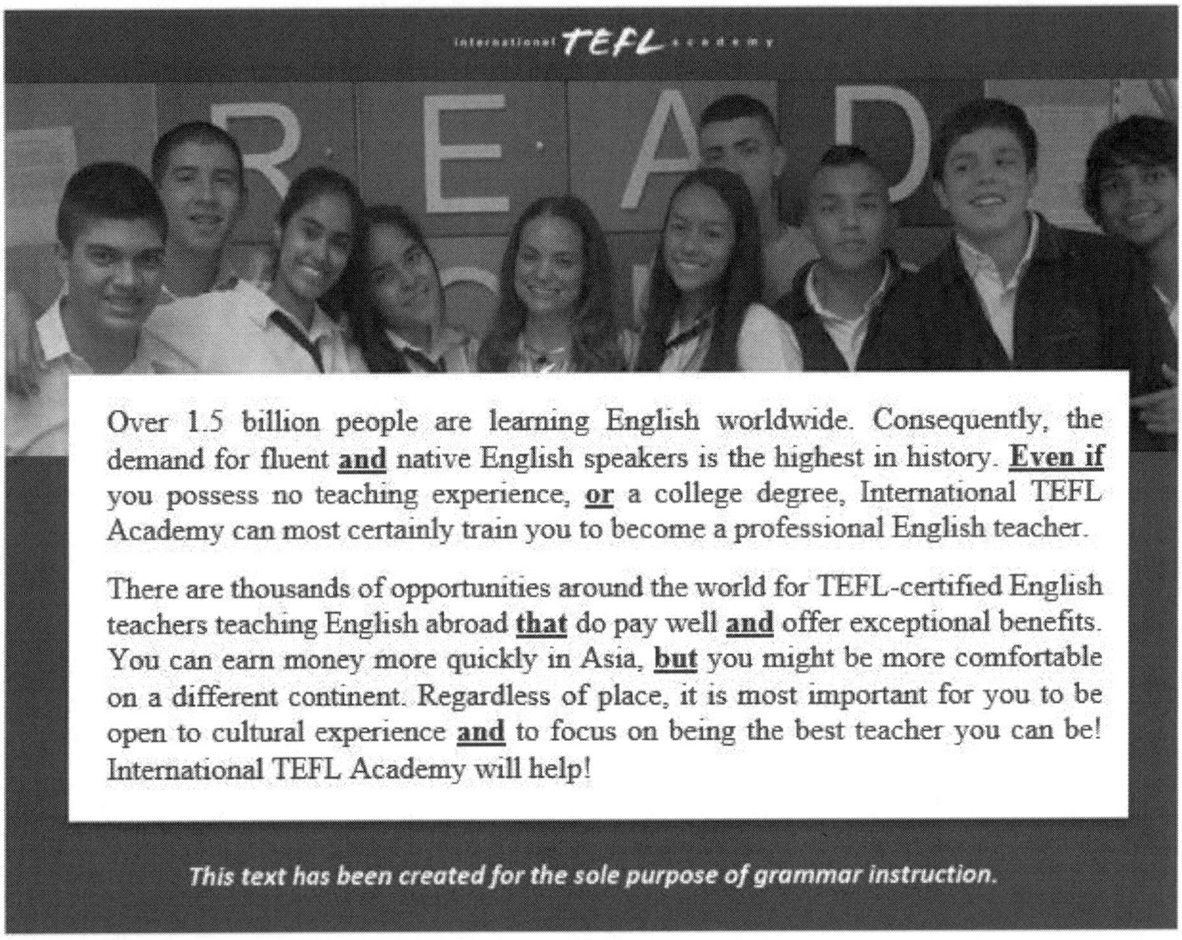

Let's look closer at some of the examples from the text.

Conjunctions connect two or more units of language (words, phrases, or clauses); they can be either coordinating conjunctions or subordinating conjunctions.

Coordinating conjunctions provide equal status for different units of language and create lists and compound sentences.

but (conjunction – coordinating)
and (conjunction – coordinating)
or (conjunction – coordinating)

Subordinating conjunctions connect two or more clauses into complex sentences.

Even if (conjunction – subordinating)
that (conjunction – subordinating)

The differences between these two types of conjunctions may be bigger than you think, so let's start by taking a closer look at each type in turn.

Conjunctions

Generally speaking, ***conjunctions*** connect two or more units of language (words, phrases, or clauses) to form a relationship between those units. However, this is a major oversimplification of the myriad roles that conjunctions can play, and the two major subcategories of conjunctions—coordinating and subordinating—are used in vastly different ways to create new and meaningful connections.

It is important to understand these two subcategories of conjunction and how they help us to create meaning in English, so let's dive in and explore coordinating conjunctions first.

Coordinating Conjunctions

Coordinating conjunctions connect two or more units of language that have equal status in a sentence (and sometimes across sentences). The seven main coordinating conjunctions in English are *for and, nor, but, or, yet, so*. (An easy way to remember them is with the mnemonic FANBOYS.) Let's look at some examples of how these conjunctions coordinate different language units.

The conjunctions *and, or* coordinate two or more words or phrases to create lists.

He was walking <u>and</u> chewing gum. (verbs)
I'll take water, milk, <u>or</u> a soda. (nouns)
The building was tall <u>and</u> imposing. (adjectives)
Was he walking quickly <u>or</u> slowly? (adverbs)
Was he walking quickly <u>or</u> running slowly? (verb phrases)
We need lots of ice, some cold drinks, <u>and</u> all of our friends! (noun phrases)

In addition, the conjunctions *and, or, but, so* can coordinate two or more independent clauses (S+V constructions that can stand alone as a sentence) to create new, expanded sentences with balanced clauses, which are called ***compound sentences***[1.8]. Let's look at them in turn.

The conjunction *and* combines two clauses to show added information.

We went to the restaurant, <u>and</u> I had a sandwich. (conjunction – coordinating)

The conjunction *or* combines two clauses to contrast different choices.

We can work together, <u>or</u> we can do it the hard way. (conjunction – coordinating)

The conjunction *<u>but</u>* combines two clauses to show contrast.

She wanted to see a movie, <u>but</u> I wanted to eat. (conjunction – coordinating)

The conjunction *so* combines two clauses to show a result (with the *so–* clause showing the result of the other clause).

We were all very tired, so everyone went home. (conjunction – coordinating)

These are just the coordinating conjunctions, which are relatively small in number. There are many more conjunctions of the subordinating variety. Let's take a look at some of them.

NOTE 1.8: For more about and examples of clauses and compound/complex sentences, see Unit 2.

Subordinating Conjunctions

Subordinating conjunctions connect two or more clauses into a new sentence called a ***complex sentence***[1.8]. Complex sentences have at least one independent clause and one or more dependent (or subordinate) clauses. Look at the following compound sentence that uses the subordinating conjunction *if.*

If you want to learn more grammar, there are many great resources available.
(dependent clause) (independent clause)

We know that the first clause is dependent because it cannot stand alone as a separate sentence; it needs to be subordinated to another clause. We know that the second clause is independent because it can stand alone as a complete sentence.

There are many subordinating conjunctions in English. Some of the most common are *after, although, because, before, if, when, while*. Note that when the independent clause comes first, no comma is used, but if the dependent clause comes first, a comma is needed.

I moved to South Korea after I finished my TEFL course.
(independent clause) (dependent clause)
After I finished my TEFL course, I moved to South Korea.
(dependent clause) (independent clause)

Here are more examples of complex sentences that include subordinating conjunctions:

Although I can't speak Russian, I can read it fairly well. (conjunction – sub.)
I want to work in Italy because my uncle lives there. (conjunction – sub.)
When you start teaching, this knowledge will be handy. (conjunction – sub.)
He was listening to the radio while he brushed his teeth. (conjunction – sub.)
I couldn't label parts of speech before I saw this book. (conjunction – sub.)

Finally, it should be noted that a word is a subordinating conjunction only if it is used to create a complex sentence—it connects two S+V clauses. Otherwise, it is some other part of speech. Take the following two sentences, which are very similar in meaning and which both use the word *before*.

I couldn't label parts of speech <u>before</u> I saw this module. (conjunction – sub.)
I couldn't label parts of speech <u>before</u> this module. (preposition)

In the first sentence, the word *before* is a subordinating conjunction because it connects two clauses (or S+V constructions) creating a complex sentence. In the second sentence, there is only one clause (S+V construction), so *before* is a preposition of time (and the sentence is simple, not complex).

This represents just a small sample of the conjunctions we use to create complex sentences. You can find a larger list of subordinating conjunctions in Appendix 3.

Conclusion

This concludes not only our section about prepositions and conjunctions but also our entire unit on words. No book could possibly teach you every nuance and form of the parts of speech of English, but we hope that this unit has you feeling more confident in your knowledge of these crucial building blocks of our English sentences. To that end, it is a good idea to go to the "Quizzes" section of the book and take the quiz on prepositions and conjunctions (as well as the other parts of speech, if you haven't already done so).

Speaking of sentences, that is the topic and title of the next unit of our book, in which we explore how the parts of speech are used to construct larger chunks of meaning via phrases, clauses, sentences, and questions. In the meantime, it is a good idea to start taking closer notice of the sentences you see and use in your everyday life. Can you identify all of the parts of speech within?

UNIT 2 SENTENCES

Introduction to Sentences

In this unit, we move away from individual words and start looking at how those building blocks are used to construct larger chunks of meaning. We will approach the concept of sentences in the English language via two main sections.

Organization of Unit

The unit contains two sections about the formation of sentences. The sections of Unit 2 are organized as follows:

1. Sentence Formation
2. Question Formation

"Sentence Formation" starts with an FAQ for new English teachers at a school in Japan, which provides a clear context for some of the section's examples. Then we consider the various types of sentences in the English language, followed by some structures that occur within and across sentences. There is an expanded section on clauses, followed by a section that explores some common mistakes in forming sentences.

"Question Formation" follows a similar pattern, starting with an EFL student exit questionnaire to provide context. We then consider the various types of questions in English and conclude with some common errors that learners demonstrate when forming questions. Now, let's explore the sections on sentence formation!

NOTE 2.1: The content in this unit is intended for use by teachers of English, not students of English as a second/foreign language. For example, one portion of the "Question Formation" section discusses the difference between subject-based and predicate-based *Wh–* questions. This is an important distinction, but it is not provided here in language that you should use with your lower level learners (but those learners should start forming questions as soon as possible). In short, the content here is designed to make you a more knowledgeable teacher, one with a more exhaustive explicit language knowledge and who is better prepared to answer student questions about the English language. It is not intended to be used as the sole basis for your future lesson plans. For ideas about how to implement the knowledge from this book into your lesson plans (and in alignment with the skills of reading, listening, speaking, and writing), see the various chapters of *The Fundamentals of Teaching English as a Foreign Language*.

2.1 Sentence Formation

Introduction

Look at the word cloud below containing terms from the unit on parts of speech. Do you recall definitions for many of these terms?

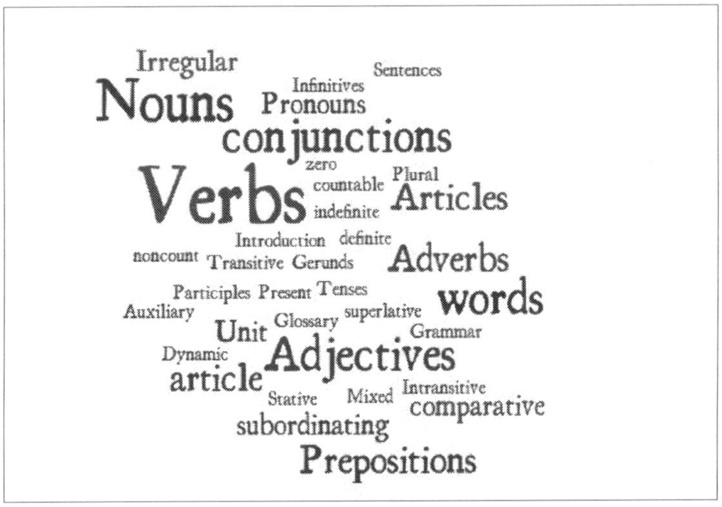

Now that you have studied all of these terms, consider the myriad ways in which we can form sentences using these different parts of speech.

This section contains information about sentence types and structure. We will start by looking at the target language in the context of a Frequently Asked Questions list for incoming teachers at a school in Japan. Then we will look specifically at categorizing sentences into four types:

1. Declarative
2. Interrogative
3. Imperative
4. Exclamatory

After that, you'll be given information about basic word order, phrases, and the two basic clause types, as well as how they fit into sentence structure, including simple, compound, complex, and compound/complex sentences. Finally, we will look at different clause types used in complex sentences.

Objectives

- Identify different sentence types in context
- Define basic word order in English
- List the elements of basic clauses in sentences
- Distinguish between simple, compound, complex, and compound/complex sentences
- Identify noun, adjective, and adverb clauses in context
- Identify correct comma usage with adjective and adverb clauses

Use in Context: FAQ for Incoming Teachers

Read the following FAQ list that a TEFL teacher wrote to help incoming teachers to her school in Japan. This FAQ is designed to help teachers prepare for their first day at work. While reading, think about the different sentence types and structures used in the FAQ.

FAQs for New Foreign Assistant Language Teachers

Yaotome Junior High School

Travel Rules Dress Code Language

What is the best way to travel to Kamo JHS on a daily basis?

Many teachers drive, but if you don't have a car, you can take the subway, bike, or walk. The subway is of course more expensive, but it is also more convenient. Get off at Yaotome Station. The school is about a 5-minute walk from the station.

I know that Japanese people have rules about wearing shoes indoors. What kind of shoes should I wear to school?

You can wear any type of shoe to school. When you get to school, you'll take off your shoes and store them in your locker after you change into your indoor shoes. Bring indoor shoes on your first day. Whatever type of shoe you wear indoors is fine, but be sure to only wear them indoors!

Is there a dress code?

There isn't an official dress code for teachers, but teachers should dress professionally. Do not wear jeans or shorts. Most Japanese teachers also dress fairly modestly.

Is it okay if I don't speak Japanese?

Yes, it's totally fine! The teachers at your school won't expect you to speak Japanese because this isn't a requirement of the JET Programme. At our school, there are two Japanese teachers of English who can help translate for you. And, you'll quickly pick up Japanese phrases that will be useful to you in your daily life here.

Identification of Sentences in Context

Let's examine the different sentence types and structures by looking at some examples from the FAQ list.

Table 2.1 Sentence Types and Structures	
Sentence Type: Function of Sentences	
Sentence Type	**Examples**
Declarative	There isn't an official dress code for teachers, but teachers should dress professionally. The school is about a 5-minute walk from the station.
Interrogative	What is the best way to travel to Kamo JHS on a daily basis? Is there a dress code?
Imperative	Bring indoor shoes on your first day. Get off at Yaotome Station.
Exclamatory	Whatever type of shoe you wear indoors is fine, but be sure to only wear them indoors! Yes, it's totally fine!
Sentence Structure: Complexity of Sentences	
Sentence Type	**Examples**
Simple	Most Japanese teachers also dress fairly modestly. The school is about a 5-minute walk from the station.
Compound	There isn't an official dress code for teachers, but teachers should dress professionally. The subway is of course more expensive, but it is also more convenient.
Complex	When you get to school, you'll take off your shoes and store them in your locker after you change into your indoor shoes. The teachers at your school won't expect you to speak Japanese because this isn't a requirement of the JET Programme.
Compound/ complex	Whatever type of shoe you wear indoors is fine, but be sure to only wear them indoors! Many teachers drive, but if you don't have a car, you can take the subway, bike, or walk.

Table 2.1 serves as an introduction that provides a glimpse of just how varied sentence structure can be. Explanations for each sentence type and structure are presented in the following sections.

Sentence Types

One basic way of understanding sentences is to categorize them into different types. In the following classification system, a sentence can be labeled ***declarative, interrogative, imperative***, or ***exclamatory***. Table 2.2 describes each sentence type with examples, a short explanation, and indication of the type of punctuation typically used.

Table 2.2 Sentence Types with Punctuation

Sentence Type	Examples	Explanation	Punctuation
Declarative	That movie was suspenseful. This chocolate cake tastes rich. I've taught English for about 3 years. She's reading.	States a fact or an opinion	Period
Interrogative	Was the movie suspenseful? Do you like the chocolate cake? How long have you taught English? Why is she reading so late?	Poses a question	Question mark
Imperative	Let's go out. Please join me for lunch. Watch your step! Don't bother her!	Gives a command or suggestion (the subject *you* is dropped but is understood)	Period or exclamation point
Exclamatory	Ruth just won the lottery! I can't believe it! We should celebrate!	Expresses excitement, shock, or surprise	Exclamation point

Sentence Structure: Word Order, Phrases, and Clauses

Another way to understand sentences is to look at sentence structure. Basic understanding of word order, phrases, and clauses is needed to fully understand sentence structure. This section describes the elements of word order, phrases, and clauses.

Word Order

Simple word order in English follows the SVO formula: *subject + verb + object.*

The *verb + object* part of the formula is also known as the predicate of a sentence. Nouns and pronouns, which are discussed in depth in Unit 1 of this book, make up the subject and object of sentences. (Subjects and objects can also consist of noun phrases.) Unit 1 also contains information about different types of verbs that can be used in this formula. It should also be noted that only transitive verbs require an object. Intransitive verbs are verbs that do not require an object, so sentences with that type of verb may be only SV, for example, *He slept.*

Word order in English can deviate from the basic SVO formula in different situations. As stated in Table 2.2, imperative sentences imply the subject *you* but do not include it, for example, *Watch your step!* Therefore, imperative sentences lack the S in the SVO formula. Two other deviations are when we form questions and when we use the passive voice. Both of these situations are discussed more in depth in their respective sections in this grammar book.

It is important to understand, for comparison, that English language reliance on word order is not the standard for all languages. There are languages with entirely different word order formulas, and some languages rely entirely on inflection of all parts of speech, rendering word order (almost) completely flexible. Table 2.3 summarizes basic word order formulas from other languages.

Table 2.3 Word Order Distribution of Languages

Basic Word Order	Proportion of Languages	Examples
Subject-[Verb-Object]	42%	English, Indonesian
Subject-[Object- Verb]	45%	Japanese, Turkish
Verb-Subject-Object	9%	Welsh, Zapotec
[Verb-Object]-Subject	3%	Malagasy
[Object-Verb]-Subject	1%	
Object-Subject-Verb	0%	

Adapted from Tomlin (1986)

Phrases

A ***phrase*** is a group of words that does not contain both a subject and a predicate. Phrases are used as a single part of speech. A phrase cannot stand alone; it must be used in a clause. The examples below show some different types of phrases used in independent clauses.

He walked <u>the long way home</u>. (noun phrase)

She drove her <u>car over the bridge</u>. (prepositional phrase)

Clauses

A ***clause*** is a group of words containing a subject and a predicate. The subject tells us who or what (person, place, thing, idea) the sentence is about, and the predicate tells us more information (actions or characteristics) about that subject. Table 2.4 gives examples of subjects and predicates.

Table 2.4 Examples of Subjects and Predicates

Subject	Predicate
The cat	meowed.
The concept	was interesting.
The mountains	are beautiful.

Independent Clauses

An ***independent clause*** is a subject and predicate, following the basic SVO word order, that can stand alone as a sentence. It contains a subject and a verb, and sometimes more information. All of the examples in Table 2.4 are independent clauses.

Dependent Clauses

A ***dependent clause*** (also called a ***subordinate clause***) also contains a subject and verb. However, a dependent clause does not constitute a complete sentence and cannot stand alone. Dependent clauses often begin with subordinating conjunctions like *since*, *although, because, while.*

(See the "Prepositions and Conjunctions" section of Unit 1 for more information about subordinating conjunctions.)

In the following examples, the addition of a subordinating conjunction means that the clause cannot stand on its own, and thus is dependent:

<u>Because</u> of the rain ...

<u>Since</u> I was three years old ...

Although I ate there often ...
While I was doing my homework ...

Sentence Structure: Degrees of Complexity

In addition to classifying sentences as different types (declarative, interrogative, imperative, and exclamatory), sentences can also be defined by structure. This section defines four basic sentence structures:

1. Simple
2. Compound
3. Complex
4. Compound/complex

Simple Sentences

A ***simple sentence*** contains a subject, verb, and sometimes an object. There is only one independent clause and no dependent clause.

Here are a few of the different patterns, based on the basic SVO formula, that simple sentences follow in English:

Bob slept. (*subject + verb*)
Bob brought my bag. (*subject + verb + direct object*)
Bob gave her a gift. (*subject + verb + indirect object + direct object*)
Bob gave a gift to her. (*subject + verb + direct object + indirect object*)

The first example contains an intransitive verb, which does not take an object. The second and third examples contain transitive verbs, which do take objects.

Note the difference between indirect and direct objects. A direct object answers the questions *who(m)* or *what*. In the second example above, the direct object *bag* tells us what Bob brought. An indirect object answers the questions *to whom, for whom, for what*. In the third and fourth examples above, the indirect object *her* answers the question *to whom*.

The tense of the verb and additional phrases, adjectives, or adverbs do not change a sentence from simple to complex. The examples below show varying degrees of complexity in simple sentences. They are all simple sentences even though the last sentence is much longer, and seemingly more complex, than the first sentence.

Hugo ran a mile today.
Hugo ran a mile today in the blistering heat.
Hugo bravely ran a mile today in the blistering heat.

Simple sentences can also appear more complex with multiple subjects and/or verbs.

My friend, my cat, and I went to the park.
I ate pizza, drank a beer, and slept.
My mother and I scrubbed and rinsed the car.

Compound Sentences

A ***compound sentence*** consists of two independent clauses joined by a comma and a coordinating conjunction: *for, and, nor, but, or, yet, so.* (See "Prepositions and Conjunctions" section in Unit 1 for more information about coordinating conjunctions.)

Hugo ran a mile today, yet he looks well rested.
Hugo ran a mile today, so he's having a big dinner tonight.
Hugo ran a mile today, but his wife prefers swimming.

Like simple sentences, compound sentences can contain independent clauses that appear more complex because of the addition of nouns, verbs, phrases, adjectives, or adverbs.

Consider the following compound sentence:

Hugo and I ran a mile today, and we will walk or run again tomorrow.

In this sentence, we see two subjects: *Hugo, I.* We also see two verbs: *walk, run.* This sentence appears more complex than the previous examples, but it is still a compound sentence.

Complex Sentences

A complex sentence contains a dependent clause attached to an independent clause. Dependent clauses (underlined below) are categorized as ***adjective clauses, adverb clauses***, or ***noun clauses***, and begin with such words as *that, who, when, why, where, whereas, if*[2.2], *because, although, before, whether*.

The lake house where we got married is being renovated.
The student who you met is going back to Brazil next week.
We're not going to the fireworks display this year because the park gets too crowded.
Although a tropical vacation sounds enticing, we need to pay off our credit cards first.
If you travel abroad, you will see your own culture with new eyes.

NOTE 2.2: Clauses containing *if* are used in conditionals. These are discussed in depth in the "Conditionals" section of Unit 4.

Compound/Complex Sentences

A ***compound/complex sentence*** contains at least two independent clauses (in italics below) as well as at least one dependent clause (underlined below). Here is one example with the two independent clauses combined with a coordinating conjunction as well as one dependent clause:

> ***We're not going to the fireworks display this year* <u>because the park gets too crowded</u>, but *I will meet you later at the restaurant.***

Dependent Clauses

Different types of ***dependent clauses*** are used in complex and compound/complex sentences. These clauses function as nouns, adjectives, or adverbs. This section describes noun, adjective, and adverb clauses and provides information about the usage of each.

As an introduction to these clauses, Table 2.5 lists keywords used in each type of clause. The following sections will give more information about the function of these keywords in dependent clauses.

Table 2.5 Keywords by Clause Type	
Words to introduce noun clauses	That; which; who; whom; whose; what; whatever; whichever; whoever; whomever; how; if; when; whenever; where; wherever; whether; why
Words to introduce adjective clauses	That; which; who; whom; whose; when; where
Words to introduce adverb clauses	After; although; as; as if; because; before; even though; if; in order that; since; so that; than; that; though; unless; until; when; where; whether; while

Adapted from A Writer's Reference *(Hacker & Sommers, 2011, p. 325)*

Noun Clauses

A ***noun clause*** is a dependent clause that functions as a noun. Compare the two sentences below to see how a clause can function as a noun.

> **I'll have the <u>salad</u>.**
>
> **I'll have <u>whatever she is having</u>.**

The first sentence contains a noun, *salad*, acting as the object of the sentence. The second sentence contains a noun clause, *whatever she is having*, acting as the object of the sentence.

Noun clauses begin with keywords, such as *that, which, who, whom, whose, what, whatever, whichever, whoever, whomever, how, if, when, whenever, where, wherever, whether, why*. (Keywords can either be subordinating conjunctions or relative pronouns, depending on their use). These clauses can act as the subject or object of a sentence or as the object of a preposition.

Subject of a Sentence

What he said is totally unacceptable.
Whenever you want to go is fine with me.

Object of a Sentence

I don't know when they are coming.
Can you tell me where he went?

Object of a Preposition

I am not responsible for what he decided to do.
I asked about why they went home.

The subordinating conjunction is often omitted in speech when we use noun clauses beginning with *that*; however, the subordinating conjunction is often included in formal writing.

I know he is happy. (subordinating conjunction omitted in speech)
I know that he is happy. (subordinating conjunction used in formal writing)

Adjective Clauses

Adjective clauses, also called ***relative clauses***, are dependent clauses that function as adjectives. Compare the following two sentences to see how a clause can function as an adjective.

The hungry child ate everything on his plate.
The child, who was very hungry, ate everything on his plate.

The first sentence contains an adjective, *hungry*, modifying the subject, *child*, of the sentence. The second sentence contains an adjective clause, *who was very hungry*, modifying that same subject.

Adjective clauses closely follow the nouns they are modifying and begin with the relative pronouns *that, which, who, whom. Who* and *whom* are used for people, *which* is used for things, and *that* can be used for people or things. These relative pronouns are sometimes used as the subject, the object, or the object of a preposition in the adjective clause. Each example below shows how two sentences can be combined using adjective clauses and the different ways in which those clauses can be written.

Relative Pronoun as Subject

I saw the man. He gave me the book.
I saw the man who gave me the book.
I saw the man that gave me the book.

Relative Pronoun as Object

The dinner wasn't very good. We had it last night.
The dinner which we had last night wasn't very good.
The dinner that we had last night wasn't very good.
The dinner we had last night[2.3] wasn't very good.

Relative Pronoun as Object of Preposition

The recital was excellent. We listened to it last week.
The recital which we listened to last week was excellent.
The recital that we listened to last week was excellent.
The recital we listened to last week[2.3] was excellent.

NOTE 2.3: The relative pronoun can be omitted in these cases.

The keywords *whose, where, when* can also be used in adjective clauses.

The student whose essay I read won the grand prize.
The city where she lives is overcrowded.
The time when I met you was the best time of my life.

Punctuation with Adjective Clauses

Essential clauses. Commas are not used if the information in the adjective clause is necessary for identification of the modified noun. These are called ***essential clauses***.

The children who are playing over there should be in class.

The subject, *children*, in the example sentence above is not specific, and the essential adjective clause, *who are playing over there*, helps us identify which children we are talking about. In this case, no commas are used.

In essential clauses, any appropriate relative pronoun may be used.

The children who (or that) are playing over there should be in class.

Nonessential clauses. Commas are used in the information if the adjective clause is not necessary for identification of the modified noun. These are called ***nonessential clauses***.

Mr. Baker, <u>whom I met yesterday</u>, is a great teacher.

The subject, *Mr. Baker*, in the example sentence above is specific because we know who Mr. Baker is even without the extra information in the adjective clause, *whom I met yesterday*. In this case, commas are used around the adjective clause to indicate that it does not contain essential information.

In nonessential clauses, the relative pronoun *that* may not be used.

Mr. Baker, <u>whom (or who) I met yesterday</u>, is a great teacher.

Self-check. Consider the following two sentences. The only difference is the presence or absence of a comma, but that comma creates a huge difference in meaning.

I hate politicians who lie.
I hate politicians, who lie.

Can you describe the difference in meaning using the above information about essential and nonessential clauses?

Answer. In the first sentence, the subject of the verb, *hate*, is *politicians who lie*, meaning that the speaker does not hate all politicians, only that subset of politicians that tells lies. The lack of comma shows us that the adjective clause, *who lie*, is essential and cannot be removed, so the first sentence cannot be broken into two separate sentences. In the second sentence, on the other hand, the subject of the verb, *hate,* is *politicians*, meaning all politicians. The comma shows us that the adjective clause, *who lie,* is nonessential, providing extra information about politicians. The second sentence can be broken into two separate sentences: *I hate politicians. Politicians lie.*

Adverb Clauses

Adverb clauses are dependent clauses that function as adverbs. Compare the following two sentences to see how a clause can function as an adverb.

I jogged <u>slowly</u>.
I jogged <u>after I ate dinner</u>.

The first sentence contains an adverb, *slowly*, modifying the verb, *jogged*. The second sentence contains an adverb clause, *after I ate dinner*, modifying that same verb.

Adverb clauses show us relationships (time, cause and effect, contrast, and condition) between ideas in a sentence and can be inserted before or after the independent clause in a sentence. Adverb clauses begin with ***subordinating conjunctions*** that help us see those relationships.

Time Relationships

Subordinating conjunctions—including *after, before, when, while, as, by the time, since, until, till, as soon as, once, as long as, so long as, whenever, every time, the first time, the last time, the next time*—can be used in adverb clauses indicating time relationships. The following sentences with underlined adverb clauses show examples of time relationships:

<u>When I got to school</u>, I was very tired.

He did his homework <u>before he played video games</u>.

<u>As soon as the rain stops</u>, I'll go outside to weed the garden.

Cause-and-Effect Relationships

Subordinating conjunctions—including *because, now that, since*—can be used in adverb clauses indicating cause-and-effect relationships. The following sentences with underlined adverb clauses show examples of cause-and-effect relationships:

She didn't watch the movie <u>because she was too sleepy</u>.

<u>Now that I'm an adult</u>, I wish I could change some things about my childhood.

<u>Since he was late to class</u>, the professor didn't let him take the quiz.

Contrasting Relationships

The subordinating conjunction *while* can be used to show a contrasting relationship between two parts of a sentence. The following sentences with underlined adverb clauses show examples of contrasting relationships.

I like milk in my coffee, <u>while my husband prefers his coffee black</u>.

<u>While my town in Colorado is very sunny</u>, some parts of the mountains are very cloudy and get more precipitation.

Conditional Relationships[2.4]

The subordinating conjunctions *if, even if, unless, whether or not, in case, only if* can be used in adverb clauses indicating conditional relationships. The following sentences with underlined adverb clauses show examples of conditional relationships.

<u>If it is too windy</u>, I won't take my umbrella.

I will ride my bike <u>even if it is raining</u>.

NOTE 2.4: Conditional clauses are discussed in more depth in the "Conditionals" section in Unit 4.

Punctuation with Adverb Clauses

Comma usage with adverb clauses is very simple and can be understood with two simple rules.

1. If the dependent adverb clause precedes the independent clause in a sentence, the adverb clause is followed by a comma.

<u>When I got to school</u>, I was very tired.

As soon as the rain stops, I'll go outside to weed the garden.
Now that I'm an adult, I wish I could change some things about my childhood.
Because he was late to class, the professor didn't let him take the quiz.

2. If the dependent adverb clause comes after the independent clause, no comma is used.
He did his homework before he played video games.
She didn't watch the movie because she was too sleepy.
I will ride my bike even if it is raining.

One exception to the second rule is when we use the subordinating conjunction *while* to show contrast.
I like milk in my coffee, while my husband prefers his coffee black.

Common Mistakes

Two of the most common mistakes native and nonnative speakers make with sentence structure are writing sentence fragments and run-on sentences. This section shows how to identify these mistakes and how to correct them.

Sentence Fragments

Sentence fragments are incomplete sentences that do not contain a subject or verb. Sentence fragments are also common when people try to use a dependent clause as a stand-alone sentence.
Incorrect: **I already know the answer. Because I learned it in school.**

The dependent clause, *because I learned it in school*, cannot stand alone; thus, it is a sentence fragment.
Correct: **I already know the answer because I learned it in school.**

To fix this sentence fragment, the independent and dependent clauses should be combined to make a complex sentence. No comma is needed because the dependent clause follows the independent clause in the sentence.

Another way to fix this sentence fragment is to delete the subordinating conjunction *because* and separate the remaining independent clauses with a period. By doing this, the cause-and-effect relationship between the clauses isn't as prominent.
Correct: **I already know the answer. I learned it in school.**

Run-on Sentences

Run-on sentences occur when two or more independent clauses are joined incorrectly.

Incorrect: **My favorite movie is *The Princess Bride* it is so funny.**

This sentence contains two independent clauses: *My favorite move is The Princess Bride* and *it is so funny*.

Incorrect: **My favorite movie is *The Princess Bride*, it is so funny.**

Adding a comma between the two independent clauses does not make it correct. This is called a ***comma splice***.

The run-on sentence can be fixed in different ways. You can add a coordinating conjunction or a subordinating conjunction to make a compound or complex sentence, as in the first two following sentences. You can also add a semicolon or a period between the two independent clauses, as in the last two following sentences. Each different solution slightly changes the relationship between the clauses.

Correct:

My favorite movie is *The Princess Bride*, and it is so funny.
My favorite movie is *The Princess Bride* because it is so funny.
My favorite movie is *The Princess Bride*; it is so funny.
My favorite movie is *The Princess Bride*. It is so funny.

Conclusion

Now that you know more about the construction of different types of sentences, we can conclude this first section in our "Sentences" unit. We hope you have learned something new about clause types and how they make up simple, compound, and complex sentences. This information will be useful for you on a daily basis in your future classroom. As you can see from the contents of this section, comma usage, sentence fragments, and run-on sentences are just some of the common mistakes you will encounter in the EFL classroom.

There are quizzes with questions about sentence formation in the "Quizzes" section, and we encourage you to go there now and take them.

The next and final section in this unit focuses on the many variations of question formation.

2.2 QUESTION FORMATION

Introduction

The image above includes several of the different varieties of question types that exist in the English language. This section will introduce four question types in the context of a student questionnaire. Then the examples from the questionnaire will be broken down to address formation and grammatical differences. Finally, this section will provide insight into common pitfalls for ESL/EFL students.

Objectives

- Identify the formation and word order of a variety of question types in context
- Compare and contrast the form of *Wh–* subject, *Wh–* predicate, yes/no, and tag questions
- Explain the meaning and intent in using tag questions, including the impact of both positive and negative sentences preceding tag questions
- Identify common mistakes made with question formation

Use in Context: An English Student Questionnaire

Read the following questionnaire administered to an international student who came to the US to study English. Pay particular attention to the different types of questions that are used throughout.

> **English Program Questionnaire**
>
> **Name:** Zhang Wei
>
> **1. What year are you in the program?** I am in my last year.
>
> **2. Why did you want to learn English?** I selected English because I want to be a language teacher in my home country. Also, English is a good language to know for almost any career in the future, isn't it?
>
> **3. How would you describe your level before beginning the program?** I was probably at an intermediate level. I had studied in primary and high school. I also went to a one-month intensive language program in the UK.
>
> **4. What have been some of your favorite classes?** Advanced Conversation was my favorite class. It was very fun and useful!
>
> **5. Did you have the opportunity to travel while in the program?** Yes! I went to Yellowstone National Park and New York City. Great experiences!
>
> **6. Did you participate in the English conversation table?** I went at first, but stopped. Most people were in level 1 classes, so it wasn't challenging enough.
>
> **7. Have you found other resources outside of class to practice English**? I like to watch American movies. I also make friends in the cafeteria. There are always lots of other international students there, and you can usually chat with them. Also, I use different apps and online sites.
>
> **8. Are you satisfied with how your language skills have developed?** I feel pretty satisfied.
>
> **9. What suggestions do you have to improve the program?** I would have liked better feedback on my work in the classes. I was not always sure how I was doing or what I should do to get better.

Identification of Question Types in Context

Let's examine the different question types by looking at some examples from our questionnaire.

Wh– Predicate Questions

What year are you in the program?
Why did you want to learn English?

Wh– Subject Questions

What have been some of your favorite classes?

Yes/No Questions

Did you have the opportunity to travel during the program?
Did you participate in the English conversation table?
Are you satisfied with how your language skills have developed?

Tag Questions

English is a good language to know for any career in the future, isn't it?

These examples serve as an introduction into the different types of questions that can be formed.

Common Question Words

Table 2.6 lists the most common question words and the type of information that is sought in each question.

Table 2.6 Common Question Words	
Question Word	**Desired Information**
Who?	person
What?	thing, action, concept
When?	time
Where?	location
Why?	reason, motive
How?	manner
More Specific Question Word (These words emphasize that the speaker is looking for more specific information.)	**Desired Information**
Whose?	ownership
Whom?	person
How much?	cost, amount (noncount)
How many?	quantity (count)

How long?	duration
How often?	frequency
How far?	distance
What kind (of)?	description
Which (one)?	choice between options

Now that you have considered question words and the information they elicit, we will take a more detailed look at question formation in the sections that follow.

Wh– Questions

This next section will explore the topic of *Wh–* question formation. The content will be broken into two main parts:

1. *Wh–* predicate questions
2. *Wh–* subject questions

Wh– Predicate Questions

Wh– predicate questions refer to a question whose answer is found in the predicate of the response. The predicate refers to the part of the sentence where the verb is found and where the verb is followed by additional information about the subject.

For example, the question *What is your professor's name?* can be answered by saying *Her name is Dr. Gates*. The information sought, *Dr. Gates*, is found in the predicate of that answer.

We usually form *Wh–* predicate questions in the following way:

Wh– question word + auxiliary or modal verb + subject + main verb.

Let's look more closely at a few examples. Notice that each question begins with one of the following question words: *who, whose, what, when, where, why, which, how*. Each of these examples follows the order shown above.

Why	**did**	**you**	**want**	**to learn English?**
(*Wh–* question word)	(auxiliary or modal verb)	(subject)	(main verb)	(rest of question)
How	**would**	**you**	**describe**	**your level … ?**
(*Wh–* question word)	(auxiliary or modal verb)	(subject)	(main verb)	(rest of question)

Keep in mind (as seen in the list of specific question words in the previous section), that when the information to be obtained through the question word is specified, we must keep that information together in the word order to emphasize this connection. This happens frequently with the question words *what, which, whose.* Read the following example:

What suggestions do you have to improve the program?

The question word is *what*, but the specific information to be obtained is *suggestions*, which is why the two should be kept together. The following is a similar question:

What year are you in the program?

Wh– Subject Questions

Wh– subject questions refer to a question whose answer is found in the subject of the response. The subject refers to the noun (person, place, thing, idea) that is doing the action of the sentence. For example, the question *Who has her book?* can be answered by saying *Max has her book.* The information sought, *Max*, is found in the subject of that answer.

We usually form *Wh–* subject questions with the following word order:

Wh– question word + main verb.

Observe how in the following example from the questionnaire, the *Wh–* question word replaces the subject of the sentence in such a way that the question is asking for the subject as its answer. In this case, when the question word is the subject, we change the structure by including the subject in the place of the *Wh–* question word. Note that *Wh–* subject questions do not contain an auxiliary verb.

What	**have been**	**some of your favorite classes?**
(*Wh–* question word)	(main verb)	(other elements)

We can see that the answer to the question will be the subject of the sentence. For example, one might answer with *Advanced Conversation was one of my favorite classes.*

Following are more examples of *Wh–* subject questions:

Who finished the homework? (I finished my homework.)
Who teaches history in this school? (Mr. Parker teaches history in this school.)
What was for homework for today? (Grammar exercises were assigned for today.)

Notice how the answer for each question can be found in the subject of the answer.

Yes/No Questions

Yes/no can be formed using auxiliary or modal verbs. All of these questions can be answered with a simple yes or no answer. By observing the interview carefully, we can see that the ESL student answers some questions with a greater degree of elaboration, but the question type in and of itself requires only a simple yes or no.

Yes/no questions follow the same word order presented in the previous section concerning *Wh–* predicate questions. However, the *Wh–* question word is removed. Notice this structure in the various question types below: *auxiliary verb (be, do, have) or modal verb + subject + main verb.*

Yes/No Questions with Auxiliary Verbs

Did	**you**	**have**	**the opportunity to travel while in the program?**
(auxiliary verb)	(subject)	(main verb)	(other elements)
Did	**you**	**participate**	**in the English conversation table?**
(auxiliary verb)	(subject)	(main verb)	(other elements)
Are	**you**	**satisfied**	**with your language skills?**
(auxiliary verb)	(subject)	(main verb)	(other elements)
Have	**you**	**found**	**other resources to practice English?**
(auxiliary verb)	(subject)	(main verb)	(other elements)

Yes/No Questions with Modal Verbs[2.4]

Could	**you**	**help**	**me with my English homework?**
(modal verb)	(subject)	(main verb)	(other elements)
Should	**I**	**take**	**an extra English course next semester?**
(modal verb)	(subject)	(main verb)	(other elements)

NOTE 2.5: Only two of many modal verbs are shown here. Learn more about the meaning and use of modal verbs in the "Modals" section of Unit 4.

Tag Questions

Tag questions do exactly as their name suggests. They are extra questions that we add or tag on to the end of statements. Tag questions are located at the end of the sentence and communicate a variety of meanings.

We can see in the following examples that the use of tag questions is more frequently seen in spoken English and used often in the informal register. Speakers can use tag questions for several reasons, as demonstrated in the examples below.

To Confirm

We use tag questions often for information that we already know the answer to, and we are simply seeking affirmation in the response.

This shirt is turquoise, <u>isn't it</u>?

To Ask for Help

Tag questions are a polite way to request information when we might need help in a particular situation.

You don't know if they're hiring, <u>do you</u>?

Invitations and Orders

One might use a tag question to politely invite someone to do something, and in most cases, these tag questions allow the responder to act, but no verbal response is necessary. Often when we are ordering someone to do something, the tone in the tag question is not polite. Both invitations and orders use the imperative/command form in the main sentence.

Turn off the lights, <u>won't you</u>? (polite)
Eat your dinner, <u>will you</u>? (not polite)

Tag Question Types

Positive Main Sentence/Negative Tag Question

As you look at the following examples, notice how tag questions that are added after a positive sentence are phrased with a negative.

English is a good language to know for any career in the future, isn't it?
You have already taken the test, haven't you?

Negative Main Sentence/Positive Tag Question

By contrast, questions tagged after a negative sentence, are phrased with the positive.

I couldn't be an interpreter or translator with just this degree, could I?
I hear they aren't doing the program this summer … that isn't true, is it?
They'll never come to my office hours, will they?

With Auxiliaries

When the main sentence uses an auxiliary verb, the same auxiliary verb is included in the tag.

This <u>isn't working</u>, <u>is</u> it?
They <u>have been</u> here before, <u>haven't</u> they?

Without Auxiliaries

When the main verb of the main sentence doesn't include an auxiliary, the tag question is created with a form of the verb *do*.

She <u>likes</u> country music, <u>doesn't</u> she?
I <u>made</u> a mistake, <u>didn't</u> I?

With Modals

When the main sentence uses a modal verb, that same modal is included in the tag.

He <u>couldn't</u> answer the professor's question, <u>could</u> he?
You <u>will</u> come to the party later, <u>won't</u> you?

***Exception: Tag Questions with* I am**

When the main sentence begins with *I am*, the verb *is/are* is used in the tag.

I'<u>m</u> a good singer, <u>aren't</u> I?

Common Mistakes

Let's take a look at some of the common mistakes made by nonnative speakers. Often it is the unique word order that questions require that can be confusing. Each example sentence below has an error that will be corrected and explained. Before reading the explanations, try to analyze the errors, and see if you are able to correct them.

Incorrect:

1. **What he was talking to you about?**
2. **Where was taken the picture?**
3. **How are ordered the books?**
4. **Where you did study?**
5. **It is true that she is leaving next year?**
6. **What do else I need to work on to get better?**
7. **I could open a travel business, could I?**

Correct:

1. **What <u>was he</u> talking to you about?**

This is a *Wh–* question. The subject should come after the auxiliary/modal verb.

2. **Where was <u>the picture taken</u>?**

This is a *Wh–* question. The main verb should come after the subject.

3. **How are <u>the books ordered</u>?**

This is a *Wh–*question. The main verb should come after the subject.

4. Where did you study?

This is a *Wh–* question. The subject should come after the auxiliary/modal verb.

5. Is it true that she is leaving next year?

This is a question that begins with the verb *be* and is also a yes/no question. The verb should come before the subject.

6. What else do I need to work on to get better?

This is a *Wh–* question in which the subject is what is being sought out by the speaker with the word *what*. The word *else* specifies or adds information to the subject and must not be separated from it.

7. I could open a travel business, couldn't I?

This is a tag question. When the sentence previous to a tag question is in the positive, the tag question should be formed with the negative, and vice versa.

Conclusion

After completing this section, you should have a better understanding of the complexities of question formation. You will not necessarily be teaching all of these complexities to your EFL students, but it is good for you, as the teacher, to be aware of how complicated question formation can be in English. It is also a good idea for you to take the quiz on question formation in the "Quizzes" section of this book.

With the conclusion of this section, we conclude Unit 2. In the next unit, we will examine the tense/aspect system of English, which includes the simple, continuous, perfect, and perfect continuous forms of the present, past, and future tenses.

UNIT 3 TENSES

Introduction to Tenses

In this unit, we move from words and sentences toward grammar, specifically the tense/aspect verb system of English. To fully explore this system, we first need to define tense and aspect and generally discuss how these facets of language construct English grammar. We will also look at the distinctions among form, meaning, and use as they pertain to language, as well as how those distinctions serve to organize the unit's sections. This will help you to better digest the information in the sections to come and assist you in applying that information to your language teaching.

Tense and Aspect

In relation to grammar, the term *tense* refers to the point or segment of time when an action occurs. Usually when we think about tenses, we think of three basic categories: the past, the present, and the future. The term *aspect* refers to the duration of an event, either within or between tenses. English has two aspects: perfect and continuous (or progressive). Tense and aspect are often combined to indicate a specific time reference, something that is probably best understood through examples of different grammatical constructions. The sections of this unit provide many such examples.

It's important to remember that some languages do not have tenses as we understand them. For example, Mandarin Chinese uses time expressions, such as yesterday or last week, to indicate time reference. A translation from Mandarin Chinese might look like, "I yesterday lunch eat pizza." In English, we have to conjugate the verb (change *eat* to *ate*) to express the same thought, "I ate pizza for lunch yesterday."

Different languages have different numbers of tenses. English has a total of 12 tense and tense-aspect combinations, summarized in Table 3.1.

Table 3.1 English Tenses				
	Simple	Continuous*	Perfect	Perfect Continuous*
Present	I do my homework on the weekends.	I am doing my homework now.	I have done my homework. Here it is.	I have been doing my homework since 6 a.m.
Past	I did my homework yesterday.	I was doing my homework when the telephone rang.	I had done my homework before I went to bed last night.	I had been doing my homework for three hours before I submitted it.
Future	If I have time, I will do my homework tomorrow.	I will be doing my homework tomorrow morning.	I will have done my homework by 11:59 p.m. next Sunday.	I will have been doing my homework for five hours by the time I finish it.

**Continuous aspect is also known as progressive. They are used interchangeably. Thus, present continuous = present progressive. Similarly, present perfect continuous = present perfect progressive.*

Form, Meaning, and Use

One common way to think about language, and to approach language instruction, is via the three dimensions of form, meaning, and use (see, for example, any textbook in the excellent *Grammar Dimensions* series, edited by Diane Larsen-Freeman, which are organized along these dimensions).

Form is related to the structure of grammar, or how it is written and pronounced. This could also be referred to as accuracy. Meaning is about what the grammar actually communicates, or what meaning is included within the grammatical structure in itself. Use signals the larger questions of when and why a structure is chosen, which could also be called situational/contextual appropriateness.

It is important to keep all three of these dimensions in focus when teaching and while proceeding through the various sections within this unit.

Organization of Unit

1. Present Simple and Present Continuous
2. Past Simple and Past Continuous
3. Future Simple and Future Continuous
4. Present Perfect and Present Perfect Continuous
5. Past Perfect and Past Perfect Continuous
6. Future Perfect and Future Perfect Continuous

Each of these sections begins with an introduction section, which includes the learning objectives of that section. Because meaningful input is so vital to language teaching in general, and grammar instruction in particular, the second part of each section presents authentic use in the guise of several real-world examples of the target structure in context. This is immediately followed by a section called "Explanation of Grammar in Context," in which the meaning of those examples is explained within the framework of the given context. This is followed by a discussion of the various forms that the structure can take, including affirmatives, negatives, and questions. You will then see further guidelines for how the structure communicates meaning, followed by additional contexts for use. This organization follows an inductive approach to language teaching, in which authentic use and meaning are primary drivers of instruction, established before explicit focus is given to form. It is our hope that this will assist you in doing the same in your classroom, thereby keeping all three of these facets of language in focus throughout your grammar instruction.

Now, let's jump in and start exploring the tenses of the English language!

NOTE 3.1: The content in this unit, as with the content for the entirety of this book, is intended for use by teachers of English, not students of English as a second/foreign language. Some of the language used is not appropriate for use with your learners (including, for example, the term *aspect* in relation to grammar, which is not a term most of our students need to know). Please keep in mind that the content here is designed to make you a more knowledgeable teacher, one with a more exhaustive explicit language knowledge and who is better prepared to answer student questions about the English language. It is not intended to be used as a sole basis for your future lesson plans. For more information about the actual instruction of grammar, including inductive/deductive teaching and the application of form/meaning/use to your EFL/ESL classroom, see Chapter 6 in International TEFL Academy's coursebook, *The Fundamentals of Teaching English as a Foreign Language*.

3.1 PRESENT SIMPLE AND PRESENT CONTINUOUS

Introduction

I am visiting Petra this coming weekend. People ride camels there.

The sentences above show an example of how the present continuous and the present simple tenses are used. In the first sentence, we see the present continuous tense, *am visiting*. This demonstrates how the present continuous tense can be used to show a future meaning or a future plan. The second sentence shows an example of the present simple tense, *ride*. This shows a general statement or fact.

In this section, we will look at both the present simple and present continuous tenses. We will start by looking at the target language in the context of a dialogue. Then we will look at timelines that explain the use of the verb tenses in the dialogue. After that, we will explore information about the form, meaning, and use of the target grammar.

Objectives

- Identify the present simple and present continuous in context
- Compare and contrast the form of the present simple and present continuous
- Classify meanings of the present simple and present continuous
- List common real-world contexts for use of the present simple and present continuous
- Identify common mistakes made with the present simple and present continuous

Use in Context: A Dialogue

Read the following dialogue between an EFL teacher in Jordan and her brother back home. They are talking on the phone. The text contains examples of the present simple (marked in bold) and the present continuous (marked in italics). Notice how the examples are used in conjunction with other tenses.

Dialogue

Jes: Hey, how**'s** everything back home?

Kevin: Well, pretty much the same as you left it. Fido *is healing* from his surgery at the vet. I finished my bar exam, and now I*'m waiting* for the result.

Jes: Congrats! I**'m** sure you did well.

Kevin: Thanks! Tell me about everything that**'s** happening there.

Jes: Well, I stayed with a local host family for the first two months, but now I **have** my own apartment. The family was very nice, but it**'s** nice to have my own space.

Kevin: What**'s** it like?

Jes: The apartment **is** on a big hill overlooking the village. I **walk** through the village to take a bus to work every day. And, someone **tells** you where to sit! Men and women can't sit beside each other unless they**'re** in the same family.

Kevin: Sounds interesting. How *are* you *feeling*? Any culture shock?

Jes: I*'m trying* to keep an open mind and **observe** instead of judging things. I **try** to remind myself that each culture **has** a reason for doing certain things.

Kevin: That**'s** smart, sounds like you*'re being* open-minded. What about the food?

Jes: Oh, amazing! It usually **takes** over two hours for people to make a meal, and then you **eat** for two more hours! After the meal, there**'s** Arabic coffee in tiny cups and then fruit and chocolates **come** later.

Kevin: The food **sounds** great!

(call to prayer sound effect)

Jes: Oh, **do** you **hear** that? Muslims **sound** the call to prayer five times a day every day.

Kevin: I **hear** it, yeah. **Does** it **bother** you?

Jes: I've become fond of it. Sorry, I have to go. I*'m leaving* to teach English now.

Kevin: It**'s** Saturday!

Jes: My Saturday class **starts** at 3. Oh, and I*'m visiting* Petra next weekend. I**'m** excited to ride a camel. I'll text you a few pictures soon.

Kevin: Wow, **have** a nice time. I'll talk to you soon. Bye.

Jes: Bye!

Explanation of Grammar in Context

Now let's have a look at the usage of the target grammar by looking at some of the sentences from the dialogue you just read. With each sentence, there is a timeline that explains the relationship between the present tenses. Next to each sentence is text in parentheses that indicates the form of the present simple or present continuous. Form is discussed more thoroughly later on in this section.

Present Simple

In general, the ***present simple*** is used to express habitual or everyday activities, or in some cases, actions that are happening right now.

I <u>walk</u> through the village to take a bus to work every day. (*walk*)

In this sentence, the speaker is expressing an action that is done habitually or every day. With this example, we understand that Jes walks through the village every day to get to the bus that takes her to work.

Each culture <u>has</u> a reason for doing certain things. (*has*)

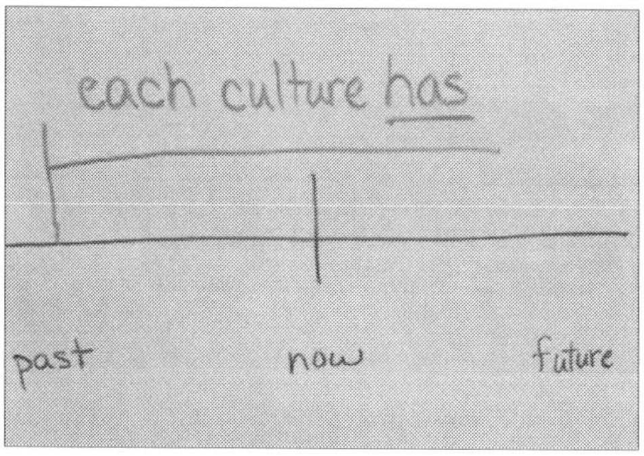

In this sentence, we see a general statement of fact and timeless truth. We understand that cultures generally have a reason for doing things and that cultural practices have roots in history. The statement is understood to be true in the past, true at present, and true in the future.

It'<u>s</u> nice to have my own space now. (*is*)

The present simple can include a form of the *be verb* + *adjective*, which usually expresses a stative meaning. In the above sentence, is shows a form of the *be* verb in the present tense, and the word *nice* is an adjective. The meaning is stative and shows a condition or situation at present that might also be true in the past and future.

My Saturday class <u>starts</u> at 3 p.m. (*starts*)

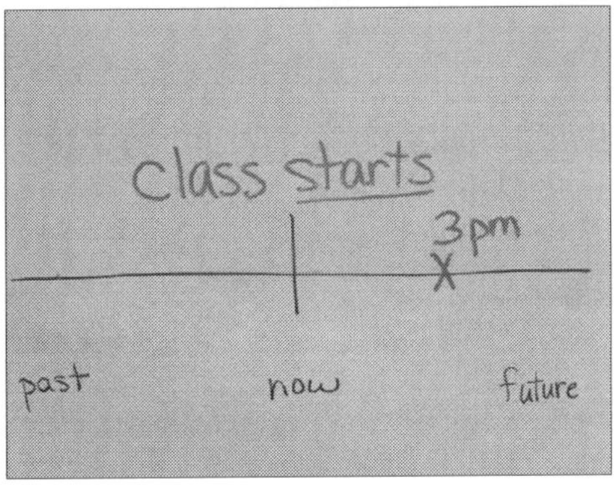

The present simple can also be used to express future time where events are on a definite schedule or timetable. This is often referred to as the ***simple present*** as future meaning/tense. These sentences usually include future time words and include specific verbs, such as *open, close, begin, end, start, finish, arrive, leave, come, return.* In the above sentence, the class is on a fixed schedule every Saturday and it will start later (in the future) at 3 p.m.

Present Continuous

With the ***present continuous***, also called the ***present progressive***, we are looking at an action that is in progress right now at the moment of speaking or generally in progress this week, this month, or this year. One key difference between the present simple and the present continuous is that the present continuous can be used only with dynamic (action) verbs and not stative verbs. To review the difference between dynamic and stative verbs, see the "Verbs" section in Unit 1.

Fido <u>is healing</u> from his surgery at the vet. (*is + healing*)

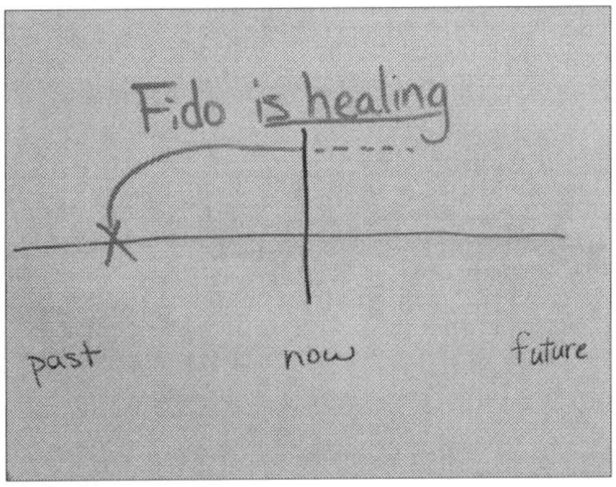

This sentence expresses an activity that is in progress at the moment of speaking. The activity of healing from surgery is temporary, and it began in the past, is continuing at present, and will probably end sometime in the future.

I finished my bar exam, and now <u>I'm waiting</u> for the result. (*am + waiting*)

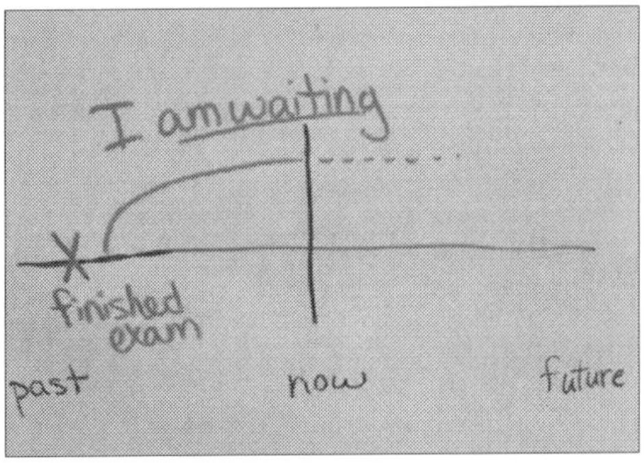

In this sentence, the present continuous expresses an action that is of a general nature where something is in progress this week, this month, or this year. At present, and over the course of a few weeks or months, Kevin is waiting for the result of the exam.

You'<u>re being</u> open-minded. (*are* + *being*)

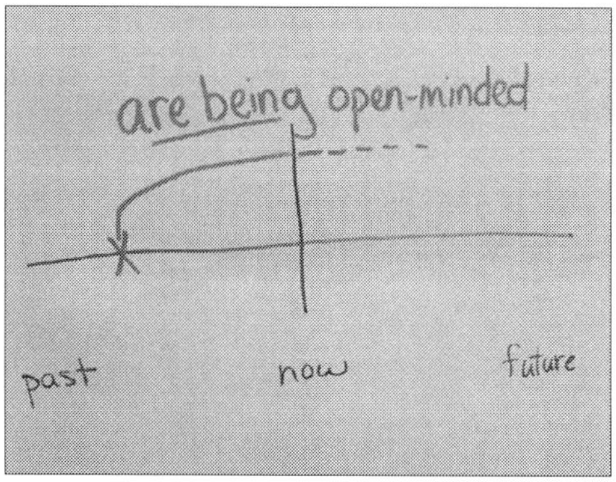

Sometimes the present continuous tense is used to describe a temporary behavior that is in progress. The *present continuous tense* + *adjective* is used. In this sentence, Jes shows a temporary behavior or characteristic. Jes is behaving in an open-minded way toward the situation at hand.

Oh, and I'<u>m visiting</u> Petra next weekend. (*am* + *visiting*)

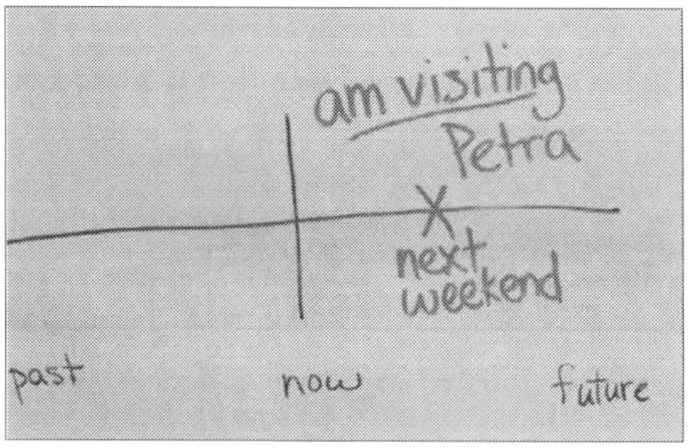

The present continuous may be used to express future time where there is a planned event or a definite intention. This is often referred to as the ***present continuous as future meaning*** tense. The future meaning is indicated by future time words or by the context. In the above sentence, Jes has a future plan to visit Petra. The words *next weekend* are specific time words that show us that this visit is a plan for the upcoming weekend.

Timeline Video

In addition to the timeline images, there is a video on International TEFL Academy's YouTube channel that depicts an EFL teacher using timelines to give explanations of a few example sentences from the "Use in Context" section. Timelines can be effective visual aids for explaining time relationships inherent in verb tenses. This video does not give an exhaustive explanation of meaning and use for the present simple and the present continuous tenses. For a more thorough explanation, please refer to the "Meaning" and "Use" parts of this section.

Present Simple and Present Continuous - https://youtu.be/uM1tozJpHXo

Form

In the sample dialogue, we saw a few examples of the present simple and the present continuous tenses. We just looked at an explanation of those tenses. Now let's focus our attention on the form. Look at the questions in the Think Box below and try to answer the questions using only your prior knowledge and the example sentences from the dialogue.

> **Think Box**
>
> Read the present simple and present continuous examples below. What do you notice about the form of the tenses? What do the present simple examples have in common? What do the present continuous examples have in common?

Present Simple Examples

I walk through the village.
My class starts at 3:00 p.m.
It takes over two hours for people to make a meal.
I am sure you did well.
The apartment is on a big hill.

Present Continuous Examples

Fido is healing.
I am leaving to teach English now.
I am trying to keep an open mind.
You are being open-minded.
Tell me about everything that is happening there.

Now that you have considered how these two tenses are formed, we will take a more detailed look at form on the following two pages.

Present Simple

Were you able to identify similarities and/or apply any terms to the sentences in the previous section? Perhaps you noticed that all the examples of present simple contain the base form of a verb. The base form of the verb is used, but be careful not to confuse the base form with the infinitive form, which uses *to* before the verb, *to visit, to wait, to have.*

subject + base verb + –s/–es in third person singular.

I walk through the village.
My class starts at 3:00 p.m.

There are two key points to consider in regard to the form of the present simple tense. The first is subject-verb agreement, which means that the third person singular takes an *–s*. The second point is in regard to irregular verbs. Irregular verbs—such as *be, have, do*—use their own conjugation patterns and should usually be taught separately. In ESL/EFL classes, a great degree of effort and time is often devoted to practicing irregular forms.

subject + a form of irregular be verb.

The apartment is on a big hill.
I am sure you did well.

Subject-Verb Agreement with Regular Verbs

I walk
You walk
She walks
He walks
It walks
We walk
They walk

Subject-Verb Agreement with Irregular *Be* Verb

I am
You are
He is
She is
It is
You are
They are

Statement and Question Formation

For your reference, Table 3.2 summarizes the form of affirmative and negative statements, yes/no questions, and *Wh–* questions. Note the conjugations for different subjects. (More detailed information about general sentence and question formation can be found in Unit 2.)

Table 3.2 Present Simple			
Affirmative Statements			
Subject	**Base Verb (+ *–s/–es* for third person singular)**	**Additional Elements**	
I/You/They	have	a great view.	
He/She/It	takes	two hours to prepare a meal.	

Negative Statements			
Subject	**Auxiliary Verb + Not**	**Base Verb**	**Additional Elements**
I/You/They	do not	have	a great view.
He/She/It	does not	take	two hours to prepare a meal.

Yes/No Questions			
Auxiliary Verb	**Subject**	**Base Verb**	**Additional Elements**
Do	I/you/they	have	a great view?
Does	he/she/it	take	two hours to prepare a meal?

Wh– Questions				
***Wh–* word**	**Auxiliary Verb**	**Subject**	**Base Verb**	**Additional Elements**
Where	do	I/you/they	have	a great view?
Why	does	he/she/it	take	two hours to prepare a meal?

Present Continuous

Now let's move on to the examples that contain the ***present continuous*** tense. Were you able to identify similarities and/or apply any terms to those sentences? Perhaps you noticed that all these examples contain the verb *be* conjugated in the present tense to *am, is*, *are*. This is followed by the present participle.

subject + be verb + present participle (base form of the verb + –ing).

I am trying to keep an open mind.
Charlie is healing from surgery.
You are being wise.

Statement and Question Formation

For your reference, Table 3.3 summarizes the form of affirmative and negative statements, yes/no questions, and *Wh–* questions. Note the conjugations for different subjects in each chart. (More detailed information about general sentence and question formation can be found in Unit 2.)

Table 3.3 Present Continuous			
Affirmative Statements			
Subject	***Be* Verb**	**Present Participle**	**Additional Elements**
I	am	trying	to keep an open mind.
He/She/It	is	healing	from surgery.
You/We/They	are	being	wise.

Negative Statements			
Subject	***Be* Verb + Not**	**Present Participle**	**Additional Elements**
I	am not	trying	to keep an open mind.
He/She/It	is not	healing	from surgery.
You/We/They	are not	being	wise.

Yes/No Questions			
***Be* Verb**	**Subject**	**Present Participle**	**Additional Elements**
Am	I	trying	to keep an open mind?
Is	he/she/it	healing	from surgery?
Are	you/we/they	being	wise?

***Wh–* Questions**				
***Wh–* word**	***Be* Verb**	**Subject**	**Present Participle**	**Additional Elements**
How	am	I	trying	to keep an open mind?
Where	is	he/she/it	healing	from surgery?
Why	are	you/we/they	being	wise?

Meaning

This section will look at how meaning is communicated through the present simple and present continuous tenses in different situations. You will recognize some of these examples from the *Explanation of Grammar in Context* section where situational usage of the target grammar was explained from the dialogue.

Present Simple

Habitual Actions or General Truths

The ***present simple*** tense shows actions, events, or states that are true in general or happen habitually.

Each culture has a reason for doing certain things.

I ride my bike to school at the same time every day, and I eat lunch in the same spot in the cafeteria.

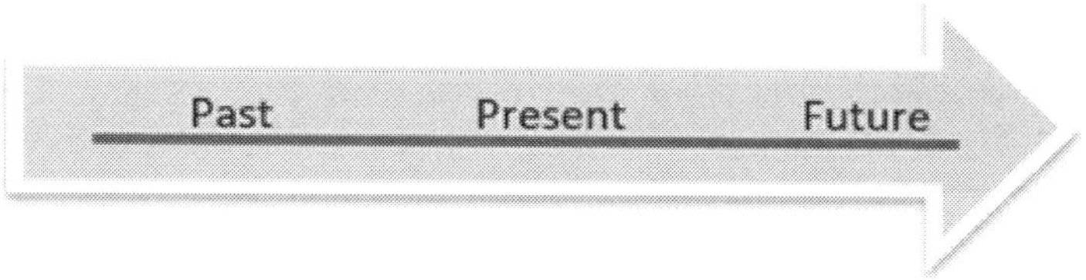

Normally, we use *adverbs* with action verbs in the present.

It *usually* takes me over an hour to drive home.

I *rarely* drink coffee after dinner because it *always* makes me stay awake too late.

In addition, we use the sense verbs—*look, sound, feel, smell, taste*— to show states, and they are used with *adjectives*, not adverbs.

To me, kimchee smells *bad*, but it tastes amazing!

Actions Happening Right Now

The present simple tense is also used with stative verbs to show actions happening right now.

She is at home now.

I believe you.

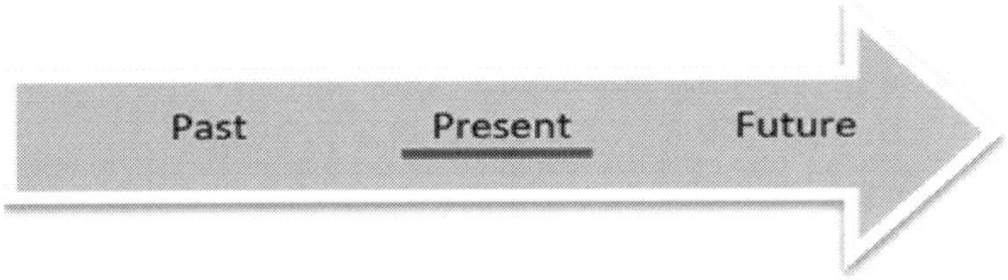

Scheduled Events

The present simple tense can also have a future meaning. This occurs with verbs—such as *open, close, arrive, leaves, departs.* In this case, there is usually a timetable or a schedule such as the opening or closing hours of a store or business, the start time of classes, or the arrival and departure times of airplanes and trains.

Our class ends at 6 this evening, but the store closes at 5.

My plane departs at 8 a.m. tomorrow.

Present Continuous

Actions or Events Happening Right Now

The ***present continuous*** shows actions or events in progress at the moment and which are not finished.

Shh! The students are taking an exam!

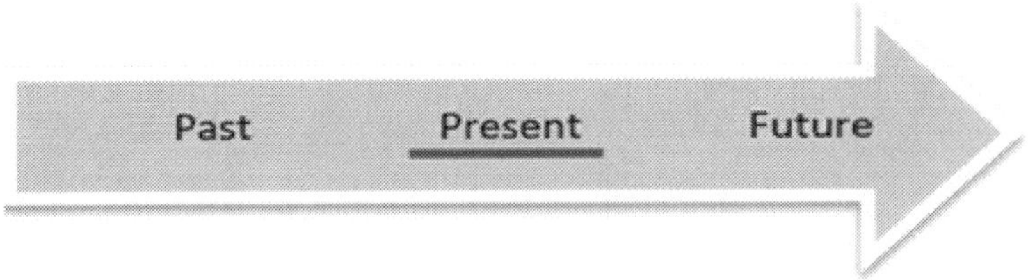

Be careful not to use nonaction verbs (stative verbs) in the present continuous tense. *Believe* is an example of a stative verb.

Correct: I **believe you**. (The present simple can be used with stative verbs.)

Incorrect: I **am believing you**. (The present continuous cannot be used with stative verbs.)

Near Future Events

The present continuous can also have a future meaning to show a future event. In this case, the present continuous is used to talk about arrangements, plans, or intentions for future events that usually more than one person is aware of.

We are having lunch next week.

We are meeting tomorrow.

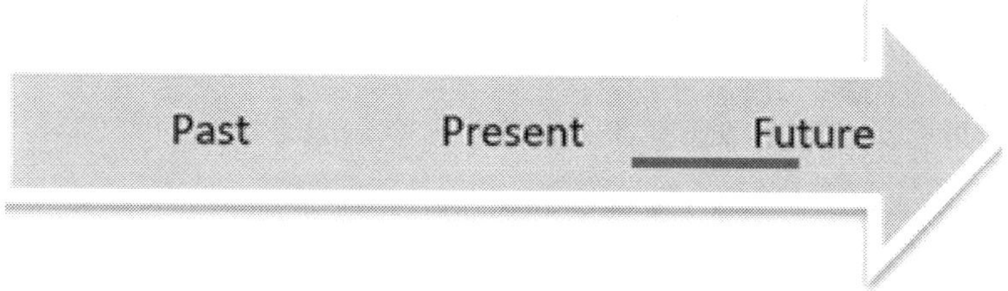

Repetition and Irritation

The present continuous can be used to show the emotion of annoyance with habits or actions. This usage is often paired with the key adverbs *always* and *constantly*.

He is *always* teasing his sister.

They are *constantly* bickering.

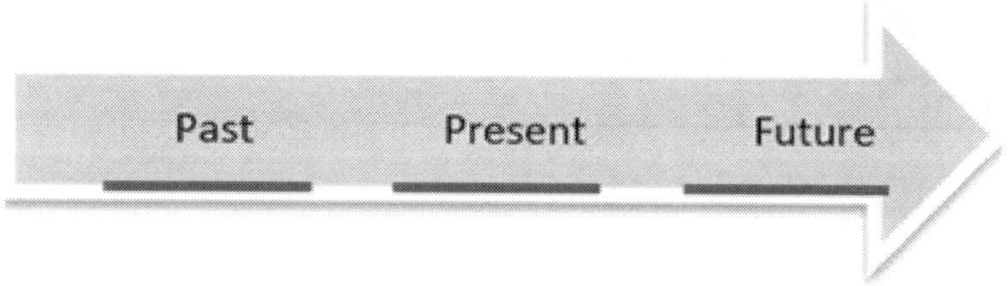

Additional Contexts for Use

This section provides examples of contexts where present simple and present continuous are commonly used. The dialogue at the beginning of this section contained examples of these two tenses in one real-world context. The following list presents some additional real-world contexts in which these tenses are commonly found.

To Communicate Rituals

We use the present simple to describe events in sequence.

Every morning, I eat breakfast, call my sister, and walk to work.

To Describe a Setting or an Object

We use the present simple to describe a place.

My office is small, but it has a good work space. I keep it messy.

To Describe a Person

We use the present simple to describe a person.

My sister is so funny! She loves to tell jokes, but she also has a serious side. She listens to classical music and always gets good grades.

To Narrate Events

We use the present continuous to narrate events as they happen.

Look! That man is walking in the middle of the street, and the cars aren't stopping!

To Describe an Image

We use the present simple to describe the state captured in a photo or work of art, and we use the *present continuous* to describe the action.

In one of Van Gogh's self-portraits, he *is wearing* a hat and *smoking* a pipe. His ear has a bandage, and he looks thoughtful and somewhat forlorn.

Common Mistakes

Let's take a look at some common mistakes made by nonnative speakers first learning these tenses.

Subject-Verb Agreement

Nonnative speakers commonly make mistakes with subject-verb agreement. The third person singular must take an *–s*.

Incorrect: **It usually take over two hours for people to prepare a meal.**

Correct: **It usually takes over two hours for people to prepare a meal.**

Incorrect Verb Tense

Some nonnative speakers just learning these two forms may mix them up and use parts of the present continuous in place of the present simple.

Incorrect: **It usually taking over two hours for people to prepare a meal.**

Correct: **It usually takes over two hours for people to prepare a meal.**

No *Be* Verb

Some nonnative speakers forget to include a form of the *be* verb with the present continuous tense.

Incorrect: **I waiting for the result.**

Correct: **I am waiting for the result.**

One reason for this error may be that native speakers can use the present continuous tense with a contraction, resulting in changing *I am* to *I'm*. When the contracted form is used, the */m/* sound is softer and quicker than the sounds around it. As a result, nonnative speakers may only hear *I waiting for the result* and not realize the contracted form was included. They then copy this pattern when they speak and erroneously omit the contraction.

Conclusion

Now that we know more about the present simple and present continuous tenses, we can conclude this first section Unit 3. We hope you have learned something new about the various meanings for these tenses and how they are used in the real world. In addition, learning common mistakes made by nonnative speakers should help you anticipate and be prepared for some of the struggles your ESL/EFL learners will face. We encourage you to take the quiz on present simple and continuous that is in the "Quizzes" section of this book to see how much you've learned.

The next section will focus on the next two verb tenses typically taught to beginning- and intermediate-level students: the past simple and the past continuous.

3.2 PAST SIMPLE AND PAST CONTINUOUS

Introduction

I was enjoying my afternoon coffee when the rains came.

The example sentence above shows a contrast between the past continuous and the past simple. In this sentence, we can see how the past continuous, *was enjoying*, demonstrates an action that was in progress or incomplete. The past simple, *came*, demonstrates a completed action with a clear ending point.

In this section, we will start by looking at both the past simple and the past continuous in the context of a blog to further establish this important contrast. After that, you will be given information about the form, meaning, and use of each tense in addition to some common errors to look for when teaching.

Objectives

- Identify the past simple and the past continuous in context
- Compare and contrast the form of the past simple and past continuous
- Classify meanings of the past simple and the past continuous
- List common real-world contexts for use of the past simple and past continuous
- Identify common mistakes made with the past simple and past continuous

Use in Context: A First-Year Teacher's Blog

Read the blog of a recent International TEFL Academy graduate who has just completed her first month of teaching in a rural elementary school in Costa Rica. The first paragraph sets up the use of the past simple (marked in bold) throughout, using a variety of both regular and irregular forms. Then the past continuous (marked in italics) is introduced at different moments in the second paragraph.

Contact me	English Classes	How I got here

"Pura Vida Interrupted"

On this particular morning in San Joaquin, the sun **rose up** just as it always **did** for however many centuries over this tiny tranquilo town, but for me it **was** my first visit to the little town of Bajo Pacuare. Because there isn't a bus there, I **walked** all day to the town down a dusty road packed with rocks and rain gutters running all down the hill. I **found** the little school and **set up** to teach the lesson. I **taught** a 30-minute English lesson on adjectives and emotions, and something funny **happened**. Just as I **began** to sing, "If you're happy and you know it", a heavy rainstorm **started**.

While it *was raining* down on the tin roof, we *were playing* a game, tossing around my participation ball. It's funny how interruptions are ironically routine here. I suppose the interruption factor **became** really clear the time I **sent** home letters to my students' parents about setting up parent teacher conferences. Back in Chicago I always **seemed** pretty professional and organized. But here I *was doing* my best to respect their time and schedules, when not a single soul **signed up** to meet with me. The first time I **met** a parent was when I *was walking* through town to explore. I **noticed** that the sweet little eyes of my students *were peering out* from their windows. All of a sudden, everyone *was inviting* me in on the fly for afternoon cafecito. I **met** almost all of my students' families. Just like the sweet rain yesterday, those interruptions *were annoying* at first, but now I see how they **helped** us connect.

Explanation of Grammar in Context

We will begin by looking at some of the examples of each of the two tenses from the blog that you just read. With each sentence, there is a timeline that explains the meaning of these past tenses. Next to each sentence is text in parentheses that indicates the form of the past simple or past continuous. Form is discussed more thoroughly later on in this section.

Past Simple

The ***past simple*** is the most basic form of the past tense in the English language. What perhaps sets it apart from other forms of the past tense is that it signifies a simple past action that occurred before the present moment and is complete. However long ago it occurred and/or the duration of the action are not significant points.

In San Joaquin, the sun <u>rose up</u> just as it always <u>did</u>. (*rose up, did*)

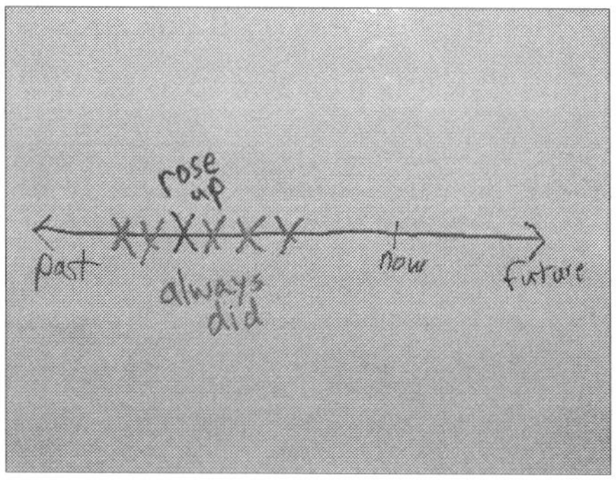

In the introductory sentence of the blog, we have two completed actions in the past. The first action describes the exact moment in the past when the sun rose. The second describes how the sun had always completed this same action habitually over a very long period. Thus we can see how the past simple can portray one completed action and also a habitual (repeated) action in the past.

I <u>walked</u> all day to the town down a dusty road. (*walked*)

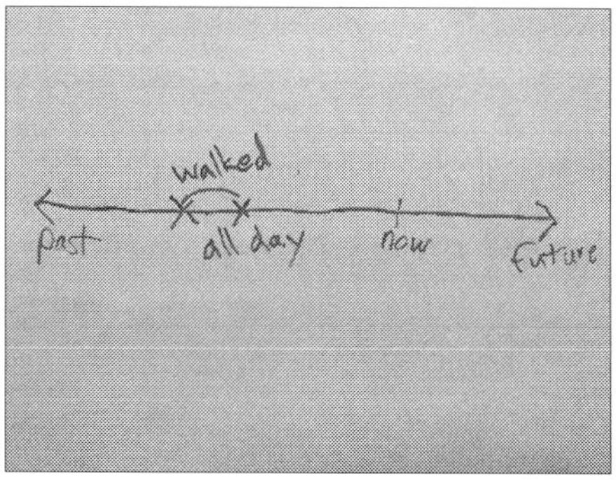

Later in the blog, the writer describes how she walked to the town where she would teach. We know that the action is completed because later in the story the writer has now arrived at the town. What makes the use of the past tense verb unique in this context is that the act of walking took place over a longer period of time, which is described by the phrase *all day.*

I <u>found</u> the little school and <u>set up</u> to teach the lesson. I <u>taught</u> a 30-minute English lesson. (*found, set up, taught*)

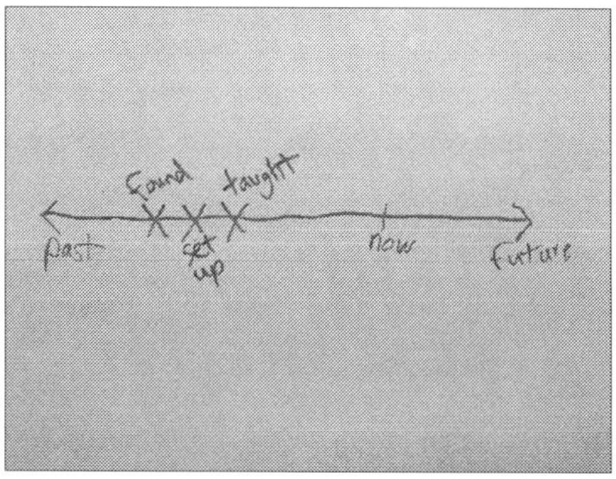

Finally, in this last segment of the first paragraph, we see many actions that happened in succession. It is evident that each verb in the simple past builds upon the next in a sequence of past events. After the writer found the school, she set up and then taught the lesson.

Past Continuous

The ***past continuous*** is used to describe ongoing events in the past. In this sense, the past continuous seems unfinished or incomplete in contrast to the completed actions represented by the simple past.

The first time I met a parent was when I <u>was walking</u> through town to explore.
(*was + walking*)

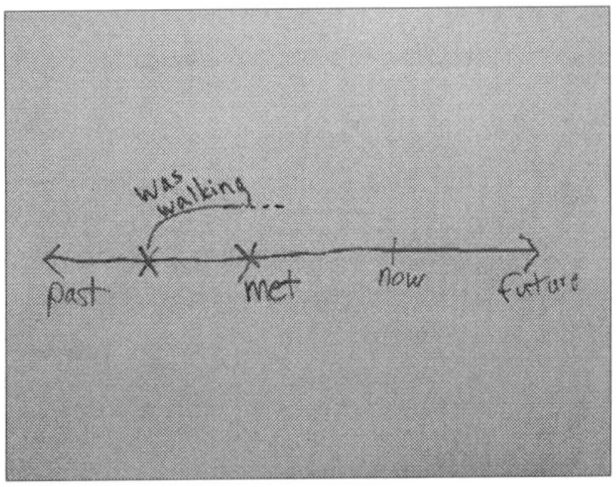

This sentence establishes one of the most frequently used combinations of the past continuous in conjunction with the past simple: to show an action that was in progress and was interrupted by a complete action in the past. The writer was continuously walking through town, which was interrupted when she met a parent.

While it <u>was raining</u> down on the tin roof, we <u>were playing</u> a game, tossing around my participation ball. (*was + raining, were + playing*)

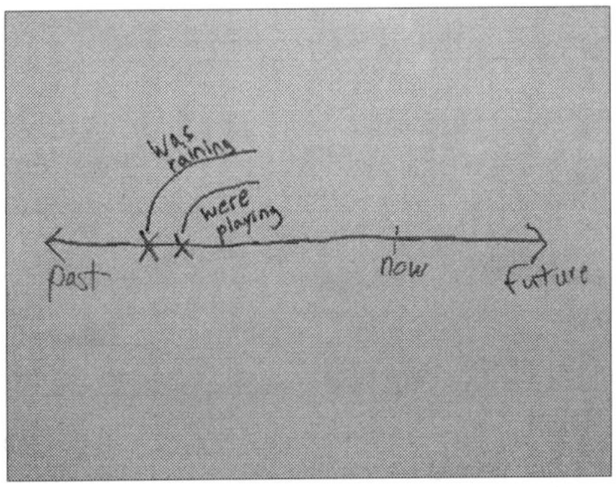

In this example sentence, we can see two simultaneous actions, both expressed through the past continuous. There is a clear overlap between the two actions, which is emphasized by the keyword *while*. The use of the past continuous to represent how it was raining AND the class was playing the game provides a clear image for two actions that began at some point in the past and continued to progress simultaneously. At some point, both actions came to completion, but the duration of time is not specified for either of these actions.

Everyone <u>was inviting</u> me in on the fly for afternoon cafecito. (*was + inviting*)

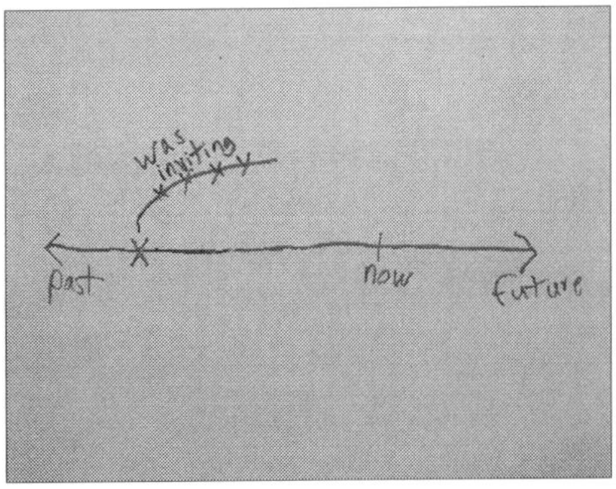

This example sentence demonstrates a repeated action as expressed through the past continuous, which began in a particular moment and continued on. As the writer describes walking through the town, she noticed that local community members were repeatedly inviting her in for coffee.

Timeline Video

In addition to the timeline images above, there is a video on International TEFL Academy's YouTube channel that depicts an EFL teacher using timelines to give explanations of a few example sentences from the "Use in Context" section. Timelines can be effective visual aids for explaining time relationships inherent in verb tenses. This video does not give an exhaustive explanation of meaning and use for the present simple and the present continuous tenses. For a more thorough explanation, please refer to the Meaning and Use parts of this section.

Past Simple and Past Continuous - https://youtu.be/MGoKbfBI1nI

Form

In the blog post, we saw a few examples of the past simple and past continuous. Now that we have looked closely at the meaning of those tenses, let's shift our attention to a focus on form. To begin, read the Think Box below and try to answer the questions using only your prior knowledge and the example sentences from the blog.

Think Box

Read the past simple and past continuous examples below. What do you notice about the form of the tenses? What do the past simple examples have in common? What do the past continuous examples have in common?

Past Simple

In San Joaquin the sun rose up just as it always did.
I walked all day to the town down a dusty road.
I found the little school and set up to teach the lesson. I taught a 30-minute English lesson.

Past Continuous

The first time I met a parent was when I was walking through town to explore.
While it was raining down on the tin roof, we were playing a game.
Everyone was inviting me in on the fly for afternoon cafecito.

Now that you have considered how these two tenses are formed, we will take a more detailed look at form.

Past Simple

Were you able to identify similarities or differences for the past simple examples? You may have noticed that the past simple is formed in two ways: regular and irregular formation. The regular formation is formed with the base form of a verb plus *–ed.* The irregular formation of past simple verbs has many variations:

subject + verb + –ed or irregular form

I watched TV yesterday.

I went to the theater last Friday.

Regular and irregular formation of the past simple is explained in detail below.

Regular Formation

We form the past simple by adding *–ed* to the ending of most words and *–d* to words that end in *–e*. Some of the words used in the example blog that follow this pattern are listed below. We can see how each verb looks before and after the past simple suffix is added.

Table 3.4 Regular Formation

Base Verb	Simple Past Form Adding *–ed* or *–d*
ask	asked
walk	walked
pound	pounded
introduce	introduced

There are some exceptions to this rule, as seen in Table 3.5.

Table 3.5 Exceptions to Regular Formation

Explanation of Exceptions to the *–ed* or *–d* Rule	Example
When the final consonant is after a short-stressed vowel, that consonant is doubled	Commit becomes commi**tt**ed
When *–l* is the final consonant after a vowel, the *l* is also doubled	Propel becomes prope**ll**ed
When the final letter is a *–y* immediately after a consonant, the *–y* is changed to *–i*	Worry becomes worried

Irregular Formation

Irregular verbs in the simple past do not follow a predictable formula; instead, they must be learned through practice and exposure. Some irregular verbs from the blog are shown in Table 3.6 contrasting the infinitive form with the irregular form in the simple past. For a more exhaustive list of irregular past tense verbs, see the "Verbs" section of Unit 1.

Table 3.6 Irregular Verbs with Infinitive	
Infinitive Verb	**Simple Past Form**
to be	was (I, he, she)/ were (you, we, they)
to have	had
to rise	rose
to get	got
to spend	spent
to give	gave
to teach	taught
to choose	chose

Statement and Question Formation

For your reference, Table 3.7 summarizes the form of affirmative and negative statements, yes/no questions, and *Wh–* questions. Note the conjugations for different subjects in each chart. (More detailed information about general sentence and question formation can be found in Unit 2.)

Table 3.7 Past Simple			
Affirmative Statements			
Subject	**Base Verb + *–ed* or Irregular Form**	**Additional Elements**	
I/You/We/They He/She/It	walked	all day.	
I/You/We/They He/She/It	taught	an English lesson.	
Negative Statements			
Subject	**Did + Not**	**Base Verb**	**Additional Elements**
I/You/We/They He/She/It	did not	walk	all day.
I/You/We/They He/She/It	did not	teach	an English lesson.

Yes/No Questions			
Did	**Subject**	**Base Verb**	**Additional Elements**
Did	I/you/we/they he/she/it	walk	all day?
Did	I/you/we/they he/she/it	teach	an English lesson?

Wh– Questions				
***Wh–* word**	**Did**	**Subject**	**Base Verb**	**Additional Elements**
Why	did	I/you/we/they he/she/it	walk	all day?
When	did	I/you/we/they he/she/it	teach	an English lesson?

Past Continuous

Now let's move on to the examples that contain the past continuous tense. Were you able to identify similarities and/or apply any terms to those sentences? Perhaps you noticed that all these examples contain the verb *be* conjugated in the past tense to *was* or *were*. This is followed by the present participle.

subject + be verb + present participle (base form of the verb + –ing)

They were waiting for me to show up.
He was watching TV.

Statement and Question Formation

For your reference, Table 3.8 summarizes the form of affirmative and negative statements, yes/no questions, and *Wh–* questions. Note the conjugations for different subjects. (More detailed information about general sentence and question formation can be found in Unit 2.)

Table 3.8 Past Continuous			
Affirmative Statements			
Subject	***Be* Verb**	**Present Participle**	**Additional Elements**
I/ He/She/It	was	walking	home.
You/We/They	were	playing	a game.
Negative Statements			
Subject	***Be* Verb + Not**	**Present Participle**	**Additional Elements**
I/ He/She/It	was not	walking	home.
You/We/They	were not	playing	a game.
Yes/No Questions			
***Be* Verb**	**Subject**	**Present Participle**	**Additional Elements**
Was	I/ he/she/it	walking	home?
Were	you/we/they	playing	a game?

***Wh–* Questions**				
***Wh–* word**	***Be* Verb**	**Subject**	**Present Participle**	**Additional Elements**
When	was	I/ he/she/it	walking	home?
Where	were	you/we/they	playing	a game?

Meaning

This section presents guidelines for how meaning is communicated through the past simple and the past continuous tenses in different situations. Important keywords and phrases for each situation are also discussed.

Past Simple

Describing Completed Events in the Past

The ***past simple*** can be used to describe a specific moment that occurred and was completed in the past at an indicated time, as referred to in the sentences with exact key phrases of time—*yesterday, last Saturday, three years ago.*

I drank coffee at the Café Britt coffee tour *yesterday*.
They planned the party *last Saturday*.
He started the job in San Jose *three years ago*.

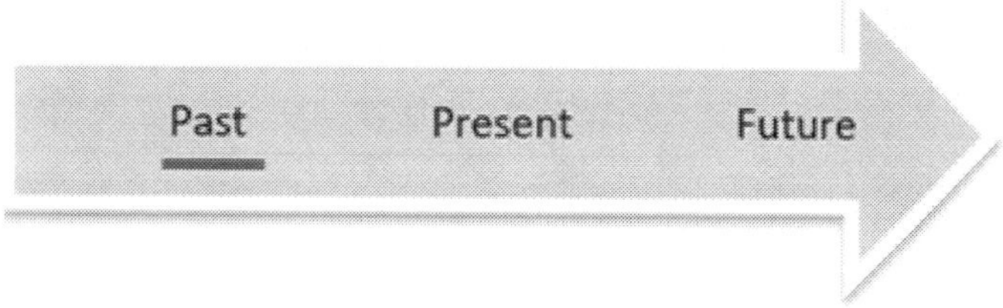

Past Habits

We can also use the past simple to refer to a personal repeated habit in the past that is generally no longer true in the present moment. It is important to note that the key phrases in these sentences—*every, when, throughout high school*— refer to periods of past time in which the actions were repeated actions.

I studied Spanish at the DILE Institute *every* summer during college.
My mother took voice lessons *when* she was a little girl.
What clubs did you participate in *throughout* your *high school* career?

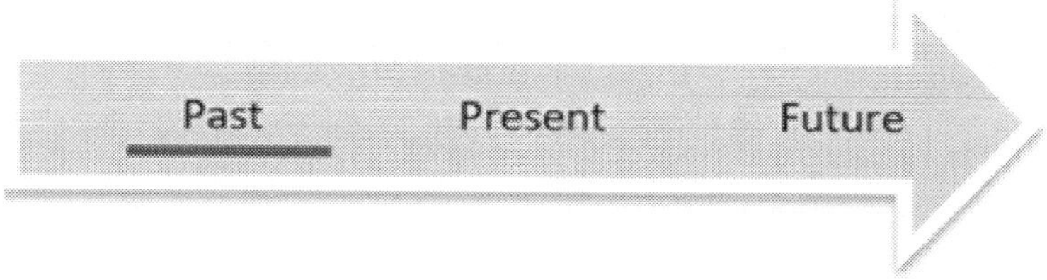

Longer Actions in the Past

It is possible that a past action has a specific moment of completion but takes a longer period of time in the past to fulfill. In this case the key phrases—*an hour, entire week, for four years*— are similar to those in point one above because the action here is also completed and at a specific time; however, the length of the action is greater.

We chatted on Skype for more than *an hour* yesterday.
It took my class the *entire week* to learn that song.
Did their engagement really last *for four years*?

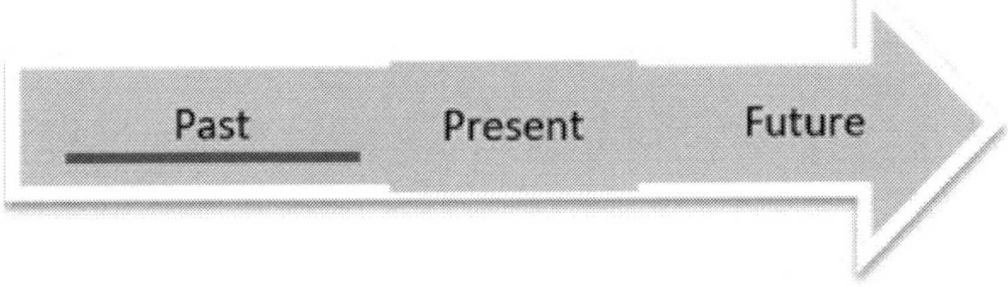

Sequence of Past Events

Finally, the past simple can be seen throughout one sentence or a group of sentences to show how the events of a story or the steps in a plan unfold in order. The key phrases—*after, when*— point out this sequence.

***After* he finished his homework, he wrote some emails and got a snack.**
***When* I heard the news, I gave my sister a call to congratulate her.**
Did you take the two aspirin *after* you ate your breakfast?

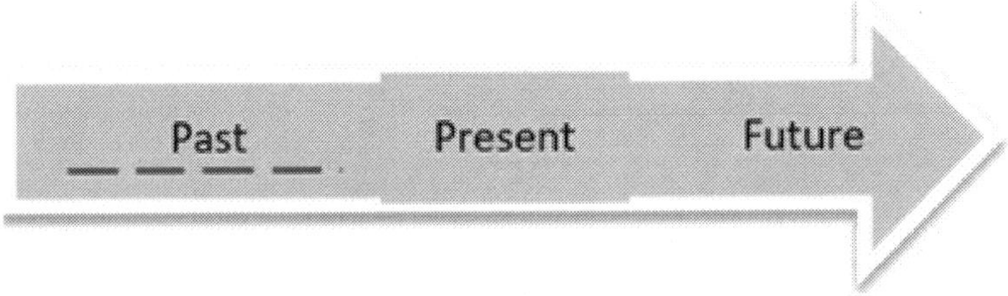

Past Continuous

Interrupted Actions in the Past

As seen in the blog at the start of this section, the past continuous works to demonstrate how one action can interrupt another in the past. In this case, the past continuous will demonstrate an ongoing action in the past that is usually interrupted by the past simple. The key words —*when, while*— are important to set up this relationship.

I was watching the news *when* my phone rang.
***While* we were waiting in line, I finished my book.**
What were you doing *when* they announced the winner?

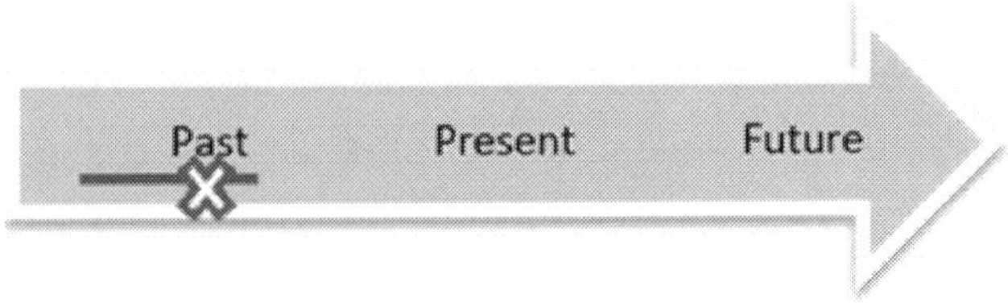

Specific Time as an Interruption

Key phrases—*what time, last night, midnight*— are used in the following examples to denote a specific time and show how the past continuous can represent a longer action that both began and continued after a particular time. In this way, time itself is the interruption to the action, and the speaker hopes to draw attention to what was in process at a specific moment.

What time was it when you were driving across the border?
Last night at about 7 I was getting my kids ready for bed.
It was almost _midnight_, and they were still trying to finish the holiday puzzle?

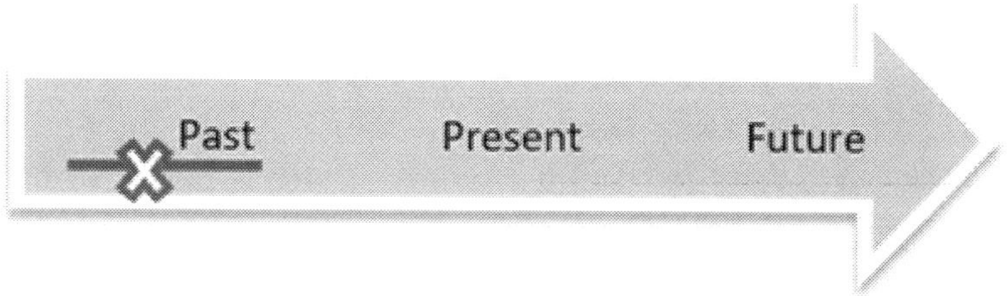

Parallel Actions

We can also use the past continuous to demonstrate two simultaneous ongoing actions. The keyword *while* is often used in this construction.

They were playing cards _while_ we were setting up the soccer game.
I was doing the laundry _while_ trying to finish some payments online.

Repetition and Irritation

Finally, the past continuous can be used to emphasize the emotion of a reader who is particularly bothered by an ongoing habit or repeated action. This is often paired with the keywords—*the whole time, constantly, always*.

He was chewing his food right in my ear _the whole bus ride._
They were constantly complaining about the lunch menu.

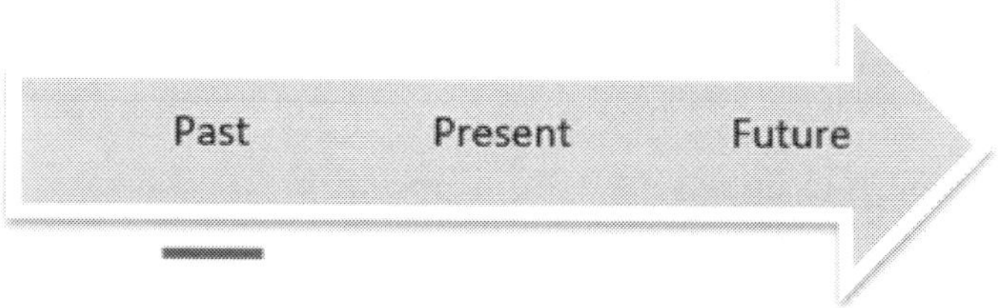

Additional Contexts for Use

This section provides examples of contexts where the past simple and the past continuous are commonly used. The blog at the beginning of this section contained examples of these two tenses in one real-world context. Following are some additional real-world contexts in which these tenses are commonly found.

Storytelling and Anecdotes

We use the past continuous to set the scene and add description.

They were getting ready for bed. Emily was talking on the phone with her best friend. Her mom was downstairs relaxing and drinking a glass of wine, and her dad was washing the dishes in the kitchen. Their dog was constantly barking.

We use the past simple to chronicle events.

Suddenly they heard a noise from the basement. A strange man entered through the cellar door and crept up the stairs. Luckily, Emily's dad grabbed the phone in the kitchen and called the police as soon as he saw him. Everyone was safe because they arrived quickly.

Description of Childhood

We use the past simple and *past continuous* to talk about childhood memories.

I went to the pool every day during the summers when I was younger.

I *was* always *arguing* with my older sister when we were kids.

Memorable Experience

We use the past simple to describe memorable experiences.

We went to Disney World last summer. The whole family had a wonderful time, and we rode most of the rides.

News Reports

We use the past simple and *past continuous* to detail sequence of events reported in the news.

The suspect went into the bank holding a gun. He held the tellers at gunpoint while they *were emptying* out their cash drawers.

Cover Letters, Job Applications, and Interviews

We use the past simple to highlight unique experiences in work history

When I was in university, I had the opportunity to volunteer in Mexico.

I taught English to children at a summer camp.

Common Mistakes

Let's take a look at some of the common mistakes made by nonnative speakers who are first learning these tenses. Often for nonnative speakers, there is not a one-to-one correlation between these tenses and a similar tense in their native language, which is why we can confuse which tense would be correct to use in various contexts.

Irregular Past Tense Verbs

Nonnative speakers commonly make mistakes with irregular past tense verbs.

Incorrect: **I <u>eated</u> dinner at 6 p.m. last night.**

Correct: **I <u>ate</u> dinner at 6 p.m. last night.**

Spelling

Nonnative (and native) speakers commonly make mistakes with the spelling of past tense verbs.

Incorrect: **The boat <u>propeled</u> through the water.**

Correct: **The boat <u>propelled</u> through the water.**

Incorrect Verb Tense

Some nonnative speakers just learning these two forms may mix them up and use the past continuous in place of the past simple.

Incorrect: **I <u>was walking</u> to town every day when I lived in Costa Rica.**

Correct: **I <u>walked</u> to school every day when I lived in Costa Rica.**

Conclusion

As you learned in this section, the past simple and past continuous can be used in a number of ways to discuss past events. One key aspect of the formation of these tenses to remember is that there are many irregular past tense verb forms for nonnative speakers to memorize. You will encounter this idea of irregular verb formation in many of the verb tenses to follow in this unit. You will also find it within the quiz on past simple and past continuous in the "Quizzes" section of the book.

The next section will move us from the past to the future and illustrate the form, meaning, and use of the future simple and future continuous verb tenses.

3.3 FUTURE SIMPLE AND FUTURE CONTINUOUS

Introduction

I will be living within a few miles of Lake Victoria. This is going to be an amazing experience!

The sentences above show an example of how the future continuous and the future simple tenses are used. In the first sentence, we see the future continuous tense, *will be living.* This demonstrates how the future continuous tense can be used to show an action that will be in progress at a time in the future. The second sentence shows an example of the future simple tense, *is going to be*. This example shows something that a person thinks will happen in the future.

In this section, we will look at both the future simple and future continuous tenses. We will start by looking at the target language in the context of a travel log. Then we will look at timelines that explain the use of the verb tenses in the travel log. After that, we will explore information about the form, meaning, and use of the target grammar.

Objectives

- Identify the future simple and future continuous aspect in context
- Compare and contrast the form of the future simple and future continuous
- Classify meanings of the future simple and future continuous
- List common real-world contexts for use of the future simple and future continuous
- Identify common mistakes made with the future simple and future continuous

Use in Context: A Travel Log

Read this travel log that an EF teacher travelling to Uganda wrote while flying on the plane to his teaching post in Jinja, Uganda. The dialogue contains examples of the future simple (marked in bold) and the future continuous (marked in italics). Notice how the examples are used in conjunction with other tenses.

My Travel photos | My English Classes | About Me

Getting Started!!

Right now I am on an airplane flying over the Atlantic Ocean. I'm on my way to teach English at an international high school in Jinja, Uganda. It **is going to be** intriguing! I *will be living* within a few miles of the Nile River and Lake Victoria! My students, many of whom speak either Luganda or Swahili at home, have studied English in school for years, but they have limited opportunities to practice their English language skills outside of school. Given this, I **will try** to create authentic speaking opportunities for them. I have already been in contact with the school administrators and other teachers about this. We **are going to use** Experiential Learning and take the students on field trips. Also, *we are going to be bringing* in guest speakers who speak English. I'm excited to try out these new things.

This time next week, I **will be in** the classroom with my students. The administrator of the school said that at this time of the year they always celebrate Uganda's Independence Day to mark the country's independence from British rule in 1962. There **will be** a parade and people **will light** candles to celebrate this occasion. I am very much looking forward to this. From what I have read, it seems that the students **are going to be** very respectful and eager to learn. We **are going to have** an amazing experience! Right now though, I **will continue** my cultural research about Uganda. Soon I **will finish** this book about the language and culture of Central Uganda's Buganda Kingdom. This should help out with my cultural understanding. The adventure begins...

Explanation of Grammar in Context

Now let's have a look at the usage of the target grammar by looking at some of the sentences from the dialogue you just read. With each sentence, there is a timeline that explains the relationship between the future tenses. Next to each sentence is text in parentheses that indicates the form of the future simple or future continuous. Form is discussed more thoroughly later on in this section.

Future Simple

The ***future simple*** with *will* or *be going to* is used to express what a person thinks will happen in the future.

This time next week, I <u>will be</u> in the classroom with my students! (*will + be*)

In this sentence, the EFL teacher is expressing that she thinks she will be in her classroom with her students by this time next week.

We <u>are going to use</u> experiential learning and take the students on field trips. (*are going to + use*)

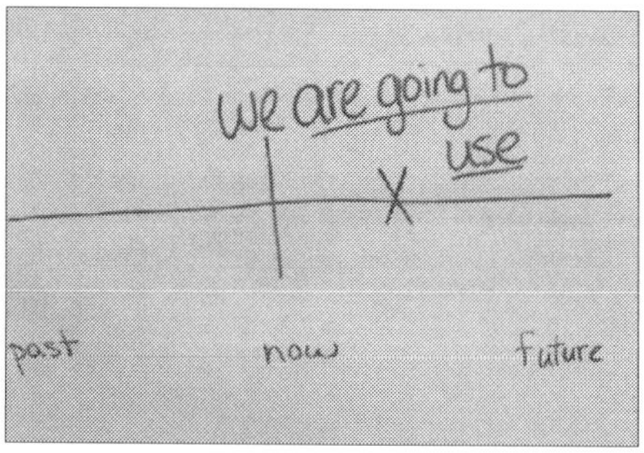

The future simple with *be going to* is usually used to talk about a future situation that is planned or in development already. In this sentence, we see the EFL teacher and the administration already have plans to use experiential learning and to take the students on field trips. These are plans that are already developing.

Right now, though, I <u>will continue</u> my cultural research about Uganda. (*will + continue*)

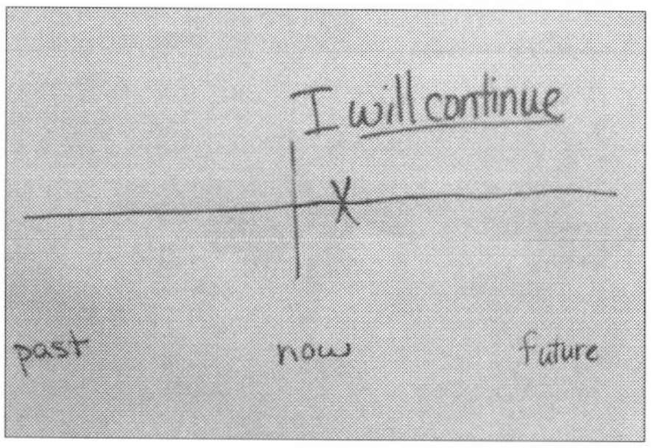

The future simple with *will* expresses a future action that is decided on at the moment of speaking. In this sentence, the EFL teacher makes an on-the-spot decision to continue her cultural research within the next few minutes.

Given this, I <u>will try</u> to create authentic speaking opportunities for them.
(*will + try*)

The future simple can also be used to express a willingness to do something or to show a desire to volunteer to do something in the future. In this case, the EFL teacher is showing a willingness to try to create authentic speaking opportunities for the students.

Future Continuous

With the ***future continuous***, also called the ***future progressive***, there is an action that will be in progress at a certain time in the future.

I <u>will be living</u> within a few miles of the Nile River and Lake Victoria!
(*will + be + living*)

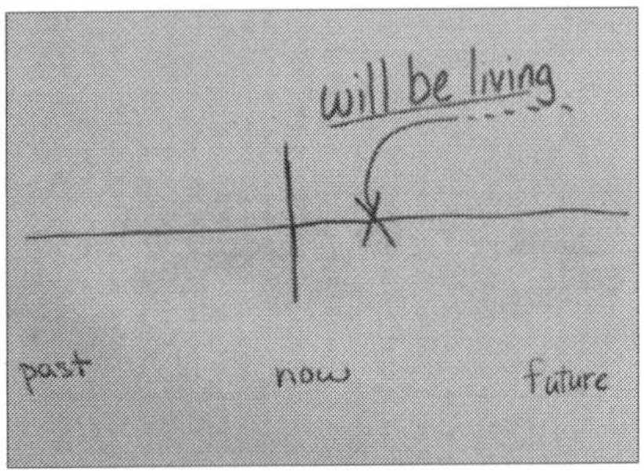

This sentence expresses an activity that will be in progress in the future. This action has already been arranged, and it is expected that it will be occurring over a specific duration in the future. We understand that the teacher will be living a few miles from the Nile River in the future, and this will happen for a certain duration.

Also, we <u>are going to be bringing</u> in guest speakers who speak English.
(*are going to + be + bringing*)

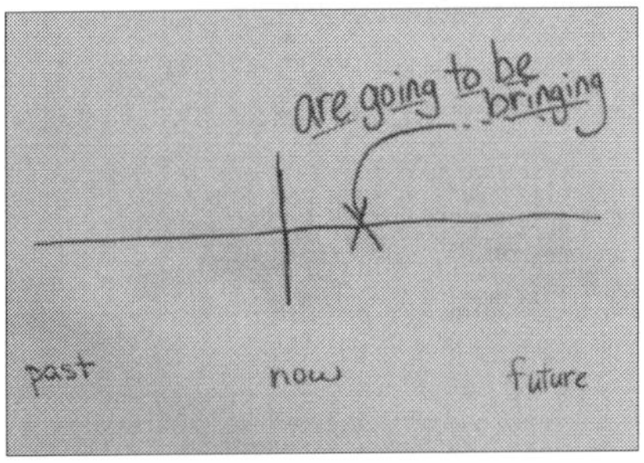

In this sentence, the future continuous expresses an action that will be in progress in the future. This action has been arranged, and it will be in progress in the future over a certain duration.

Timeline Video

In addition to the timeline images above, there is a video on International TEFL Academy's YouTube channel that depicts an EFL teacher using timelines to give explanations of a few example sentences from the "Use in Context" section. Timelines can be effective visual aids for explaining time relationships inherent in verb tenses. This video does not give an exhaustive explanation of meaning and use for the future simple and future continuous tenses. For a more thorough explanation, please refer to the "Meaning" and "Use" parts of this section.

Future Simple and Future Continuous - https://youtu.be/5-Zrmqyo-Ls

Form

In the sample travel log, we saw a few examples of the future simple and the future continuous tenses, and this was followed by an explanation of the meaning of some of those sentences. Now let's focus our attention on the form. Look at the questions in the Think Box below and try to answer the questions using only your prior knowledge and the example sentences from the travel log.

> **Think Box**
> Read the future simple and future continuous examples below. What do you notice about the form of the tenses? What do the future simple examples have in common? What do the future continuous examples have in common?

Future Simple Examples

People will light candles to celebrate this occasion.
This time next week, I will be in the classroom with my students!
Right now, though, I will continue my cultural research about Uganda.
It is going to be intriguing!
It seems that the students are going to be very respectful and eager to learn.
We are going to have an amazing experience!

Future Continuous Examples

I will be living within a few miles of the Nile River.
They will be having a cultural celebration when I arrive.
We are going to be bringing in guest speakers who speak English.
I am going to be learning a great deal about Ugandan life and culture.

Now that you have considered how these two tenses are formed, we will take a more detailed look at form on the following two pages.

Future Simple

Were you able to identify similarities and/or apply any terms to the sentences in the previous section? Perhaps you noticed that all the examples of future simple contain *will* plus the base form of the verb or *be going to* plus the base form of the verb.

subject + will + base form of verb

People will light candles to celebrate this occasion.

This time next week, I will be in the classroom with my students!

Right now though, I will continue my cultural research about Uganda.

subject + be going to + base form of verb

It is going to be intriguing!

It seems that the students are going to be very respectful and eager to learn.

We are going to have an amazing experience!

Statement and Question Formation

For your reference, Table 3.9 summarizes the form of affirmative and negative statements, yes/no questions, and *Wh–* questions. Note the conjugations for different subjects. (More detailed information about general sentence and question formation can be found in Unit 2.)

Table 3.9 Future Simple

Affirmative Statements

Subject	**Will or Be Going to**	**Base Verb**	**Additional Elements**
I/You/We/They He/She/It	will	try	to create authentic speaking opportunities.
I	am going to	use	Experiential Learning.
He/She/It	is going to	use	Experiential Learning.
You/We/They	are going to	use	Experiential Learning.

Negative Statements

Subject	**Will + Not or Be Going to + Not**	**Base Verb**	**Additional Elements**
I/You/We/They He/She/It	will not	try	to create authentic speaking opportunities.
I	am not going to	use	Experiential Learning.
He/She/It	is not going to	use	Experiential Learning.
You/We/They	are not going to	use	Experiential Learning.

Will Yes/No Questions

Will	**Subject**	**Base Verb**	**Additional Elements**
Will	I/you/we/they he/she/it	try	to create authentic speaking opportunities?

Be Going to Yes/No Questions

***Be* Verb**	**Subject**	**Going to**	**Base Verb**	**Additional Elements**
Am	I	going to	use	Experiential Learning?
Is	he/she/it	going to	use	Experiential Learning?
Are	you/we/they	going to	use	Experiential Learning?

Will *Wh–* Questions				
***Wh–* word**	**Will**	**Subject**	**Base Verb**	**Additional Elements**
When	will	I/you/we/ they he/she/it	try	to create authentic speaking opportunities?

Be Going to *Wh–* Questions					
***Wh–* word**	***Be* Verb**	**Subject**	**Going to**	**Base Verb**	**Additional Elements**
When	am	I	going to	use	Experiential Learning?
Where	is	he/she/it	going to	use	Experiential Learning?
Why	are	you/we/t hey	going to	use	Experiential Learning?

Future Continuous

Now let's move to the examples that contain the future continuous tense. Were you able to identify similarities and/or apply any terms to those sentences? Perhaps you noticed that these examples contain the *be* verb conjugated in the present tense to *am, is, are.* This is followed by *going to be* plus the present participle. Alternatively, you may have noticed that this tense can be formed with *will* followed by the *be* verb and the present participle.

subject + will + be + present participle (base form of the verb + ing)

I will be living within a few miles of the Nile River.

They will be having a cultural celebration when I arrive.

(*subject + be verb + going to be + present participle (base form of the verb + ing)*

We are going to be bringing in guest speakers who speak English.

I am going to be learning a great deal about Ugandan life and culture.

Statement and Question Formation

For your reference, Table 3.10 summarizes the form of affirmative and negative statements, yes/no questions, and *Wh–* questions. Note the conjugations for different subjects in each chart. (More detailed information about general sentence and question formation can be found in Unit 2.)

Table 3.10 Future Continuous			
Affirmative Statements			
Subject	**Will + Be or Be Verb + Going to be**	**Present Participle**	**Additional Elements**
I/You/We/They	will be	living	near the Nile River.

He/She/It			
I	am going to be	bringing	guest speakers.
He/She/It	is going to be	bringing	guest speakers.
You/We/They	are going to be	bringing	guest speakers.
Negative Statements			
Subject	**Will + Not + Be or Be Verb + Not + Going to Be**	**Present Participle**	**Additional Elements**
I/You/We/They He/She/It	will not be	living	near the Nile River.
I	am not going to be	bringing	guest speakers.
He/She/It	is not going to be	bringing	guest speakers.
You/We/They	are not going to be	bringing	guest speakers.

Yes/No Questions				
***Will* or *Be* Verb**	**Subject**	**BE or Going to be**	**Present Participle**	**Additional Elements**
Will	I/you/we/they/ he/she/it	be	living	near the Nile River?
AM	I	going to be	bringing	guest speakers?
Is	he/she/it	going to be	bringing	guest speakers?
Are	you/we/they	going to be	bringing	guest speakers?

***Wh–* Questions**					
***Wh–* Word**	**Will or Be Verb**	**Subject**	**Be or Going to Be**	**Present Participl e**	**Additional Elements**
When	will	I/you/we/they he/she/it	be	living	near the Nile River?
Why	am	I	going to be	bringing	guest speakers?
How	is	he/she/it	going to be	bringing	guest speakers?
When	are	you/we/they	going to be	bringing	guest speakers?

Meaning

This section will look at how meaning is communicated through the future simple and future continuous tenses in different situations. You will recognize some of these examples from the "Explanation of Grammar in Context" section where situational usage of the target grammar was explained from the travel log.

Future Simple

To Express Future Time

In general, the future simple tense uses *will* or *be going to* to express future time, whether that time is specifically stated or the time is indefinite. Notice the placement of the word *not* in the negative form. (Note that in speaking, */going to/* is often pronounced */gonna/*. This point can be explicitly taught to your students.)

I will not be at home tomorrow.

I am going to be at work.

To Express a Prediction

More specifically, the future simple tense uses *will* or *be going to* to make a prediction about what the speaker thinks will occur in the future or things that are expected to occur, including general truths, habits, states, activities, or future facts. Weather predictions are common in this situation. (Note that the negative usage *will not* is contracted to *won't*, which is a point that can be reviewed with students when teaching this tense.)

I hope that it won't rain while I am walking to my friend's house.

The weather report said that the sky is going to be clear.

Be careful! You will fall if you don't tie your shoe.

This is going to be an amazing experience!

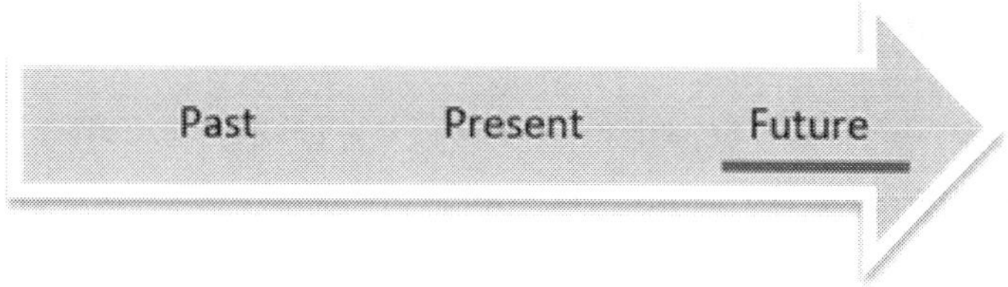

To Express a Prior Plan

The future simple tense uses *be going to* to express a prior plan that the speaker intends to do or has already decided to do or is in development.

I am going to meet my new friend at her house in the village. She is going to make Ugandan tea.

We are going to use experiential learning and take students on field trips.

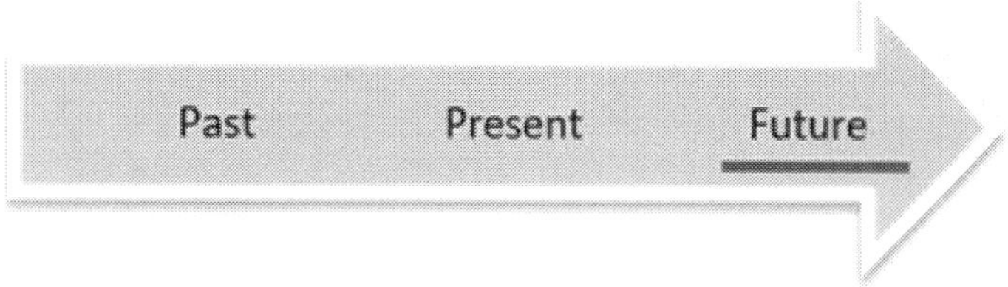

To Express a Future Action Decided at the Moment

We can use *will* to show a future action that is decided on at the moment of speaking. This action is often a quick or spontaneous decision.

On the way, I will stop at the bank and get some Ugandan shillings.
Now, I will finish the book I brought about the language and culture of Central Uganda's Buganda Kingdom.

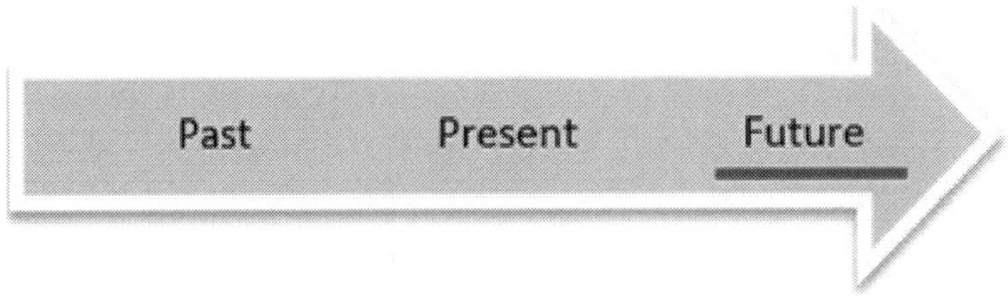

To Express Willingness

The future simple tense uses *will* to express that a person is willing to do something or that a person wants to volunteer to do something.

I will help you with your English homework.
Who is knocking at the door? I will answer it.

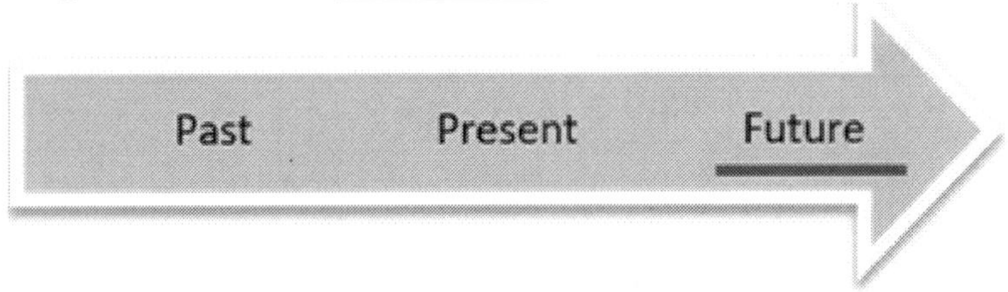

Future Continuous

Actions in Progress in the Future Interrupted by Other Events

The future continuous shows a future action that will be in progress in the future or an action that will be ongoing in the future. These continuous future actions are often interrupted by another event that will occur in the future. A specific time phrase—such as *when, at this time, next week, later this year*—is often used in conjunction with this tense.

I am going to be teaching *next week at this time*. My schedule looks full.
She will be cooking *when* I arrive.

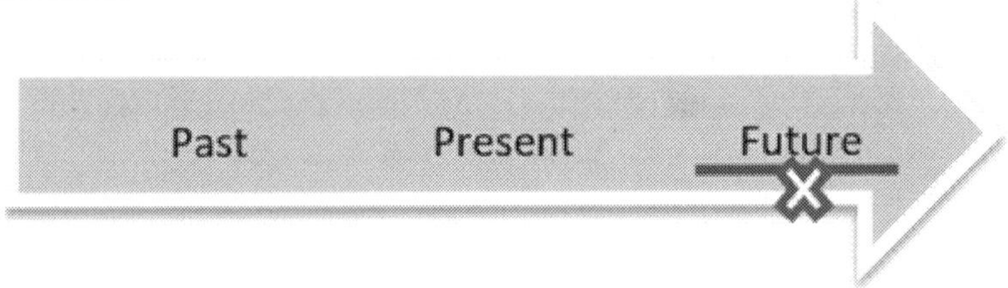

Predicting Actions That Will Be in Progress in the Future

The future continuous shows a prediction of a future action that will be in progress in the future or an action that will be ongoing in the future.

> **Someday cell phone companies will be offering more affordable packages, especially for smartphones.**
>
> **In the future, doctors are going to be using more natural and alternative practices, including quantum medicine and biofeedback.**

Additional Contexts for Use

This section provides examples of contexts where future simple and future continuous tenses are commonly used. The travel log at the beginning of this section contained examples of these two tenses in one real-world context. Following are some additional real-world contexts in which these tenses are commonly found.

To Plan a Trip

We use the future simple with *be going to* to plan trips, and we can use *future continuous* to give general descriptions of those plans.

> **I am going to visit my family in Minnesota next month. Since it is winter now, we are going to go sledding and skiing. We*'ll be flying* down mountains all weekend!**

To Write a Business Plan

We can use the future simple with *will* to express future events occurring at an indefinite time, and we can use *be going to* to express future events that are planned. Both of these can be used in writing a business plan.

> **Next month, my partner and I are going to purchase the empty building on the corner of 3rd Street.**
>
> **We will begin renovations to convert it into a coffee shop.**

To Engage in Fortune Telling

We use the future simple with *will* or *be going to* to foretell something that we believe will happen in the future or to foretell a general truth that will be true in the future. We can also use the *future continuous* to predict an action in progress at a specific future date/time.

> **She says that you are going to have a lot of children in the future.**
>
> **You will do amazing things in your lifetime.**
>
> **When you turn 50 years old, you *will be living* in a mansion.**

Common Mistakes

Let's take a look at some common mistakes made by nonnative speakers first learning these tenses.

Time Clauses

When there are two clauses in a sentence, one clause that is a dependent time clause and one clause that is an independent clause[3.2], nonnative speakers commonly make the mistake of using the future simple tense in both clauses, but the present simple should be used in the dependent time clause.

Incorrect: **I will use public transportation when I will arrive in Uganda.**

Correct: I **will use public transportation when I arrive in Uganda**.

Be Verb

Some nonnative speakers forget to include a form of the *be* verb with the future continuous tense.

Incorrect: **I will working at that time.**

Correct: **I will be working at that time.**

Will and *Be Going to*

Some nonnative speakers forget to include the future words *will* or *be going to* to express the future in the future simple or future progressive tenses. This often stems from the lack of a modal verb like *will* in students' native languages.

Incorrect: **I be working at that time.**

Correct: **I will be working at that time.**

Incorrect: **I help you tomorrow.**

Correct: **I will help you tomorrow.**

NOTE 3.2 : Learn more about sentence clauses in the "Sentence Formation" section of Unit 2.

Conclusion

We now conclude our section on the future simple and future continuous tenses. In addition to understanding the meaning and use of these tenses, it is important to recognize the two different forms, *will* and *be going to*, are used interchangeably at times and are slightly distinguished from each other in meaning in other situations. It is also important to test your knowledge on these structures by taking the relevant quiz in the "Quizzes" section of the book.

The next section will lead us into the perfect aspect with an introduction to the present perfect and the present perfect continuous tenses.

3.4 PRESENT PERFECT AND PRESENT PERFECT CONTINUOUS

Introduction

Rio has been waiting to get on the subway for two hours.

The example sentence above shows the basics of the perfect aspect in English. In this sentence, we see that the present perfect continuous tense, *has been waiting*, demonstrates a relationship between a time in the past and now.

This section illustrates the perfect aspect in the English language, specifically looking at the present perfect and present perfect continuous tenses. We will start by looking at the target language in the context of an email. Then we will look at timelines that explain the use of aspect in the email. After that, you'll be given information about the form, meaning, and use of the target grammar.

Objectives

- Identify the use of the present perfect and present perfect continuous in context
- Compare and contrast the form of the present perfect and present perfect continuous
- Classify meanings of the present perfect and present perfect continuous
- List common real-world contexts for use of the present perfect and present perfect continuous
- Identify common mistakes made with the present perfect and present perfect continuous

Use in Context: An Email Home

Read the following email an EFL teacher in Japan sent to her parents. The text contains examples of the present perfect (marked in bold) and the present perfect continuous (marked in italics). Notice how the underlined examples are used in conjunction with other tenses like the present simple, the present continuous, the past simple, and the future simple.

New Message

To momanddad@email.com Cc Bcc

Subject Week Three in Japan!

Mom and Dad,

Well, I'm here! I'**ve been** here for about 3 weeks now, and I'm slowly adjusting. All of the teachers at school are really nice, even if we can't communicate very well. They*'ve been helping* me with a lot of things, like getting a cellphone and setting up my utilities. I really need their help because I can't do a lot of things by myself with the language barrier. I'**ve set up** my own utilities before, but never in another language! When I first got to my apartment, I didn't know how anything worked! I wasn't able to wash my clothes because I couldn't figure out the washing machine! But, one of my neighbors showed me how to do it, and I'**ve run** the machine a few times all by myself since then. I still **haven't figured out** exactly what the buttons say, but I just remember which ones to push. You both know that I'**ve** always **had** a pretty good memory. For the past few days, I*'ve been trying* to memorize some characters (kanji) in the Japanese writing system. I put a poster on the wall in my apartment for extra practice. I need to go to work now, so I'll write more soon.

Love,
Karen

P.S. I'**ve attached** a picture of the buttons on my washing machine, so you can see why I*'ve been having* so many problems!

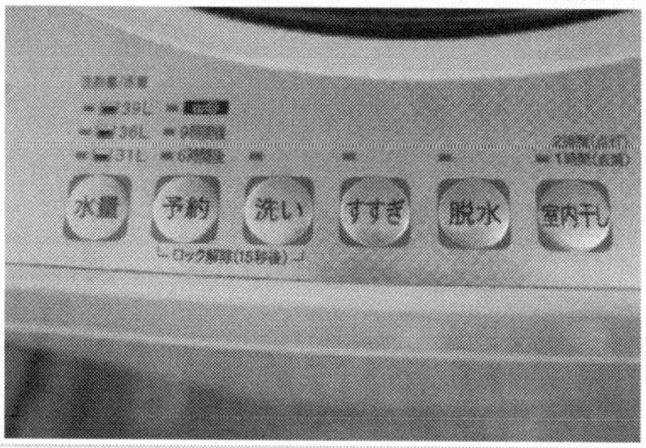

Sans Serif

Send

Explanation of Grammar in Context

Let's examine the usage of the target grammar by looking at some of the sentences from the email you just read. With each sentence, a timeline explains the relationship between the past and the present. Next to each sentence is text in parentheses that indicates the form of the present perfect or present perfect continuous. Form is discussed more thoroughly later on in this section.

Present Perfect

With the ***present perfect,*** we can understand that in the present, we have a connection to a past action or experience.

I'<u>ve been</u> here for three weeks now. (*have + been*)

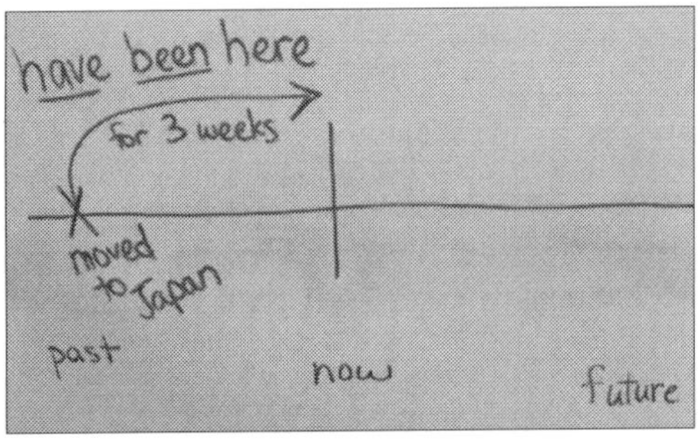

In this sentence, the speaker is expressing an action that started in the past and continues into the present. In this example, we know the exact point in the past when the action started. The teacher moved to Japan three weeks before the email was written, and this sentence shows us that the teacher is still in Japan at the time of writing the email.

I'<u>ve set up</u> my own utilities before, but never in another language! (*have + set up*)

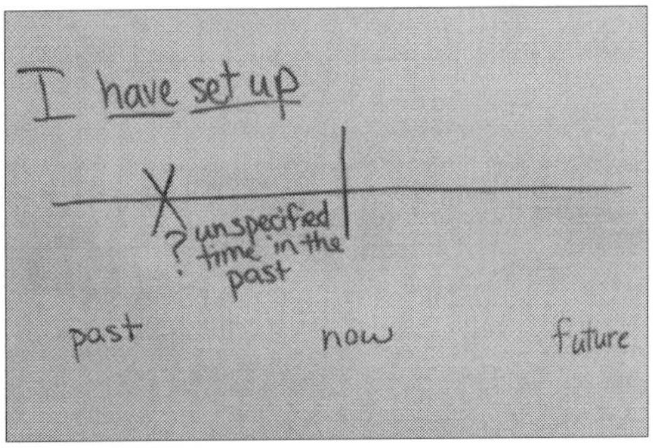

In this sentence, the speaker is expressing an action that happened in the past, but it's not clear exactly when that happened. We do not know when the speaker set up her own utilities, so the present perfect is used to show that action at an unspecified time in the past. It is not important when this action happened in the past because the experience of that action is what is important to the current time of writing the email.

I'<u>ve run</u> the machine a few times all by myself since then. (*have + run*)

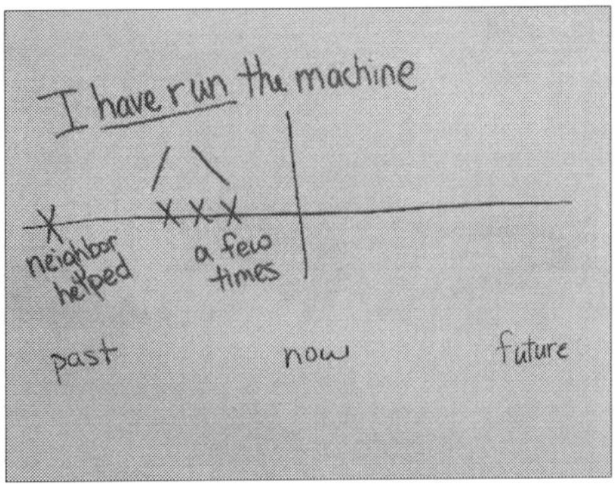

In this sentence, the speaker is expressing the repetition of a past action that is important to the current conversation (or email). The sentence shows us that the teacher has successfully run her machine a few times since her neighbor showed her how to use it, and we assume that this action will likely be repeated in the future.

Present Perfect Continuous

With the ***present perfect continuous***, we are again looking at a relationship between the past and the present and showing something that started in the past and is still happening or is still true now. One key difference between the tenses is that the present perfect continuous can be used only with dynamic (action verbs) and not stative verbs. Stative verbs cannot be used in any continuous tense. (More information on stative and dynamic verbs can be found in the "Verbs" section in Unit 1.)

They'<u>ve been helping</u> me with a lot of things. (*have + been + helping*)

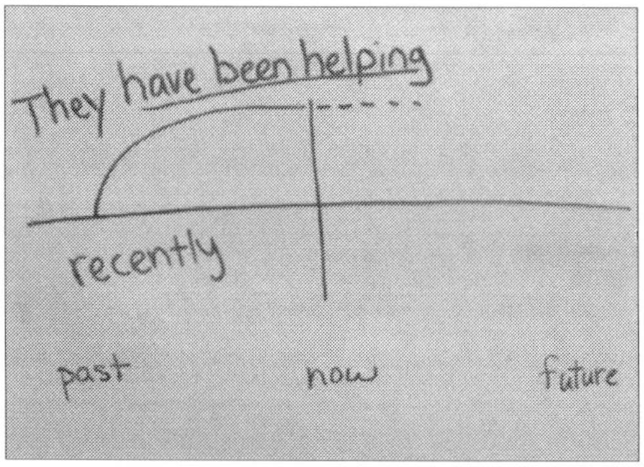

This sentence shows us that the Japanese teachers have been repeatedly helping the teacher with things she needs to set up for her new life in Japan. The sentence also indicates that this will probably continue happening into the future.

For the past few days, I'<u>ve been trying</u> to memorize some characters in the Japanese writing system. (*have + been + trying*)

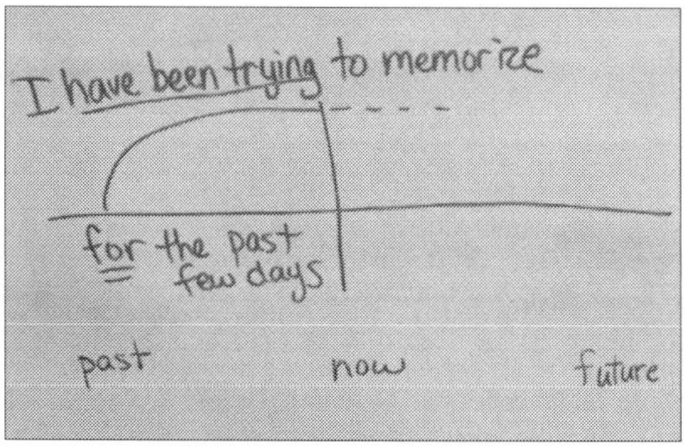

This sentence expresses an action that has taken place recently and is likely to continue. In this case, we see the teacher's recent attempts of trying to memorize something. The use of the present perfect continuous suggests that the teacher will continue this action into the future.

I'<u>ve been having</u> so many problems. (*have + been + having*)

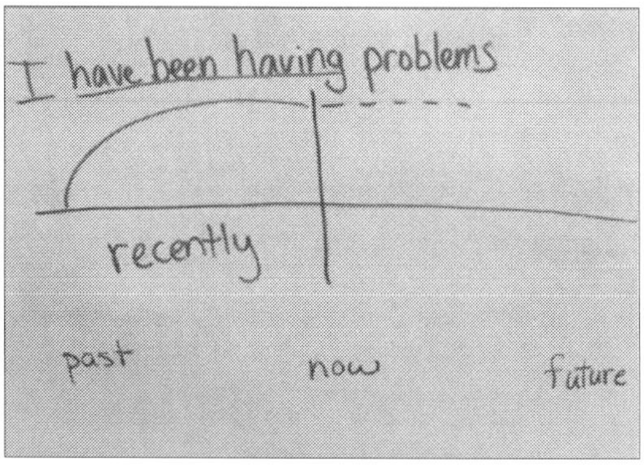

Again, this sentence shows something that has been happening repeatedly in the recent past and will presumably continue to occur.

Timeline Video

In addition to the previous timeline images, there is a video on International TEFL Academy's YouTube channel that depicts an EFL teacher using timelines to give explanations of a few example sentences from the "Use in Context: An Email Home" section. Timelines can be effective visual aids for explaining time relationships inherent in verb tenses. This video does not give an exhaustive explanation of meaning and use for the present perfect and present perfect continuous tenses. For a more thorough explanation, please refer to the "Meaning" and "Use" parts of this section.

Present Perfect and Present Perfect Continuous - https://youtu.be/M1LA6YoHs_M

Form

In the sample email, we saw a few examples of the present perfect and the present perfect continuous. Now that we have looked closely at the meaning of those tenses, let's shift our attention to a focus on form. To begin, read the Think Box below and try to answer the questions using only your prior knowledge and the example sentences from the email.

> **Think Box**
>
> Read the present perfect and present perfect continuous examples below. What do you notice about the form of the tenses? What do the present perfect examples have in common? What do the present perfect continuous examples have in common?

Present Perfect Examples

I'<u>ve set up</u> my own utilities before, but never in another language!
I <u>have been</u> here for three weeks now.
I <u>have run</u> the machine a few times all by myself since then.

Present Perfect Continuous Examples

They <u>have been helping</u> me with a lot of things.
I <u>have been trying</u> to memorize some characters in the Japanese writing system.
I <u>have been having</u> so many problems.

Now that you have considered how these two tenses are formed, we will take a more detailed look at form in the following sections.

Present Perfect

Were you able to identify similarities and/or apply any terms to the sentences in the previous section? Perhaps you noticed that all the example present perfect sentences contain the auxiliary verb *to have,* followed by a past participle. For this tense, the auxiliary verb is conjugated in the present, *has* or *have*. The following past participle is formed in one of two ways. If the verb is regular, *–ed* is added to the infinitive form, *visit + –ed -> visited.* If the verb is irregular, the irregular past participle form is given, *be -> been: subject + have/has + past participle (verb + –ed or irregular form).*

He has visited Mexico several times.

They have lived in Chicago since 2003.

Statement and Question Formation

For your reference, Table 3.11 summarizes the forms of affirmative and negative statements, yes/no questions, and *Wh–* questions. Note the conjugations for different subjects. (More detailed information about general sentence and question formation can be found in Unit 2.)

Table 3.11 Present Perfect Statement and Question Formation

Affirmative Statements				
Subject	**Have or Has**	**Past Participle**	**Additional Elements**	
I/You/They	have	lived	in Japan.	
He/She/It	has	taught	English.	
Negative Statements				
I/You/They	have not (have never)	lived	in Japan.	
He/She/It	has not (has never)	taught	English.	
Yes/No Questions				
Have or Has	**Subject**	**Past Participle**	**Additional Elements**	
Have	I/you/they	lived	in Japan?	
Has	he/she/it	taught	English?	
***Wh–* Questions**				
***Wh–* Word**	**Have or Has**	**Subject**	**Past Participle**	**Additional Elements**
Where	have	I/you/they	lived	in Japan?
When	has	he/she/it	taught	English?

Present Perfect Continuous

Now let's move on to the examples that contain the ***present perfect continuous*** tense. Were you able to identify similarities and/or apply any terms to those sentences? Perhaps you noticed that all these examples also contain the auxiliary verb *to have* conjugated in the present tense. Like the present perfect tense, the auxiliary verb is followed by a past participle, but in this case, it is always the past participle of the verb *to be*. The past participle *been* is then followed by a present participle. Present participles are formed by adding *–ing* to the base form of a verb.

subject + have/has + been + present participle (verb + –ing).

She has been watching TV for over four hours.

They have been waiting since this morning.

Statement and Question Formation

For your reference, Table 3.12 summarizes the form of affirmative and negative statements, yes/no questions, and *Wh–* questions. Note the conjugations for different subjects in each chart. (More detailed information about general sentence and question formation can be found in Unit 2.)

Table 3.12 Present Perfect Continuous Statement and Question Formation				
Affirmative Statements				
Subject	**Have or Has**	**Been + Present Participle**	**Additional Elements**	
I/You/They	have	been trying	to memorize Japanese characters.	
He/She/It	has	been studying	Japanese.	
Negative Statements				
Subject	**Have or Has + Not**	**Been + Present Participle**	**Additional Elements**	
I/You/They	have not	been trying	to memorize Japanese characters.	
He/She/It	has not	been studying	Japanese.	
Yes/No Questions				
Have or Has	**Subject**	**Been + Present Participle**	**Additional Elements**	
Have	I/you/they	been trying	to memorize Japanese characters?	
Has	he/she/it	been studying	Japanese?	
***Wh–* Questions**				
***Wh–* word**	**Have or Has**	**Subject**	**Been + Present Participle**	**Additional Elements**
How	have	I/you/they	been trying	to memorize Japanese characters?
Where	has	he/she/it	been studying	Japanese?

Meaning

This section presents guidelines for how meaning is communicated through the present perfect and present perfect continuous tenses in different situations. You will recognize some of these examples from the "Explanation of Grammar in Context" section above where situational usage of the target grammar was explained from Karen's email. Commonly used adverbs —including *since*, *for*, *ever*, *never*, *still*, *already*, *yet*—are also noted for each situation. (To review rules of placement for adverbs in sentences, see the section on "Articles, Adjectives, and Adverbs" in Unit 1.)

Present Perfect

Action for Unspecified Time in the Past

The present perfect can also be used to show something that happened or did not happen at a time in the past that is not specified and often shows achievements, experience, or uncompleted actions we are expecting. It is often used with *ever, never, still, already, yet.*

I have taught children, teens, and adults in many different settings. (achievement)
Have you *ever* visited Canada? (experience)
He has *never* eaten sushi. (experience)
They *still* haven't finished their homework. (uncompleted expected action)
She has *already* seen that movie. (experience)
I haven't gotten my brother's response *yet.* (uncompleted expected action)

Duration of Action until Now

The ***present perfect*** is used to describe a situation or action that started in the past and continues to the present (used with stative verbs), often used with *since* to indicate the point in time that the action started and *for* to indicate the period of time that the situation has been true.

I have been here *for* three weeks now.
She has lived in Japan *since* 2003.

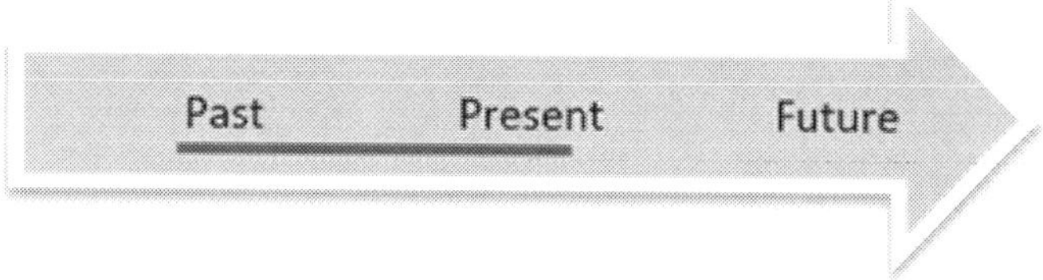

It is important to note that if the time in the past is specified and important to the context, the past simple tense is used

Unspecified Past Time: Present Perfect
She has already seen that movie.
Have you ever visited Canada?
I have taught children.
Specific Past Time: Past Simple
She saw that movie last week.
Did you visit Canada last year?

I <u>taught</u> children two years ago.

Recent Events

We can use the present perfect to show that an action was completed in the very recent past, often used with *just*.

I <u>have</u> *just* <u>entered</u> all of the data into the spreadsheet.

Repetitive Past Actions Likely to Be Repeated

The present perfect is also used to show that an action was repeated in the past and is likely to be repeated, often used with *so far*, *a few times*, *many times*, *since*, *for*.

I <u>have read</u> four books *so far* this year.
I <u>have run</u> the machine *a few times* by myself since then.
She <u>has analyzed</u> that painting *many times*.
They <u>have eaten</u> pasta for dinner almost every day *for* the past week.

Present Perfect Continuous

Duration of Action Until Now

The ***present perfect continuous*** describes an action or situation that began in the past and continues until now (used with dynamic verbs), often used with *since* to indicate the point in time that the action started and *for* to indicate the period of time that the situation has been true.

He <u>has been doing</u> his homework *since* 8:00.
She <u>has been riding</u> her bicycle *for* half an hour.
I <u>have been teaching</u> here *for* ten years.

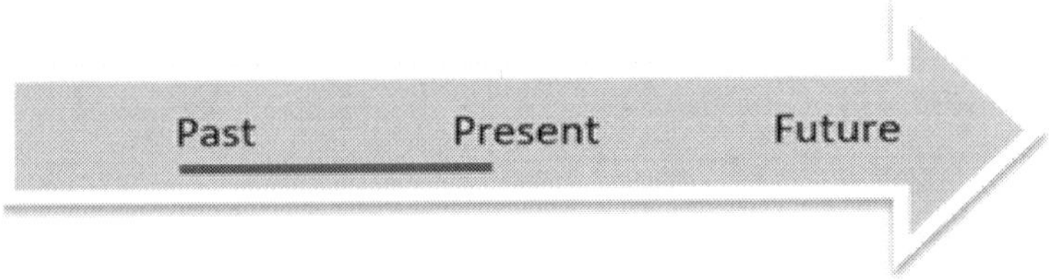

Recent Events

The present perfect continuous also shows recent events or actions, often used with *recently* and *lately*.

They have been studying a lot *recently*.

***Lately*, she has been riding her bike to work.**

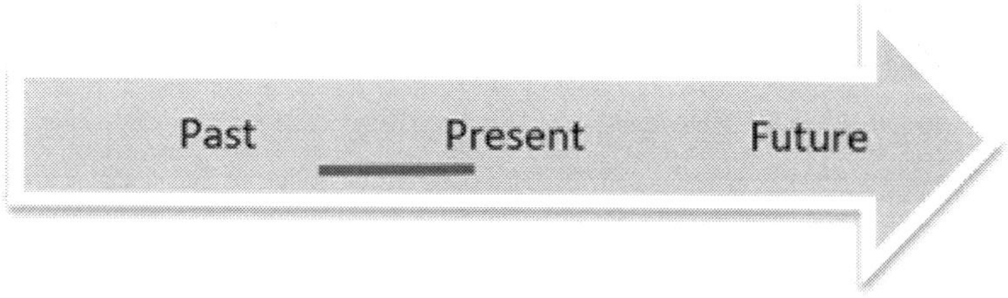

Some verbs—including *live*, *work*, *teach*—can be used with the present perfect or present perfect continuous and will maintain the same meaning.

I have been teaching here for ten years. (present perfect continuous)

I have taught here for ten years. (present perfect)

Additional Contexts for Use

This section provides examples of contexts where present perfect and present perfect continuous are commonly used. The email at the beginning of this section contained examples of these two tenses in one real-world context, an email home. Following are additional real-world contexts in which these tenses are commonly found.

News Reports

We use the present perfect when we want to describe recent events in news reports, which gives the reporting a more present feel.

The president has left for an official visit to China.

Cover Letters, Job Applications, and Interviews

We use the present perfect when we want to describe experience or achievement, which stresses the present knowledge and abilities that past experience has bestowed.

I have overseen multiple projects.

New Encounters

We use the present perfect when we want to get to know another person by conversing about experiences and achievements to find common ground.

It's nice to meet you. Have you ever eaten here before?

Postcards/Travel Communications
We use the present perfect and the *present perfect continuous* when writing home during travel. We often want to express which planned activities are completed and which lay ahead.

We have visited four countries on the trip so far, but we haven't arrived in Italy yet.

We*'ve been traveling* for three weeks so far.

Letter/Email to an Old Friend
We use the present perfect continuous when we want to catch someone up on our recent life and activities.

We love it in China! We have been getting settled in our new home, and the kids have been taking Chinese lessons three times a week. I haven't been keeping up with the Giants, however, because their games aren't on TV here.

Common Mistakes

Let's take a look at some common mistakes made by nonnative speakers first learning these tenses as well as a mistake made by native speakers.

Incorrect Past Participle Form

Both native and nonnative speakers occasionally use the incorrect form of the past participle, especially when the form is irregular.

Incorrect: **Even though he works with dangerous animals, he's never been bit by one.**

Correct: **Even though he works with dangerous animals, he's never been bitten by one.**

Incorrect: **She's an amazing swimmer; she's never been beat in this event.**

Correct: **She's an amazing swimmer; she's never been beaten in this event.**

Incorrect Verb Tense

Some nonnative speakers just learning the form will mistakenly refer to an event that took place at a specific time in the past using the present perfect. Both of these examples should instead be written in the past simple.

Incorrect: **He's written five essays last month.**

Correct: **He wrote five essays last month.**

Incorrect: **They've gone shopping on Saturday.**

Correct: **They went shopping on Saturday.**

Stative versus Dynamic Verbs

Some nonnative speakers try to use stative verbs with the present perfect continuous, but we use dynamic verbs only with this tense. Both of these examples should instead be written in the present perfect.

Incorrect: **I <u>have been knowing</u> her since elementary school.**

Correct: **I <u>have known</u> her since elementary school.**

Incorrect: **She <u>has been owning</u> that house for five years.**

Correct: **She <u>has owned</u> that house for five years.**

Conclusion

We now conclude our section on the present perfect and present perfect continuous tenses. It is important to recognize that the perfect aspect can be a particularly difficult facet of English for students of EFL/ESL. This is especially true for students whose first language does not contain this aspect. We encourage you to go to the "Quizzes" section of the book and take the quiz on present perfect and present perfect continuous while the information is fresh in your mind.

In the next section, we will continue to look at the perfect aspect, but within the past tense, as we consider the past perfect and the past perfect continuous tenses.

3.5 PAST PERFECT AND PAST PERFECT CONTINUOUS

Introduction

Susan was late for class. When she arrived, the exam <u>had already begun</u>.

The sentence above shows an example of the perfect aspect in English, used within the past tense. The text, *had already begun,* contains the past perfect tense, demonstrating a relationship between two occurrences in the past (*arrived* and *begun*), ordering one before the other, chronologically.

This section looks at the past perfect and past perfect continuous tenses. We will start by looking at the target language in the context of a teacher's testimonial about traveling abroad. Then we will look at timelines that explain the use of perfect aspect in the past tense. After that, you'll be given information about the form, meaning, and use of the target grammar.

Objectives

- Identify the use of the perfect aspect in the past tense within context
- Compare and contrast the form of the past perfect and past perfect continuous
- Classify meanings of the past perfect and past perfect continuous
- List common real-world contexts for use of the past perfect and past perfect continuous
- Identify common mistakes made with the past perfect and past perfect continuous

Use in Context: A Teacher's Testimonial

Read the following recollection from a TEFL program website that an EFL teacher has written about his first job search. The text contains examples of the past perfect (marked in bold) and the past perfect continuous (marked in italics). Notice how the examples are used in conjunction with other tenses like the past simple and the past continuous.

ABC TEFL SCHOOL*

Teacher Testimonials!

REAL TESTIMONIALS FROM REAL PEOPLE LIKE YOU WHO ARE TEACHING ENGLISH ABROAD

Contact Us | Prices | Services | Testimonials

"Bienvenidos a España" - My Experience in Spain

Moving to Spain was a huge learning experience for me. I finished my TEFL certification course in the summer of 2012 and moved immediately to Madrid. I was excited to start teaching in a new country, one that I **had** always **dreamed** of visiting. I **had** never **been** to Spain before, and now I was moving there to live and teach!

After I arrived by plane, I took the Metro to the tourist apartment I **had rented** online. I **had tried** to look for long-term apartments from the USA, but it was difficult to find details or see what the apartments looked like (this was before I knew about AirBNB!). It **had** also **been** difficult to find a teaching job because most of the schools were closed in the summer, and I **had heard** that schools in Spain tend to hire at the last minute, anyway. Luckily, I was financially prepared because *I'd been saving* money very carefully. I *had been working* two jobs for the three years previous, and I'**d started** a separate savings account just for travel. I knew that I could stay in Madrid for several months without a job, if I had to, but I hoped it wouldn't come to that.

After I arrived, I contacted a number of language schools, and many were interested in interviewing me. One school was ready to hire me immediately, but they informed me that they would not be able to complete visa paperwork for me (they **had tried** to get work visas for Americans many times before, with no luck). They offered to pay me my salary in cash, "under the table," a possibility that I **had not** truly **considered** before arriving. I **had** always **thought** that getting work visas to teach English would be easy, but I saw that I had a difficult decision to make.

Explanation of Grammar in Context

Let's examine the usage of the target grammar by looking at some of the sentences from the teacher's testimonial. With each example, a timeline explains the relationship between the past events in the sentence. Form is discussed more thoroughly later on in this section.

Past Perfect

With verbs used in the ***past perfect,*** we can understand that the action occurred before another action in the past. Thus, the past perfect is not used as a standalone tense but must be used in relation to another past tense verb or within a general past context.

I took the Metro to the tourist apartment I <u>had rented</u> online. (*had + rented*)

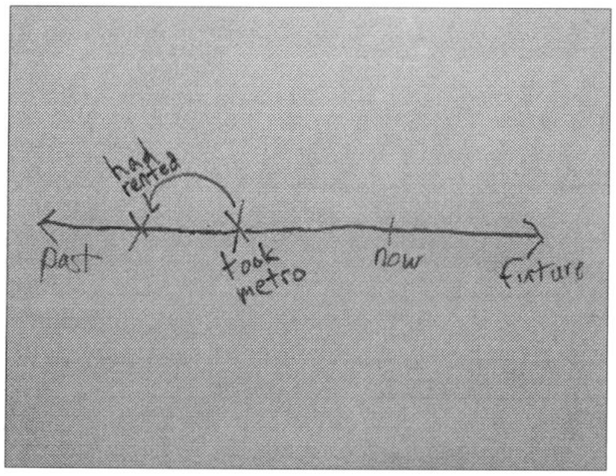

In this sentence, we know that both actions (*took* and *rented*) happened in the past, but because *rented* is in the past perfect tense, we know that it happened first chronologically. Regardless of position within a sentence—whether or not it is the first verb in the sentence order—the past perfect signals that an action occurred before any other actions that appear in the past simple or continuous. Thus, even though the verb *took* appears first in the sentence, the action, *rented,* happened first chronologically.

They informed me that they would not be able to complete visa paperwork for me (they <u>had tried</u> to get work visas for Americans many times before, with no luck). (*had + tried*)

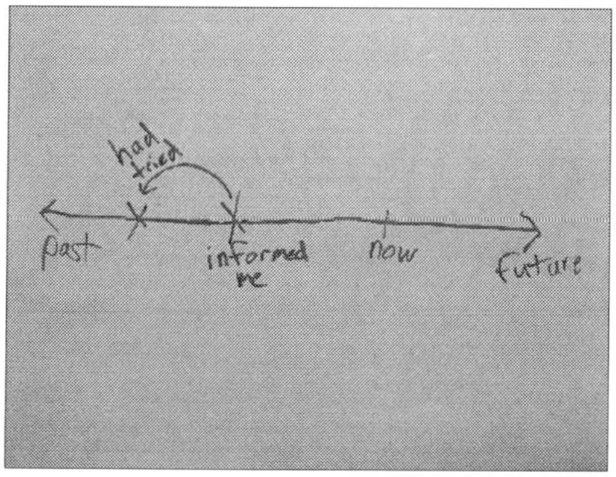

This sentence communicates repetition of an action that occurred before another action in the past. The sentence starts with an action in the past, *informed*, and then uses the past perfect, *had tried*, to show that a repeated action happened previously.

I <u>had</u> always <u>thought</u> that getting work visas to teach English would be easy.
(*had* + *thought*)

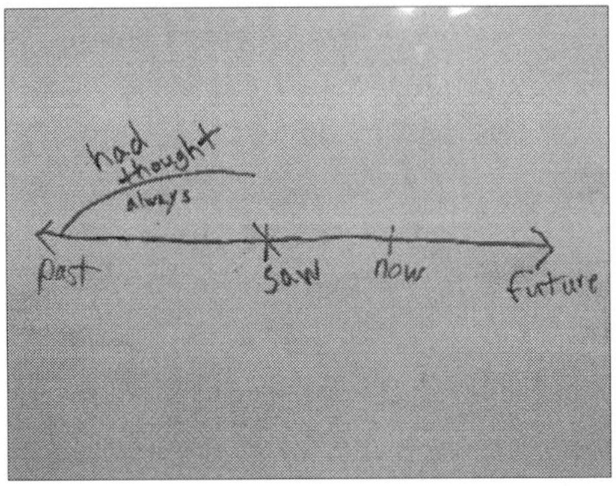

This sentence communicates that something was true for a period leading up to another past action. In this case, the writer thought that something was true before he had to make a difficult decision. The past perfect, *had thought*, shows us that this opinion always existed before the decision, but it did not continue after the decision.

Past Perfect Continuous

With the ***past perfect continuous***, we are again looking at a relationship between two verbs in the past, showing something that started in the past and was happening or was still true up to another action or time in the past (and may or may not have continued). It can explain the cause of another action or state, or it can be used with *for* or *since* to show duration of time.

I was financially prepared because I'<u>d been saving</u> money very carefully.
(*had* + *been* + *saving*)

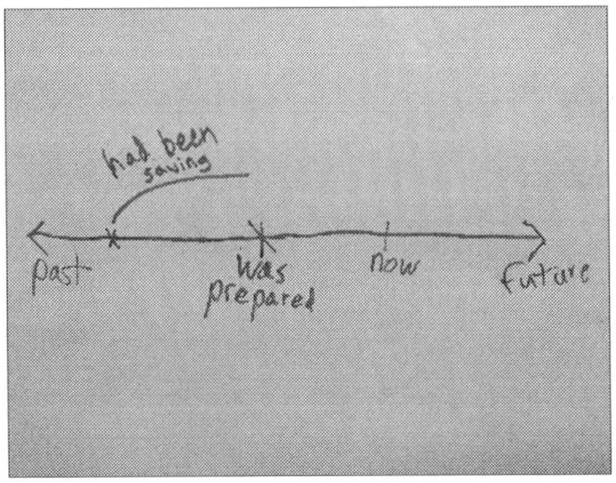

This sentence shows an action that was in progress before a state of being in the past, and it explains the cause of that state. The action, *saving*, began at some point before the author was *financially prepared*, and the action explains the cause for that state of being.

I <u>had been working</u> three jobs for the three years previous (before I moved).
(*had* + *been* + *working*)

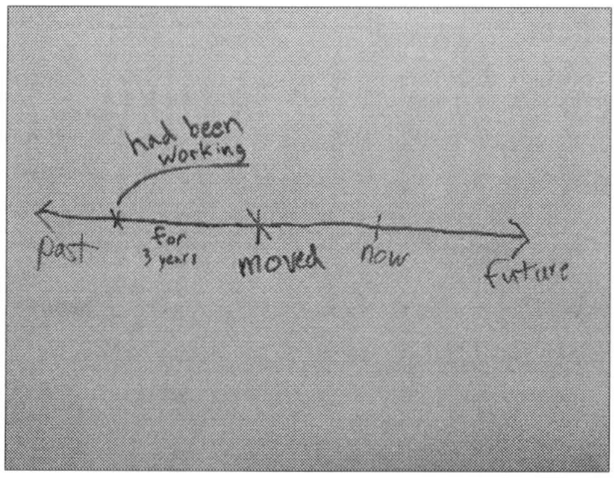

This sentence expresses the duration of time of an action that was in progress before another action in the past. The action, *working three jobs*, was in progress for three years before the author moved to Spain. This usage of the past perfect is most commonly used with *for* or *since* and a time marker.

Timeline Video

In addition to the timeline images above, there is a video on International TEFL Academy's YouTube channel that depicts an EFL teacher using timelines to explain a few example sentences from the "Use in Context" section. Timelines can be effective visual aids for explaining time relationships inherent in verb tenses. This video does not give an exhaustive explanation of meaning and use for the past perfect and past perfect continuous tenses. For a more thorough explanation, please refer to the "Meaning" and "Use" parts of this section.

Past Perfect and Past Perfect Continuous - https://youtu.be/-1hwo55BMFY

Form

In the teacher's testimonial, we saw a few examples of the past perfect and the past perfect continuous. Now that we have looked closely at the meaning of those tenses, let's shift our attention to a focus on form. To begin, read the Think Box below and try to answer the questions using only your prior knowledge and the example sentences from the testimonial.

Think Box

Read the past perfect and past perfect continuous examples below. What do you notice about the form of the tenses? What do the past perfect examples have in common? What do the past perfect continuous examples have in common?

Past Perfect Examples

I took the Metro to the tourist apartment I <u>had rented</u> online.
I <u>had</u> never <u>been</u> to Spain before, and now I was moving there to live and teach!
I <u>had</u> always <u>thought</u> that getting work visas to teach English would be easy.

Past Perfect Continuous Examples

Luckily, I was financially prepared because I <u>had been working</u> two jobs for the three years previous, and <u>I'd been saving</u> money very carefully.

Now that you have considered how these two tenses are formed, we will take a more detailed look at form in the following section.

Past Perfect

Were you able to identify similarities and/or apply any terms to the sentences in the previous section? Perhaps you noticed that all the example past perfect tenses contain the auxiliary verb *had* (the past tense of *have*) followed by a past participle. As with present perfect, the past participle is formed in one of two ways. If the verb is regular, *–ed* is added to the infinitive form, *visit + –ed -> visited.* If the verb is irregular, the irregular past participle form is given, *be -> been: subject + had + past participle (verb + –ed or irregular form).*

He <u>had visited</u> Thailand only once before he moved there last year.

We <u>had known</u> each other for years when we got married.

Statement and Question Formation

For your reference, Table 3.13 summarizes the form of affirmative and negative statements, yes/no questions, and *Wh–* questions. Note that these sentences are used to demonstrate how to form the past perfect tense alone, out of context, and therefore they do not contain additional clauses with the past simple for time reference. Sentences like these that contain a single verb phrase in the past perfect are generally used within a larger past tense context, like the example testimonial. (More detailed information about general sentence and question formation can be found in Unit 2.)

Table 3.13 Past Perfect Statement and Question Formation				
Affirmative Statements				
Subject	**Had**	**Past Participle**	**Additional Elements**	
I/You/We/They He/She/It	had	taught	in Europe.	
Negative Statements				
Subject	**Had + Not or Never**	**Past Participle**	**Additional Elements**	
I/You/We/They He/She/It	had not (had never)	taught	in Europe.	
Yes/No Questions				
Had	**Subject**	**Past Participle**	**Additional Elements**	
Had	I/you/we/they/he/she/it	taught	in Europe?	
***Wh–* Questions**				
***Wh–* Word**	**Had**	**Subject**	**Past Participle**	**Additional Elements**
Where	had	I/you/we/they he/she/it	taught	in Europe?

Past Perfect Continuous

Now let's move on to the examples that contain the ***past perfect continuous*** tense. Were you able to identify similarities and/or apply any terms to those sentences? Perhaps you noticed that all these examples also contain the auxiliary verb *had* (*have* in the past tense). Like the past perfect tense, the auxiliary verb is followed by a past participle, but in this case, it is always the past participle of the verb *to be*. The past participle *been* is then followed by a present participle. Present participles are formed by adding *–ing* to the base form of a verb.

subject + had + been + present participle (verb + –ing).

She <u>had been walking</u> in the rain, so her hair was wet.

They <u>had been waiting</u> so long when they finally got the news!

Statement and Question Formation

For your reference, Table 3.14 summarizes the form of affirmative and negative statements, yes/no questions, and *Wh–* questions. Note the conjugations for different subjects. Again, note that these examples are decontextualized; when used in discourse, they would typically be used in relation to other events in the past. (More detailed information about general sentence and question formation can be found in Unit 2.)

Table 3.14 Past Perfect Continuous Statement and Question Formation				
Affirmative Statements				
Subject	**Had**	**Been + Present Participle**	**Additional Elements**	
I/You/We/They He/She/It	had	been learning	the language.	
Negative Statements				
Subject	**Had + Not**	**Been + Present Participle**	**Additional Elements**	
I/You/We/They He/She/It	had not	been learning	the language.	
Yes/No Questions				
Had	**Subject**	**Been + Present Participle**	**Additional Elements**	
Had	I/you/we/they he/she/it	been learning	the language?	
***Wh–* Questions**				
***Wh–* word**	**Had**	**Subject**	**Been + Present Participle**	**Additional Elements**
How	had	I/you/we/they he/she/it	been learning	the language?

Meaning

This section presents guidelines for how meaning is communicated through the past perfect and past perfect continuous tenses in different situations. Note the relation of the target grammar to other grammatical features (usually the past simple) in the example sentences. Commonly used adverbs—*since*, *for*, *ever*, *never*, *still*, *already*, *yet*—are also noted for each situation. (To review rules of placement for adverbs in sentences, see the section on "Adjectives, Articles, and Adverbs" in Unit 1.)

Past Perfect

Action Completed Before another Action or Time in the Past

The past perfect describes something that happened or did not happen before another time in the past, an action that is not specified that often shows achievements, experience, or uncompleted actions relative to another point in the past, often used with *ever, never, still, already*, *yet*.

I had taught teens and adults. (experience)
Had you *ever* visited Russia before you moved there? (experience)
She had *never* eaten sushi before, and I think she liked it. (experience)
They *still* hadn't finished their homework when I got home!
(uncompleted expected action)
We'd *already* seen all of the movies that were out, so we played a game instead.
(experience)
I was worried because I hadn't heard from you *yet*. (uncompleted expected action)

Past perfect is often used in complex sentences with adverb clauses that show time relationships. If *before* or *after* is used, the time relationship is usually already clear, so the past perfect may not be necessary to order the events.

I had eaten *before* I arrived. = I ate before I arrived.

However, if the ambiguous time marker *when* is used, the time relationship is not clear, so the past perfect may be necessary to order the events.

***When* he arrived, the test started. ≠ When he arrived, the test had started.**

In the first sentence, it appears as if the two actions happened at the same time. But with the past perfect in the second sentence, we know that the test started before he arrived.

(More information about complex sentences and adverb clauses can be found in the "Sentence Formation" section of Unit 2.)

Duration of Action until Another Point in the Past

The past perfect also shows a situation or action that started in the past and continued to another point in the past (used with stative verbs), often used with *since* to indicate the point in time that the action started and *for* to indicate the period of time that the situation had been true.

She had lived in Prague *since* 2003.

We had loved each other *for* 10 years when we finally got married.

Past Perfect Continuous

Duration of Action from One Point in the Past to Another

The past perfect continuous demonstrates a situation or action that started in the past and continued to another point in the past (used with dynamic verbs), often used with *since* to indicate the point in time that the action started and *for* to indicate the period of time that the situation has been true.

We had been looking for him *for* three hours when he finally called.

I was angry because I'd been waiting *since* 8 o'clock that morning.

An Event or Action Recent to Another Past

The past perfect continuous also describes an activity that was in progress just before another event or time in the past, often explaining a cause of a past state.

My hair was wet because I'd been walking in the rain.

Additional Contexts for Use

This section provides some examples of contexts where past perfect and past perfect continuous are commonly used. The testimonial at the beginning of this section contains examples of these two tenses in one real-world context, a description of past travels. Following are additional real-world contexts in which these tenses are commonly found.

Personal Anecdotes

We use the past perfect and the *past perfect continuous* when we want to describe a personal story and need to order the events or causes of actions or states.

> **My hair was messy because I'd biked to work, and my eyes were red, so they thought I'*d been crying*. They had never had a teacher that looked so crazy before!**

Cautionary Tales

We use the past perfect when we want to describe a past state of being and the events or actions that led to it.

> **I had never lived alone before, and I hadn't studied the language or learned enough about the culture.**

Past Regrets

We use the past perfect when we want to imagine how things could have been or would be different if we could somehow change the past.

> **If I had set my alarm, I wouldn't have been fired.**
> **I wouldn't be an English teacher if I hadn't been born in the USA.**

Fictional Writing

We use the past perfect and the *past perfect continuous* when we want to convey fictional stories in books and short stories with older past events compared to a more recent time in the past.

> **He walked slowly into the house. He had never been here before, and he wasn't sure if he would be welcome. The first time he had seen this house, he wasn't old enough to reach the doorknob. He *had been having* nightmares about this house ever since that first sighting.**

(For more information on and examples of these types of sentences, see the "Conditionals" section in Unit 4.)

Common Mistakes

Let's take a look at some common mistakes made by nonnative speakers first learning these tenses as well as a mistake made by native speakers.

Incorrect Form of Past Participle

Both native and nonnative speakers occasionally use the incorrect form of the past participle, especially when the form is irregular.

Incorrect: **I was hungry because I <u>hadn't ate</u>.**
Correct: **I was hungry because I <u>hadn't eaten</u>.**

Overuse of the Past Perfect

Some nonnative speakers just learning the form will overuse the past perfect. When the past narrative is straightforward, the past simple should be used.

Incorrect: **Yesterday, I <u>had woken up</u> at 6 a.m., and I <u>had eaten</u> breakfast at 6:30.**
Incorrect: **I <u>had felt</u> awful because I <u>hadn't slept</u> very much.**

Except for the last verb, which requires the past perfect to be ordered before the others, the verbs in the narrative should use the past simple.

Correct: **Yesterday, I <u>woke up</u> at 6 a.m., and I <u>ate</u> breakfast at 6:30.**
Correct: **I <u>felt</u> awful because I <u>hadn't slept</u> very much.**

Conclusion

In this section, we looked closely at the perfect aspect as it pertains to actions completed in the past. We hope you now have a better understanding of how the past simple works with the past perfect and past perfect continuous to show us these time relationships in the past. We also hope you take any corresponding quizzes on these structures. This can be found in the "Quizzes" section of the book.

The next section will focus on the least used and, perhaps, most complex verb tenses in the English language, the future perfect and future perfect continuous.

3.6 Future Perfect and Future Perfect Continuous

Introduction

By the time I finish my TEFL Certification, I will have written five full lesson plans.

The sentence above shows an example of the future perfect tense, *will have written.* This verb tense shows an action that will be completed in the future before another action or time in the future.

In this section, we will look at the future perfect and future perfect continuous tenses. We will start by looking at the target language in the context of an email. Then we will look at timelines that explain the use of the verb tenses in the email. After that, we will look at information about the form, meaning, and use of the target grammar.

Objectives

- Identify the future perfect and future perfect continuous aspect in context
- Compare and contrast the form of the future perfect and future perfect continuous
- Classify meanings of the future perfect and future perfect continuous
- List common real-world contexts for use of the future perfect and future perfect continuous
- Identify common mistakes made with the future perfect and future perfect continuous

Use in Context: An Email

Read this email that an EFL teacher in Honduras wrote to her friend back home. The email contains examples of the future perfect (marked in bold) and the future perfect continuous (marked in italics). Notice how the examples are used in conjunction with other tenses.

New Message

To Nora@email.com Cc Bcc

Subject Love from Honduras!

Dear Nora,

I can't wait for you to visit me next month at my teaching post in Siguatepeque, Honduras. By the time you get here, I *will have been teaching* here for a whole school year! I can't wait to take you to some beautiful tourist places such as Lago de Yojoa and the city of La Ceiba which is on the Caribbean Coast. Let's also not forget that you have to visit my classroom. As you know, I have been teaching English to fifth graders at a bilingual school. We are preparing a play for the end of the year celebration. By the time the performance date arrives, we *will have been preparing* every day for six weeks. The play is about peace, and the students are so excited to perform for their families and friends. They have been working so hard to memorize their lines. It would be so cool if you could make it in time to see the play. The picture I am sending you is of Pulhapanzak Waterfall near Lago de Yojoa. It is my favorite spot, and I am going there again this weekend with my coworker. If the conditions are right, you can see a rainbow around the waterfall. I hope we can visit it when you come. By the time we go together, I **will have visited** that lovely spot three times already. But, don't worry! I will never get sick of that view! Just think, by this time next month, you **will** already **have seen** all these wonderful things in Honduras. Get here soon!

Sincerely,

Jessica

Explanation of Grammar in Context

Now let's have a look at the usage of the target grammar by looking at some of the sentences from the email you just read. With each sentence, a timeline explains the relationship between the future tenses. Next to each sentence is text in parentheses that indicates the form of the future perfect or future perfect continuous. Form is discussed more thoroughly later on in this section.

Future Perfect

The ***future perfect*** is used to express an action, state, or event that will happen before a certain time in the future or before another event in the future. We often use this tense with phrases or clauses that include *by* or *by the time*. In other words, this tense is used to show a time relationship between two situations. Note that this form is not used as often as other future forms.

By the time we go together, I will have visited that lovely spot three times already.
(*will* + *have* + *visited*)

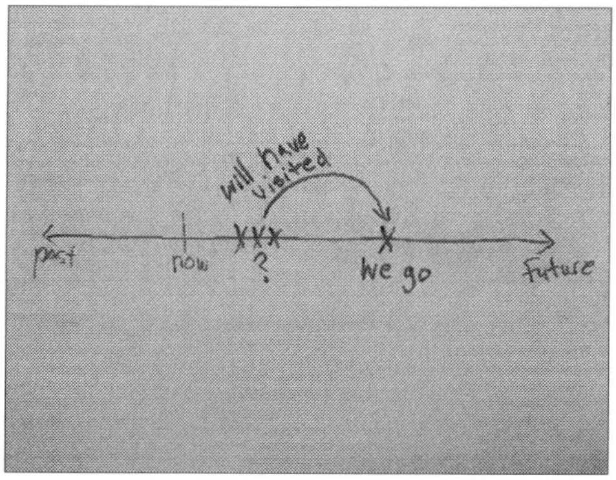

In this sentence, the TEFL teacher is expressing that when she visits the waterfall with her friend, she will have already been there three times. In other words, she will have gone there three times by herself before going there with her friend.

Just think, by this time next month, you will *already* have seen all these wonderful things in Honduras. (*will* + *have* + *seen*)

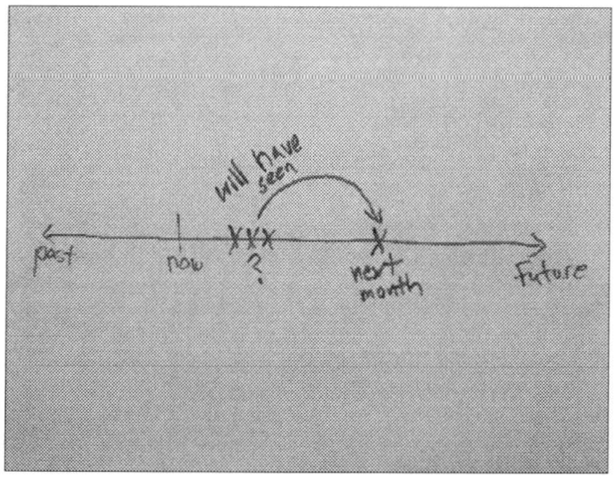

This sentence shows that one action will happen in the future before another specific time in the future. In this case, the friend will see many wonderful things in Honduras before this time next month. The adverb *already* is commonly used with this tense along with other adverbs—including *always, never, only, just, ever, still.*

Future Perfect Continuous

The ***future perfect continuous***, also called the ***future perfect progressive***, emphasizes the duration of an activity that will be in progress before another time or event in the future. This tense emphasizes that one future event is ongoing or continuous and is often incomplete. Just as with the future perfect tense, this tense is used to show a time relationship between two situations. Time clauses starting with *by the time* are often used with this tense, and this time clause uses the present simple verb tense. Like other continuous tenses, this tense cannot be used with verbs that have a stative meaning. Note that the future perfect continuous is not used as often as other future forms.

By the time you get here, I <u>will have been teaching</u> here for a whole school year!
(*will* + *have* + *been* + *teaching*)

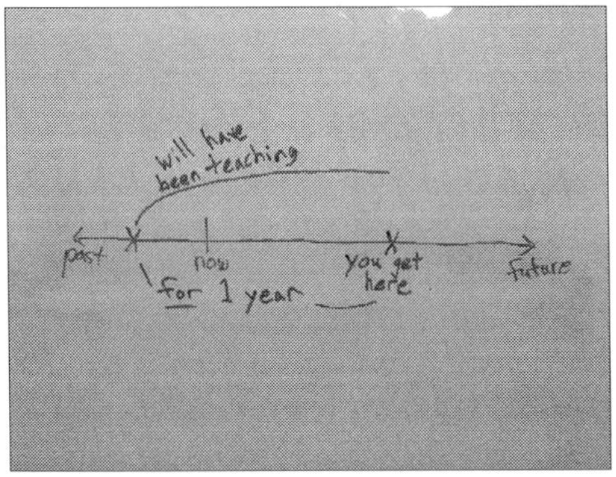

This sentence expresses an activity that will have been ongoing for a whole year before another action in the future. The teacher will have been teaching for a whole year before her friend Nora gets to Honduras. Notice that in the time clause starting with *by the time*, the present simple verb *get* is used.

By the time the performance date arrives, we <u>will have been preparing</u> every day for six weeks. (*will* + *have* + *been* + *preparing*)

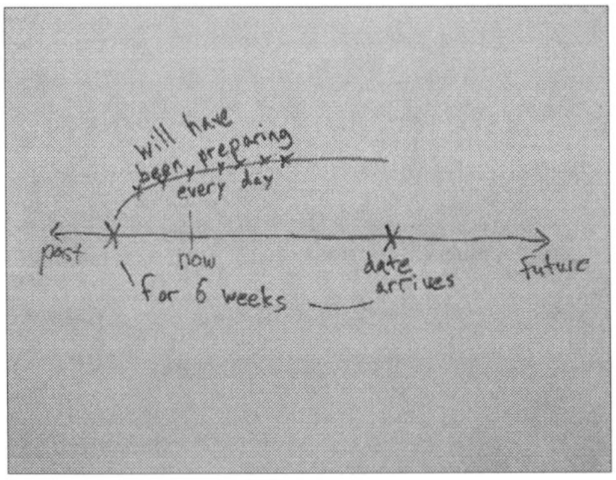

This sentence expresses an activity that will have been ongoing every day for six weeks before another action in the future. The teacher and the students will have been preparing every day for six weeks before the performance date arrives. Notice that in the time clause starting with *by the time*, the present simple verb *arrives* is used.

Timeline Video

In addition to the timeline images above, there is a video on International TEFL Academy's YouTube channel that depicts an EFL teacher using timelines to explain a few example sentences from the "Use in Context" section. Timelines can be effective visual aids for explaining time relationships inherent in verb tenses. This video does not give an exhaustive explanation of meaning and use for the future perfect and future perfect continuous tenses. For a more thorough explanation, refer to "Meaning" and "Use" in this section.

Future Perfect and Future Perfect Continuous - https://youtu.be/zKBfy5SGp9E

Form

In the sample email, we saw a few examples of the future perfect and the future perfect continuous tenses. We then looked at an explanation of some example sentences. Now let's shift our attention to the form of these verbs. Look at the questions in the Think Box below and try to answer the questions using only your prior knowledge and the example sentences from the email.

> **Think Box**
> Read the future perfect and future perfect continuous examples below. What do you notice about the form of the tenses? What do the future perfect examples have in common? What do the future perfect continuous examples have in common?

Future Perfect Examples

By the time we go together, I will have visited that lovely spot three times already.
Just think, by this time next month, you will already have seen all these wonderful things in Honduras.

Future Perfect Continuous Examples

By the time you get here, I will have been teaching here for a whole school year!
By the time the performance date arrives, we will have been preparing every day for six weeks.

Now that you have considered how these two tenses are formed, we will take a more detailed look at form.

Future Perfect

Were you able to identify similarities and/or apply any terms to the sentences in the previous section? Perhaps you noticed that all the examples of future perfect contain *will* and *have* followed by a past participle.

subject + will + have + past participle

By the time we go, I will have visited that lovely spot three times already.
Just think, by this time next month, you will have seen all these wonderful things in Honduras.

In addition to *will, be going to* can also be used with the future perfect. However, this is less common: *subject + be going to + have + past participle*.

Statement and Question Formation

For your reference, Table 3.15 summarizes the form of affirmative and negative statements, yes/no questions, and *Wh–* questions. Note the conjugations for different subjects in each chart. (More detailed information about general sentence and question formation can be found in Unit 4.)

Table 3.15 Future Perfect Statement and Question Formation

Affirmative Statements				
Subject	**Will**	**Have**	**Past Participle**	**Additional Elements**
I/You/We/They He/She/It	will	have	visited	that spot three times already.
Negative Statements				
Subject	**Will + Not**	**Have**	**Past Participle**	**Additional Elements**
I/You/We/They He/She/It	will not	have	visited	that spot three times already.
Yes/No Questions				
Will	**Subject**	**Have**	**Past Participle**	**Additional Elements**
Will	I/you/we/ they he/she/it	have	visited	that spot three times already?

***Wh–* Questions**					
***Wh–* word**	**Will**	**Subject**	**Have**	**Past Participle**	**Additional Elements**
How	will	I/you/we/they he/she/it	have	visited	that spot three times already?

Future Perfect Continuous

Now let's move to the examples that contain the ***future perfect continuous*** tense. Were you able to identify similarities and/or apply any terms to those sentences? Perhaps you noticed that these examples contain *will, have,* and *been* followed by a present participle.

subject + will + have + been + present participle

By the time you get here, I will have been teaching here for a whole school year!

By the time the performance date arrives, we will have been preparing every day for six weeks.

In addition to *will, be going to* can also be used with the future perfect continuous. However, this is less common: *subject + be going to + have + been + present participle.*

Statement and Question Formation

For your reference, Table 3.16 summarizes the form of affirmative and negative statements, yes/no questions, and *Wh–* questions. Note the conjugations for different subjects in each chart. (More detailed information about general sentence and question formation can be found in Unit 2.)

Table 3.16 Future Perfect Continuous Statement and Question Formation

Affirmative Statements				
Subject	**Will**	**Have**	**Been + Present Participle**	**Additional Elements**
I/You/We/They He/She/It	will	have	been teaching	here for a year.

Negative Statements				
Subject	**Will + Not**	**Have**	**Been + Present Participle**	**Additional Elements**
I/You/We/They He/She/It	will not	have	been teaching	here for a year.

Yes/No Questions				
Will	**Subject**	**Have**	**Been + Present Participle**	**Additional Elements**
Will	I/you/we/ they he/she/it	have	been teaching	here for a year?

***Wh–* Questions**					
***Wh–* word**	**Will**	**Subject**	**Have**	**Been + Present Participle**	**Additional Elements**
When	will	I/you/we/they he/she/it	have	been teaching	here for a year?

Meaning

This section will look at how meaning is communicated through the future perfect and future perfect continuous tenses in different situations. You will recognize some of these examples from the "Explanation of Grammar in Context" section where situational usage of the target grammar was explained from the email.

Future Perfect

Completed Action Before Another Future Action

The future perfect tense is used to express an action or event that will be completed before another time or event in the future. Often a phrase or time clause starting with *by the time* is used with this tense. If a time clause (e.g., *by the time we go*) is used, a present simple tense verb is used in that clause. The adverb *already* is commonly used with this tense along with other adverbs, including *always, never, only, just, ever, still.*

By the time **we go together, I will have visited that lovely spot three times *already.***

Just think, *by this time next month*, you will *already* have seen all these wonderful things in Honduras.

He will have tried many different Chinese dishes *by the time* his parents visit him next month.

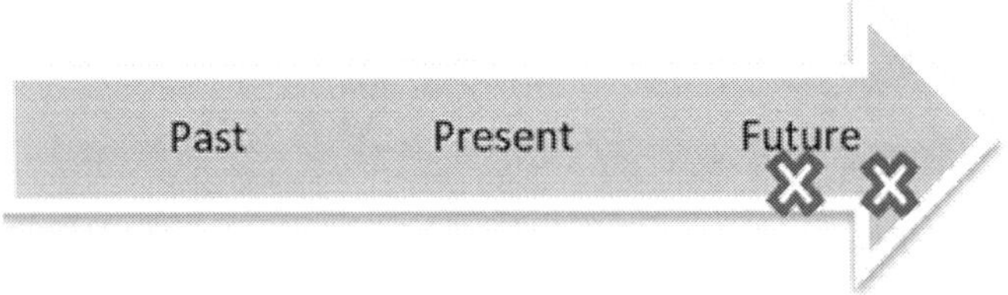

Duration of Ongoing Action or State Before Another Future Action

The future perfect tense is also used, mainly with stative verbs, to express an ongoing action or state in progress before another action or event in the future.

By the time I see you, I will have been in Honduras for one school year.

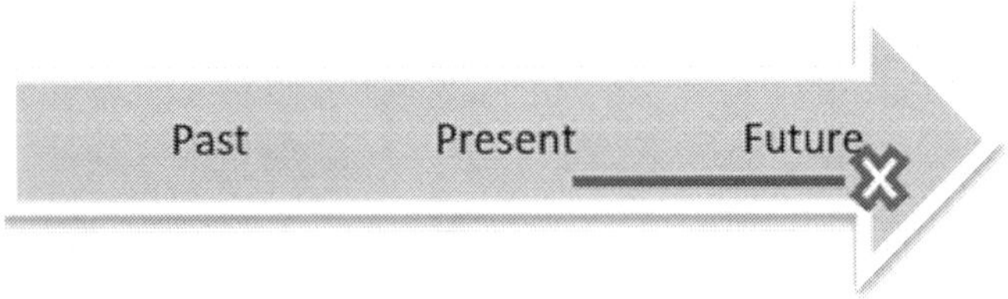

Future Perfect Continuous

Duration of Ongoing Action Before Another Future Action

The future perfect continuous shows the duration of an activity, state, or event (used with dynamic and not stative verbs) that will be in progress for a duration of time before another time or event in the future. Often a phrase or time clause starting with *by the time* is used with this tense. If a time clause is used, as in the first and second examples below, the present simple tense verb is used in the time clause.

By the time **the performance date arrives, we will have been preparing every day for six weeks.**

By the time **you get here, I will have been teaching here for a whole school year!**

By the end of **the workday, he will have been standing behind his computer for eight solid hours.**

Reason for Something in the Future

The future perfect continuous can also show a cause and effect relationship between two events or situations. In this case, the future perfect continuous shows the cause.

Dad will be tired when he arrives home because he will have been driving for over nine hours.

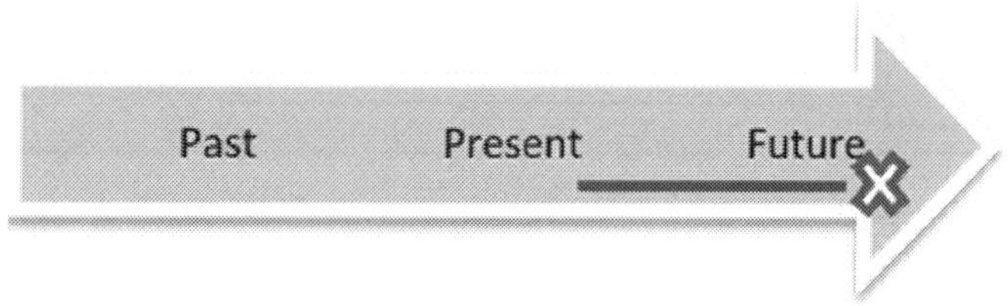

Just as with the present perfect tense, sometimes the future perfect and the *future perfect continuous* have the same meaning as in the following two sentences. This is the case when using such verbs as *live*, *work*, *teach*, *practice*.

When Dr. Mohindra retires next year, he will have practiced medicine for 40 years.
When Dr. Mohindra retires next year, he *will have been practicing* medicine for 40 years.

Additional Contexts for Use

This section provides examples of contexts where the future perfect and future perfect continuous tenses are used. The email at the beginning of this section contained examples of these two tenses in one real-world context. Following are some additional real-world contexts in which these tenses can be found.

To Talk about Goals or Intentions for the Future

We can use the future perfect to talk about a goal that is to be completed in the future before another time in the future, and the *future perfect continuous* to place a duration on activities in progress at a future time.

By the time he is 30 years old, he will have completed his master's degree and he *will have been working* in the private sector for several years already.

To Talk about Possible Future Inventions, Explorations, and Discoveries

We can use the future perfect to talk about things that we think will have been invented, explored, or discovered before a time in the future, and the *future perfect continuous* to place a duration on activities in progress at that time.

In 100 years from now, humans *will have* already *been living* on the moon for many years and astronauts will have found a way to reach distant planets.

To Talk about Business Plans, Hopes, or Predictions

We can use the future perfect to talk about the plans or sales that a business or company plans or predicts to make by a specific time in the future.

By the end of the year, the sales will have surpassed their target goal.

Common Mistakes

Let's take a look at some common mistakes made by nonnative speakers first learning these tenses.

Time Clauses

Some sentences use mixed verb tenses, meaning that they use two different verb tenses in the same sentence to show time relationships between clauses in a complex sentence. This can be confusing for English language learners. Students often try to use the same verb tense in both clauses.

Incorrect: **By the time he will have been 30 years old, he will have finished his master's degree.**

Correct: **By the time he is 30 years old, he will have finished his master's degree.**

Stative Verbs

Some students forget that stative verbs cannot be used in continuous tenses. With stative verbs, simply use the future perfect instead of the future perfect continuous.

Incorrect: **She will have been having her teaching certification for five years.**

Correct: **She will have had her teaching certification for five years.**

Conclusion

You should now have a better understanding of the future perfect and future perfect continuous tenses. Remember that these tenses are not used as often as other tenses in English, and you may never be asked to teach these tenses in your EFL classes. However, it is still important that you understand the form, meaning, and use of the future perfect and future perfect continuous to round out your knowledge of the 12 tenses in English. Now take any corresponding quizzes on these structures in the "Quizzes" section of the book.

With the conclusion of this section, we conclude Unit 3. In the next unit, we will examine a few additional grammar points that did not fit into our other units but are important for EFL teachers to be aware of and understand.

UNIT 4
ADDITIONAL GRAMMAR POINTS

Introduction to Additional Grammar Points

In this unit, the final unit of our grammar book, we consider some additional grammar points of the English language. The sections within represent language points that are important for learners of EFL/ESL but which may not have fit neatly into any other section and/or which we feel deserve separate attention.

Organization of Unit

1. Active and Passive Voice
2. Modal Verbs
3. Conditionals

The first section introduces the concept of voice in grammar and considers the difference between active and passive grammar constructions. The second section explores the subset of auxiliary verbs known as modal verbs, and all of the various usages therein. The third section expands upon the subset of complex sentences known as conditionals.

As with every unit in the book, each section begins with an introduction, which includes the relevant learning objectives. We then find a meaningful real-world text in which the target structures are used in context, followed by "Explanation of Grammar in Context," in which the meaning of those examples is explained. Next comes a discussion of the various forms that the structure can take, as well as further guidelines for how the structure communicates meaning and is used. Now, let's dive into some additional grammar!

NOTE: 4.1: The content in this section is intended for use by teachers of English, not ESL/EFL students. For example, while passive voice is an important concept for a teacher to understand, and we want our learners to be able to understand and use passive constructions, the term itself (*passive voice*) is not something you should spend time teaching in your classroom. In other words, the content here is designed to make you a more knowledgeable teacher. It is not intended to be used as a sole basis for lesson plans. For ideas about how to implement the knowledge from this book into your lesson plans see the various chapters International TEFL Academy's coursebook *The Fundamentals of Teaching English as a Foreign Language*.

4.1 ACTIVE AND PASSIVE VOICE

Introduction

1. One day, Fido bit me.   2. Right after that, Fido was bitten by me!   3. Fido doesn't bite me anymore.

The above sentences all have the same subject, *Fido*, and verb, *bite*, but Fido is not always the agent, or doer, of the action. That is because sentence 2 has a different voice than sentences 1 and 3.

This section introduces the concept of voice in the English language and demonstrates active and passive constructions. First, you will read an email that contains feedback about why a passage that was originally written in active voice should be changed to use the passive voice. After that, you will find information about the form, meaning, and use of passive voice.

Objectives

- Identify active and passive voice in context
- Compare and contrast the form of active and passive voice in various tenses
- Describe how active and passive voice are used to assign agency to a sentence's subject or object
- List common real-world contexts for use of the passive voice
- Identify common mistakes made with the passive voice

Use in Context: Email Feedback from a Professor

Read the following email from Dr. Smith, a professor of linguistics, to Sarah, one of his EFL graduate students. Sarah has completed a classroom-based research study and is writing about the project as part of her master's thesis. Dr. Smith has some important feedback about some of that writing.

Re: Process section

SarahW@college.edu

Re: Process section

Sarah-

I think your methods are good, but you use the **active voice** and should use the ***passive voice*** for this text. Here is an example from your chapter:

I **developed** three different grammar assessments. I **gave** these assessments at three different intervals. Each assessment **contained** an identical number of items, and I **allowed** the students as much time as needed to complete them. As our university research protocol **requires**, a faculty member **is keeping** the results of the assessments in a secure location, where he **will keep** them for a period of two years.

Here is how it should be written:

Three different grammar assessments ***were developed***. These assessments ***were given*** at three different intervals. Each assessment contained an identical number of items, and the students ***were allowed*** as much time as needed to complete them. As ***required*** by our university research protocol, the results of the assessments ***are being kept*** in a secure location, where they ***will be kept*** for a period of two years.

The second version is much better because the emphasis is on the materials and the processes, not the researcher/author.

Dr. Smith

Send

Meaning in Context

Let's look more closely at some of the sentences from the professor's email to Sarah. With each sentence, there is an arrow that demonstrates the difference between active and passive voice, which changes the direction of the action in a sentence.

Active Voice

For sentences in ***active voice***, the subject of the sentence is the agent, or doer, of the action. The object of the sentence is the receiver of the action.

I developed three different grammar assessments.
⟶

In this sentence, the subject, *I*, is the agent, the doer of the action, and the object, *three different grammar assessments*, is the receiver of the action.

A faculty member is keeping the results of the assessments.
⟶

In this sentence, the subject, *A faculty member*, is the agent/actor, and the object, *the results of the assessments*, is the receiver of the action.

He will keep them for a period of two years.
⟶

Here, the subject, *He*, is the agent/actor, the doer of the future action, and the object, *them*, is the receiver of the action.

Passive Voice

For sentences in ***passive voice***, the agency is reversed; the subject of the sentence is not the doer of the action, but the receiver of the action, or thing upon which the action is applied. Thus passive voice is possible only with transitive verbs. Note that in these example sentences, the agent is not named, but it could be via an optional *by* phrase (shown in parentheses).

Three different grammar assessments were developed. (*by me*)
⟵

In this sentence, the subject, *Three different grammar assessments*, is the receiver of the development. The agent/actor, *I*, is not included, but it could be via the phrase *by me*.

The results of the assessments are being kept in a secure location.
(*by a faculty member*) ⟵

In this sentence, the subject, *The results of the assessments*, is the receiver of the verb, *to keep*. The agent/actor, *a faculty member*, is not included, but it could be via a *by* phrase.

They will be kept for a period of two years. (*by a faculty member*)

Here again, the subject, *They* (the results), is the future receiver of the action, and the agent/actor is unnamed.

Form: Active and Passive Voice

In the example email, we saw several examples of active voice that were transformed into passive voice. Now that we have looked closely at the meaning of those examples, let's focus on the form of active and passive voice. Most of this section focuses on examples in active voice, so we will very briefly review that form before considering passive in greater depth.

Active Voice

Active voice follows a standard sentence pattern and is used in every tense/aspect combination.
subject + *verb* + *object*

> **Germany makes some great cars.**
> **I broke the window.**
> **We will care for your child with love and attention.**

Passive Voice

Passive voice uses the auxiliary *to be* verb and a past participle (and is very rare in the past/present/future perfect continuous forms).
subject + *to be* + *past participle* (*verb* +–*ed* or *irregular form*)

> **Some great cars are made in Germany.**
> **The window was broken.**
> **Your child will be cared for with love and attention.**

The illustration below summarizes the difference in form between the active and passive voice caused by the change in the direction of the action. Note the *by* phrase in parentheses. This phrase is used in certain situations that are detailed in the next two sections on meaning and use.

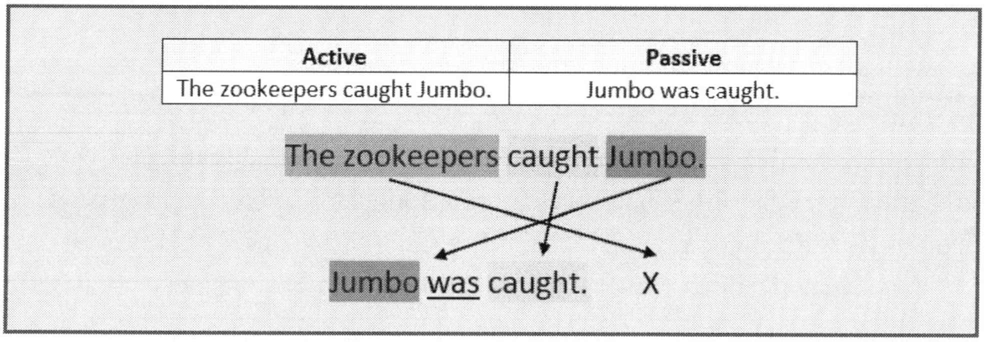

Statement and Question Formation

For your reference, Table 4.1 summarizes the passive form of affirmative and negative statements, yes/no questions, and *Wh–* questions. Note the different tenses of past/present/future. (More detailed information about general sentence and question formation can be found in Unit 2.)

<table>
<tr><th colspan="5">Table 4.1 Passive Voice Forms</th></tr>
<tr><th colspan="5">Affirmative Statements</th></tr>
<tr><th>Subject</th><th>Auxiliary Be Verb</th><th>Past Participle</th><th colspan="2">Additional Elements</th></tr>
<tr><td>Prizes</td><td>are</td><td>given</td><td colspan="2">to the winners.</td></tr>
<tr><td>The gifts</td><td>were</td><td>wrapped</td><td colspan="2">by the store clerk.</td></tr>
<tr><td>Winners</td><td>will be</td><td>chosen</td><td colspan="2">at random.</td></tr>
<tr><th colspan="5">Negative Statements</th></tr>
<tr><th>Subject</th><th>Auxiliary Be Verb + Not</th><th>Past Participle</th><th colspan="2">Additional Elements</th></tr>
<tr><td>Runners-up</td><td>are not</td><td>given</td><td colspan="2">prizes.</td></tr>
<tr><td>My car</td><td>was not</td><td>cleaned</td><td colspan="2">to my satisfaction.</td></tr>
<tr><td>We</td><td>will not be</td><td>treated</td><td colspan="2">this way!</td></tr>
<tr><th colspan="5">Yes/No Questions (For verb constructions in which the active voice does not require an auxiliary verb)</th></tr>
<tr><th>Auxiliary Be Verb</th><th>Subject</th><th>Past Participle</th><th colspan="2">Additional Elements</th></tr>
<tr><td>Is</td><td>passive voice</td><td>used</td><td colspan="2">in this field?</td></tr>
<tr><td>Was</td><td>the problem</td><td>found</td><td colspan="2">in time?</td></tr>
<tr><th colspan="5">Yes/No Questions (For verb constructions in which the active voice requires an auxiliary verb)</th></tr>
<tr><th>Auxiliary Verb</th><th>Subject</th><th>Auxiliary Be Verb</th><th>Past Participle</th><th>Additional Elements</th></tr>
<tr><td>Have</td><td>you</td><td>been</td><td>helped?</td><td></td></tr>
<tr><td>Were</td><td>they</td><td>being</td><td>harassed?</td><td></td></tr>
<tr><td>Will</td><td>my assistance</td><td>be</td><td>needed</td><td>any further?</td></tr>
<tr><th colspan="5">Wh– Questions</th></tr>
<tr><th>Wh– word</th><th>Auxiliary Be Verb</th><th>Subject</th><th>Past Participle</th><th>Additional Elements</th></tr>
<tr><td>What</td><td>is</td><td></td><td>needed</td><td>to finish the project?</td></tr>
<tr><td>Where</td><td>were</td><td>my keys</td><td>found?</td><td></td></tr>
<tr><td>Who</td><td>will be</td><td></td><td>chosen</td><td>by the judges?</td></tr>
</table>

Meaning

At the beginning of this section, we saw examples of active voice turned into passive voice. This is commonly done in academic writing, especially in descriptions of scientific processes, because we want to focus on the processes and materials themselves, not the scientists or doers of the actions. Now, let's take a look at some other reasons one might use the passive voice.

Unknown/Unimportant Agent

We use the passive voice in situations where the person or thing who performs the action is unknown, unimportant, or obvious. Most of these uses do not include a *by* phrase after the verb. The *by* phrases (in parentheses) in the following examples are optional.

Several samples were collected and stored (*by researchers*).
Many American jobs are being outsourced abroad (*by American companies*).
Ferraris are made in Italy (*by auto workers*).
My car was stolen (*by someone/a thief*)!

Focus on Receiver of Action

We also use the passive when we want to focus the attention of our sentence on the recipient (or the receiver) of the particular action and verb, thus making it the subject of the sentence. We often use a *by* phrase to add information about that subject/recipient.

That artwork was painted by my grandmother.
Only 5 to 10 new vocabulary words can be retained by your students in any lesson.

Avoidance of Mentioning Agent

In addition, the passive is used when we want to avoid mentioning the agent (or doer of the action) altogether. This is often done when we do not want to place responsibility or blame, and *by* phrases are therefore intentionally omitted.

Some things were said last night that probably shouldn't have been.
Mistakes have been made in this process, but we continue to move ahead.
The homework hasn't been done yet.

Additional Contexts for Use

This section provides examples of contexts where passive voice is commonly used. The email we saw earlier contained examples of the passive within an academic text. Following are some additional real-world contexts in which the passive is commonly found.

Describing a Process or Method

We use the passive voice when we want to focus on an object and how it is made/processed.

Coffee beans are grown in warm, humid climates. Once the beans are ripe, they are harvested. Then the beans are cleaned and dried.

Describing Location/Position and Part/Whole Relationships

We use the passive voice when we want to describe geographical location and placement.

Spain is located in the south of Europe and is divided into 17 autonomous regions. The Pyrenees mountain range is found there.

Political Speeches

The passive voice is used when a politician or leader wishes to avoid placing blame.

Lots of promises have been made, but those promises haven't always been kept.

News Reports

We sometimes use the passive voice when we cannot yet name the doer of the action/crime.

The bank was robbed last night at 10 p.m.

Common Mistakes

Here are some common mistakes made by nonnative speakers when constructing sentences in the passive voice.

Intransitive Verbs

Nonnative speakers occasionally try to use passive voice with intransitive verbs (it is only possible with transitive verbs).

Incorrect: **The sun was risen at 5:30 a.m. today.**

Correct: **The sun rose at 5:30 a.m. today.**

Incorrect: **An idea was occurred to me.**

Correct: **An idea occurred to me.**

Overuse of Passive Voice

It is possible to overuse the passive, even in contexts in which it is common. For example, in the passage from the example email at the beginning of the section (from Dr. Smith to Sarah), one sentence from the original passage was left unchanged; each assessment contained an identical number of items. The reason is the active version already uses a material, not a person, as its subject. Furthermore, the passive version would be awkward.

Incorrect: **An identical number of items was contained on each assessment.**

Correct: **Each assessment contained an identical number of items.** (sounds better active)

Conclusion

Now that we know more about passive and active voice, we can conclude this first section in our unit on additional grammar points. We hope you have learned something new about the formation, meaning, and the usage of the passive voice. The passive voice is used in very specific circumstances, and this is why EFL students can overuse the construct when first learning this grammar point. We also hope that you take the quiz on active and passive voice in the "Quizzes" section of the book.

The next section in this unit on additional grammar points will elaborate on different types of modal verbs.

4.2 MODAL VERBS

Introduction

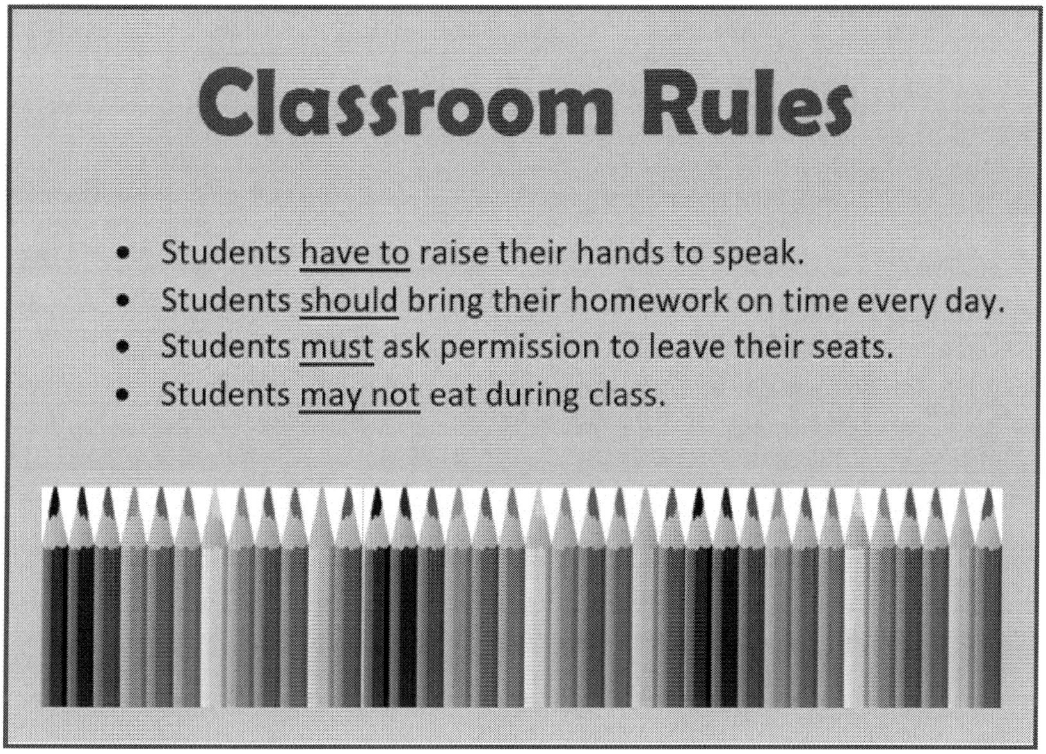

This image shows the use of various modal verbs. Modal verbs show degrees of necessity and certainty. One common situation where modals are used is in classroom rules. In these rules, the underlined modal verbs show degrees of necessity. This section introduces the concept of modal verbs in the English language and demonstrates modal constructions. First, you will read a teacher's journal entry that uses modal verbs in context. After that, you'll be given information about the form, meaning, and use of modal verbs.

Objectives

- Identify modal verbs in context
- Classify modal verbs to express degrees of necessity and certainty
- Distinguish between modal meanings for affirmative and negative forms
- Distinguish between modal meanings for past, present, and future forms
- Identify common mistakes made with modal verbs

Use in Context: A Teacher's Journal Entry

Read the following journal entry written by an EFL teacher named Jasmine. She has just completed her first day of teaching kindergarten in Macau, and she is reflecting on how the day went. Notice the use of underlined modal verbs in conjunction with the *italicized verbs* they are helping

Dear Journal,

It is a big relief to have finished my first day of teaching in Macau. It is both more rewarding and more challenging than I expected. The kindergarteners are so sweet. They only understood a few words of English which made it really challenging to communicate anything, even basic rules. The first day I tried to go over basic classroom rules. Here is a list of the rules that I presented:

- Students **have to** *raise* their hands to speak.
- Students **should** *bring* their homework on time every day.
- Students **must** *ask* permission to leave their seats.
- Students **may not** *eat* during class.

Well, the students stared at me with blank faces. I do not think they understood any of the words or sentences. I **should have** *used* visuals or pictures and more gestures to demonstrate the meaning of each rule.

One of the students was crying. Her mother told me that she was scared, especially because it is hard for her to understand English. I tried to comfort her, but I only made her cry more. I **should have** *had* a puppet or something fun to make her laugh. I, myself, wanted to cry at one point, but I kept telling myself "I **can** *do* this. I **must not** *give up.*"

Luckily, she did stop crying when we started learning the alphabet. We focused on the letter "a" and its sound today. I showed several pictures that start with "a." Then I showed students how to write the letter. We used playdough to form the letter "a." We also sang a song with "a" words. For homework the students **are supposed** *to complete* a worksheet where they **must** *color* all of the pictures that start with "a". Thankfully, teaching the lesson went well. I **will have to** *work* more on classroom management, though. I am hopeful that tomorrow **may** *go* more smoothly and that each day **might** *get* easier.

Identification of Modal Verbs in Context

Modal verbs are used with other verbs in English to express ideas that the main verb does not express on its own. Mainly, modal verbs express necessity and certainty. Modals can also express polite requests, preferences, and suggestions. Let's identify the different types of modal verbs used in the journal entry from the example text. The modal verbs are underlined followed by the italicized verbs they are helping.

Table 4.2 Modal Verbs

Type of Modal	Example from Journal Entry
Modals of necessity	Students **have to** raise their hands to speak. Students **should** bring their homework on time every day. Students **must** ask permission to leave their seats. Students **may not** eat during class. I **should have** used visuals or pictures ... I **must not** give up. For homework the students **are supposed to** complete a worksheet ... they **must** color all of the pictures ...
Modals of certainty	I **can** do this. I am hopeful that tomorrow **may** go more smoothly ... and that each day **might** get easier...

After reading the examples from the context of the journal entry, can you understand the difference in meaning between the two main categories of modal verbs: necessity and certainty? The following parts of this section will elaborate on these meanings and how to form sentences using modal verbs. After reading the following sections, come back to these examples to check your understanding of the meaning of modals of necessity and certainty.

Overview of Basic Modal Verbs

Some of the main ***modal auxiliary verbs*** in English are *can, could, had better, may, might, must, ought to, shall, should, will, would*. Modal verbs are a subset of the auxiliary verbs (or helping verbs) of English, and in the teaching of ESL/EFL, they are commonly called modals and they express a speaker's attitude.

We will classify modal verbs into two main categories:

1. ***Modals to express degrees of necessity:*** Here, modal verbs convey that the speaker thinks something is necessary, advisable, permissible, possible, or probable, and the strength of those attitudes is shown.
2. ***Modals to express degrees of certainty:*** Here, modal verbs are used to speculate the certainty or uncertainty of something.

Modals of Necessity

Modal verbs that express degrees of necessity range from obligation (necessity) to no obligation (no necessity). Here, modals can take different forms, including ***simple modals*** with the base form or perfect modals with *have*. Modals of necessity are used to talk about obligations, advice, expectations, and suggestions.

Here is a delineation of several different examples of modal verbs of necessity. Pay attention to how the modals range in degree of necessity, from total obligation or necessity (100%) to no necessity (0%), as well as the way they are used in their present and past forms. The modal verbs are underlined followed by the *italicized verbs* they are helping.

Obligation or Necessity (100%)

The strongest modals of necessity represent a total obligation.

He must *work* late.

He has to *work* late.

Of these verbs, only *has to* can be used in the past tense.

He had to *work* late.

Advice

We also use modal verbs to give advice.

We should *allow* extra time.

We ought to *allow* extra time.

We can use some of these modals in the past form to lament past decisions.

We **should have** *allowed* extra time.

Expectation

Some modals establish expectation or an outside pressure to do something.

You are supposed to *take off* your shoes.

You are to *take off* your shoes.

They can also establish that expectation in the past.

You <u>were supposed to</u> *take off* your shoes.

Suggestion

Other modal verbs provide suggestion, which lacks the strength of obligation/expectation/advice.

They <u>could</u> *study* longer.

They <u>might</u> *study* longer.

These can be used to show the suggestion in the past as well.

They <u>could have</u> *studied* longer.

No Obligation or Necessity (0%)

Finally, the negative form of *have to* shows a lack of necessity.

She <u>doesn't have to</u> *buy* more.

This has the same meaning in the past form.

She <u>didn't have to</u> *buy* more.

This lack of necessity (*don't have to*) should not be confused with negative necessity or the obligation not to do something, *must not*. This distinction, as well as other modal nuances, are described in more depth below.

Meaning and Form: Modals of Necessity

Let's have a closer look at ***modals of necessity.*** The explanations here will provide a deeper understanding of specific ways that these modals construct meaning, including the strength of various modals and how the negative and past forms can change the meaning in unexpected ways. We also consider some modal-like expressions or phrasal verbs. The modal verbs are <u>underlined</u> followed by the *italicized verbs* they are helping.

Strength of Modals

The modal verbs *must* and *have to* are similar in that they show a very strong obligation. In general, *must* is more formal and shows the strongest obligation.

Students <u>must</u> *come* to class on time.

Students <u>have to</u> *come* to class on time.

To offer advice in the present, use *should* or *ought to*. These mean that it would be a good idea to do something.

Students <u>should/ought to</u> *eat* in the cafeteria because the food is healthy.

The modal *had better* is used to offer advice and is similar to *should* or *ought to*, but it has a stronger meaning. Use *had better* to give a warning that something bad could happen if the advice is not followed.

The teacher <u>had better</u> *avoid* talking about sensitive subjects such as politics (otherwise the students could be offended or angry).

The modals *could/might* are used to make polite suggestions about the present or future.

Students <u>could/might</u> *bring* an apple or flower for the teacher on the first day.

Past and Negative Forms

The past tense of *have to* shows a strong obligation in the past. Note that there is no past tense of *must* as a modal of necessity (*had to* is used in its place), nor is there a past form of *had better*.

Students <u>had to</u> come to class on time.

To offer advice in the past, use *should have/ought to have + past participle*. This uses hindsight and suggests that the action did not happen.

Students <u>should have/ought to have</u> *eaten* in the cafeteria yesterday.

The negatives *should not have/ought not to have* suggest that the action did happen.

Students <u>should not have/ought not to have</u> *eaten* at that vendor yesterday.

Could have/might have + past participle are also used to make polite suggestions about a past opportunity or possibility, but with the benefit of hindsight. In this case, the action didn't actually happen.

Students <u>could have/might have</u> *brought* an apple or flower for the teacher on the first day (but they didn't).

To show that something is not necessary (but is allowed) in the present, use *don't/doesn't have to*.

Students <u>don't have to</u> *take off* their shoes when they enter the classroom.

To show that something was not necessary in the past, use *didn't have to*.

Students <u>didn't have to</u> *take off* their shoes when they entered the classroom.

While *must* and *have to* have similar meanings, note that their negative forms, *must not* and *don't have to,* have very different meanings.

Students <u>must not</u> *smoke* in class (it is against the rules).

Students <u>don't have to</u> *smoke* in class (but they can if they want to).

Modal-like Expressions

There are modal-like expressions or phrasal modals that have meanings similar to or equivalent to the meanings of modals. One such example is the phrase *be allowed to.*

Students are allowed to *drink* water in class.

The modal-like expression *have got to* is used in conversation and informal writing. It has a similar meaning to *have to* and it is often contracted.

I have got to *go* now.
I've got to *go* now.

Another modal-like expression or phrasal modal is *be supposed to*. This shows an expectation.

Students are supposed to *ask* permission to use the bathroom during class.

In the past, this expression suggests that the action didn't happen, while the negative suggests that the action did happen.

She was supposed to *ask* permission to use the bathroom during class, but it was an emergency situation.
She wasn't supposed to *use* the bathroom without permission, but it was an emergency situation.

To express a strong expectation in a very formal way, use a form of *be to + base form.*

Teachers are to *attend* the teacher meeting every week.

Next, let's consider a different type of modal verb, modals of certainty.

Modals of Certainty

Let's look at modal verbs that express degrees of certainty. These modals express different degrees of certainty; they are used to speculate based on logic and facts. A person may show great certainty with a word such as *must*, but less certainty will be shown with words such as *may* or *might*.

Have a look at Table 4.3 to see different examples of modals for speculation. Pay attention to how the modals range in degree of certainty from more certainty to less certainty. Also, pay attention to how the modals are used to speculate about the present, past, and future.

Table 4.3 Modals of Certainty (Modal verbs are bold and underlined followed by the italicized verbs they are helping.)	
Degree of Certainty	**Speculations (Present)**
More certainty (approximately 90% certainty)	She **<u>must</u>** *be* right. She **<u>must not</u>** *be* right. (negative form)
Less certainty (approximately 50% certainty)	She **<u>could</u>** *be* right. She **<u>may not</u>** *be* right. (negative form)
Degree of Certainty	**Speculations (Past)**
More certainty (approximately 90% certainty)	She **<u>must have</u>** *been* right. She **<u>could not have</u>** *been* right. (negative form)
Less certainty (approximately 50% certainty)	She **<u>may have</u>** *been* right. She **<u>might not have</u>** *been* right. (negative form)
Degree of Certainty	**Speculations (Future)**
More certainty (approximately 90% certainty)	She **<u>should</u>** *finish* the project soon. She **<u>ought to</u>** *finish* the project soon.
Less certainty (approximately 50% certainty)	She **<u>may</u>** *finish* the project soon. She **<u>might not</u>** *finish* the project soon. (negative form)

Meaning and Form: Modals of Certainty

Let's have a closer look at modals of certainty. The specific explanations here will provide a deeper understanding of specific ways these modal verbs can be used. Pay particular attention to how the progressive tense and negative form are used. The modal verbs are <u>underlined</u> followed by the *italicized verbs* they are helping.

Present

We use modals to show degrees of certainty by speculating based on logic and facts. To speculate about the present and to show a high degree of certainty (approximately 90%), use *must*, *have to*, or *have got to*.

The answers <u>must/have got to/have to</u> *be* correct.

To speculate about the present and to show less certainty (approximately 50%), use *may, might*, *could*.

The answers <u>may/might/could</u> *be* correct.

Any of these modals can also be used in the progressive form using *be* + *present participle* (*–ing*).

She <u>might</u> *be organizing* another language class.

The modal verbs *can't/couldn't* can be used to show negative speculations.

The answers <u>can't/couldn't</u> *be* correct.

Must not has a similar meaning but can be used to show a little less certainty.

The answers <u>must not</u> *be* correct.

Could/couldn't can also be used to form questions of uncertainty.

<u>Could</u> the answers *be* correct?
<u>Couldn't</u> the answers *be* correct?

Past

To speculate about the past and to show a high degree of certainty, use *must have/had to have* + *past participle*.

She <u>must have/had to have</u> *been* in class.

To suggest an impossibility in the past, use the negative form *couldn't have* + *past participle*.

She <u>couldn't have</u> *been* in class.

To show less certainty in the past, use the negative form *must not have* + *past participle*.

She <u>must not have</u> *been* in class.

For questions, use *could have* + *past participle*.

<u>Could</u> she <u>have</u> *been* in class?

To speculate about the past and show less certainty (about 50%), use *may have/might have/could have* + *past participle*.

She <u>may have/might have/could have</u> *been* in class.

Future

To show a high degree of certainty about a future action or event, use *should/ought to* + *base form*.

More studies and experiments <u>should/ought to</u> *help* us find a cure.

To show less certainty about a future action or event, use *may/might/could*.

More studies and experiments <u>may/might/could</u> *help* us find a cure.

To show less certainty and a negative meaning, use *may/might* + *not/never* + *base form*.

More studies and experiments <u>may/might not/never</u> *help* us find a cure.

Aside from necessity and certainty, there are various other uses for modal verbs, which we will look at next.

Further Uses for Modal Verbs

Let's look at a few other uses of modal verbs, including polite requests, making suggestions, and expressing preference. The modal verbs or phrases are <u>underlined</u> followed by the *italicized verbs* they are helping.

Polite Requests

Modals are commonly used to make polite requests. The subject of these requests is usually *I* or *you*. To request permission in a polite way, we use *May I*, *Could I*, and *Might I* (note that *Might I* is less common and more formal). *Can I* is also used to request permission, but it is less formal and less polite.

<u>May I</u> *use* the bathroom please?
<u>Could I</u> *use* the bathroom please?
<u>Can I</u> *use* the bathroom please?

Would you, *could you*, *will you* are used to make polite requests. *Would you* is more common and often considered more polite. *Could you* means both "will you" and "are you able to" do something.

<u>Would/Could you</u> please *close* the door?
<u>Will you</u> please *close* the door?

We also use *Would you mind* + *present participle* and *Would you mind if I* + *past simple* to make requests and ask for permission in a formal way.

<u>Would you mind</u> *closing* the window?
<u>Would you mind if I</u> *closed* the window?

Making Suggestions

We commonly use the phrases *let's*, *why don't*, *shall we*, *shall I* to make suggestions. *Let's* is a contraction of *let us*. It is followed by the simple form of the verb and is used to suggest something.

<u>Let's</u> *hold* our class outside tomorrow.

Why don't is used mostly in speaking to make a friendly suggestion. It means "let's do something" or "do you agree that we should do something?"

<u>Why don't</u> we *hold* our class outside tomorrow?

Shall is used with *I* or *we* in questions to make a suggestion or to ask if someone agrees with a suggestion. This is more formal and less common. *Shall we* can be used as a tag question after *let's*. In some English varieties, this use is considered more formal.

Shall we *hold* the class outside tomorrow?

Let's *go* outside, shall we?

Expressing Preference

To show a preference, we can use *would rather* followed by the simple form of the verb. Notice the use of the word *than*. To express a negative meaning, use *would rather + not* followed by the main verb in the simple form.

I would rather *hold* the class outside than inside.

I would rather not *hold* the class outside.

Would rather can be used in the past form to show a preference in the past. Use *would rather + have + the past participle*.

I would rather have *held* the class outside yesterday since the weather was so nice.

Would rather can be used in the progressive form to show a preference in the present moment. Use *would rather + be + the present participle (–ing)*.

I would rather *be holding* the class outside right now.

When using *would rather*, we often contract the modal verb *would*, especially when speaking.

I'd rather *be holding* the class outside right now.

Common Mistakes

Here are some common mistakes made by nonnative speakers when first learning how to construct sentences with modal verbs.

Incorrect Verb Form

Nonnative speakers occasionally use the incorrect form of the verb after a modal. Remember, the base form of the verb is used after modals in the present or future tenses.

Incorrect: **I can driving a car.**

Correct: **I can drive a car.**

Incorrect: **I might to leave soon.**

Correct: **I might leave soon.**

Incorrect Conjugation

Nonnative speakers also sometimes conjugate the modal to agree with different subjects. However, modal verbs always have the same form regardless of subject. (Exceptions to this rule occur with modal-like expressions, such as *have to* and *be supposed to*.)

Incorrect: **She mights ride her bike to school.**

Correct: **She might ride her bike to school.**

Incorrect Meaning

Some modals have different meanings in the past, present, or future and/or with negation. Occasionally, nonnative speakers will mistake these meanings. One common mistake in meaning is with the modal *could*. In the present, *could* refers to something that is somewhat certain. In the past and with the negative form, *could have* refers to something that we are pretty certain was not the case.

She could be right. (about 50% certain)

She could not have been right. (about 90% certain)

Conclusion

This concludes our section on modal verbs. We hope that you are now more familiar with how to form these modal constructions and how these modals affect the meaning of their companion verbs in terms of showing degrees of necessity and certainty. Keep in mind that modals can also indicate polite requests, suggestions, and preferences. These concepts are included in the "Quizzes" section, and we encourage you to go there as soon as possible.

The next section in this unit on additional grammar points will discuss specific types of complex sentences called conditionals. Many conditional sentences contain modal verbs, so keep the information that you learned in this section about modals in mind, as it will aid in your understanding of conditionals.

4.3 Conditionals

Introduction

If I hadn't gotten a TEFL certificate, I wouldn't have decided to teach overseas.

The example sentence above shows a specific type of complex sentence that conveys a conditional meaning. In this sentence, the third conditional is used to show an unreal situation in the past that is contrary to reality. In this case, the teacher did get a certificate and did decide to teach overseas. The third conditional shows what would have happened in that unreal situation.

This section contains information about many types of conditional statements. We will start by looking at examples of conditionals within the context of a TEFL job board. Then, we will discuss the fundamentals of zero, first, second, third, and mixed conditionals.

Objectives

- Identify conditional statements in context
- Distinguish between meanings for and formulaic elements of zero, first, second, third, and mixed conditionals

Use in Context: Excerpt from a TEFL Job Board

Read the following excerpt from a TEFL job board. This website has general information about jobs in Cambodia and some comments listed by users of the site. While reading, try to identify conditional statements used in the comments section.

Jenny & Bec's TEFL Job Board!

Explore our TEFL teaching and volunteer positions and start your travel dream today!

CONTACT US!

Browse Jobs by Region:

Asia	Europe	Middle East	Latin America

TIPS FOR GETTING A JOB IN CAMBODIA

Education Requirements | Typical Hiring Process | Cost of Living | Types of Jobs
Peak Hiring Months | Visas | Average Monthly Pay | Certifications

Comments Section:

■		I heard that if you are hired by a company, they will help you get a visa. Is this true?
■		Wow! A BA/BS isn't required? This isn't the case in a lot of other countries
■		I worked in Cambodia 10 years ago. If I had read this information before I went there, I would have had a better experience looking for a job. I was very uninformed.
■		Be careful about working hours. If you teach for 30 hours a week, prep time is not included.
■		Hmm...no flight reimbursement. :(
■		I've always wanted to live there! If I had a TEFL certificate, I would definitely be applying for jobs right now.

This website and job post are completely fictional and used solely for the purpose of grammar instruction.

Identification of Conditionals in Context

Conditional statements are complex sentences that typically contain an *if* clause. Table 4.4 identifies the different types of conditional statements used in the comments section from the example text.

Table 4.4 Types of Conditional Statements

Type of Conditional Statement	Example Sentence from Website Comments
Zero conditional	If you teach for 30 hours a week, prep time is not included.
First conditional	If you are hired by a company, they will help you get a visa.
Second conditional	If I had a TEFL certificate, I would definitely be applying for jobs right now.
Third conditional	If I had read this information before I went there, I would have had a better experience looking for a job.

Now, let's look at the examples to identify the basic time frame and plausibility of each statement.

Zero Conditional

If you teach for 30 hours a week, prep time is not included.

This sentence is showing us a basic truth in the present. The writer believes this to be fact: if you work 30 hours per week, prep time is never included.

First Conditional

If you are hired by a company, they will help you get a visa.

This sentence is showing us a possibility in the future. The writer sees a plausible result: you will get visa help from a company whenever they hire you.

Second Conditional

If I had a TEFL certificate, I would definitely be applying for jobs right now.

This sentence is showing us a present possibility, but unlike the zero and first conditional examples, this possibility is unreal. This is because the writer does not currently have a TEFL certificate. The writer is simply imagining the possibilities.

Third Conditional

If I had read this information before I went there, I would have had a better experience looking for a job.

Like the second conditional example, this sentence shows us an unreal situation. The difference is that this situation is about the past and therefore is impossible to change. The writer had not read this information before moving to Cambodia.

The following sections expand on the meaning of each type of conditional statement, and the form of each type is also presented. Remember, since these are complex sentences, they follow the punctuation rules presented in the "Sentence Formation" section of Unit 2.

Zero Conditionals

Meaning

Zero conditionals show general truths. This conditional is also called the ***real conditional*** because it describes things that are always true. The zero conditional usually shows a cause and effect relationship. The example below clearly shows this cause and effect relationship with a true statement about water.

If you heat water to 100 degrees Celsius at sea level, it boils.

As we know, this is a scientific fact. Every time we do the first action, the second action follows.

Form

The words *if* and *when* are commonly used interchangeably to begin the dependent clause for zero conditionals.

I get very sleepy at work *if* I don't sleep well.
I get very sleepy at work *when* I don't sleep well.

The present simple is used in both the independent and dependent clauses.

My son cries when he is hungry.
(independent clause) (dependent clause)

As you learned about complex sentences in Unit 2, the punctuation changes, depending on the position of each clause: the dependent clause is followed by a comma if it comes first in the sentence.

When he is hungry, my son cries.
(dependent clause) (independent clause)
My son cries when he is hungry.
(independent clause) (dependent clause)
If the sun shines in the winter, the snow melts.
(independent clause) (dependent clause)
The snow melts if the sun shines in the winter.
(independent clause) (independent clause)

zero conditional = general truths
dependent clause: *If/When + noun + present simple verb + comma*
+
independent clause: *noun + present simple verb*
OR
independent clause: *noun + present simple verb*
+
dependent clause: *If/When + noun + present simple verb*

First Conditionals

Meaning
First conditionals show real possibilities, which means that we see possible situations and their probable results. This is also called the ***future real conditional*** because we see a cause that leads to a possible future event. The example below shows a possible action (earn enough money) and a possible future result of that action (open a savings account).

If I earn enough money, I will open a savings account.

The speaker here is communicating a future intention given a possible future event. We are unsure whether the speaker will indeed earn enough money, but if she does, the second event (open an account) will follow.

Form
First conditionals contain a dependent *if* clause that contains a present simple verb. They also contain an independent clause that shows the possible future event with a *future simple verb*. (The future simple is normally used in the first conditional, but modals such as *may, might, could* can also be used if the outcome is less certain.[4.2]) Just like other complex sentences, the position of clauses can change, and with that the punctuation changes.

If I don't take out the trash tonight, I*'ll forget* tomorrow morning.
I*'ll forget* to take out the trash tomorrow morning if I don't do it tonight.
If I get a day off, I *will go* on a hike.
I *will go* on a hike if I get a day off.

first conditional = real possibility
dependent clause: *if + noun + present simple verb + comma*
+
independent clause: *noun + future simple verb*
OR
independent clause: *noun + future simple verb*
+
dependent clause: *if + noun + present simple verb*

NOTE 4.2: Refer to the Modals section to review the meanings attached to different modals of certainty.

Second Conditionals

Meaning

Second conditionals show unreal possibilities, which means that they describe hypothetical situations in the present or future and their probable unreal results. The following example shows the hypothetical situation of winning the lottery and a possible result (buying houses) to this unreal situation:

If I won the lottery, I would buy a house for each of my family members.

The use of the past simple form (*won*) tells us that the conversation is hypothetical. The speaker has not won the lottery and doesn't believe that he will; he simply wants to discuss imaginary possibilities.

Form

Second conditionals contain a dependent *if* clause with a past simple verb. The independent clause showing the possible unreal result contains a modal, either *would* or *could*, that is followed by the base form of a verb.

If he had more time, he could continue helping with the project.
He could continue helping with the project if he had more time.
If I were[4.3] in Mexico, I would be speaking Spanish on a daily basis.
I would be speaking Spanish on a daily basis if I were[4.3] in Mexico.

second conditional = unreal possibility
dependent clause: *If + noun + past simple verb + comma*
+
independent clause: *noun + modal + base verb*
OR
independent clause: *noun + modal + base verb*
+
dependent clause: *If + noun + past simple verb*

NOTE 4.3: *Were* is used for singular and plural subjects following *if* in dependent clauses for second conditionals.

Third Conditionals

Meaning
Third conditionals show hypothetical past situations and their probable unreal results. These situations are seen as impossible because they are contrary to what actually happened in the past. Third conditionals are often used to show a sense of regret about a situation in the past. The following example shows regret about a past situation:

If Cindy had woken up on time, she would have been on time for work.

Cindy actually did not wake up on time and, as a result, was late for work. This use of the third conditional shows what would have been the probable result if she had woken up on time. Changing the modal *would* to *could* or *might* changes the speaker's/writer's certainty[4.3] of that result.

Form
Third conditionals contain a dependent *if* clause with had + past participle. The independent clause showing the unreal result contains a modal (*would/could/might*) followed by *have + past participle*.

If I had known your address, I could have dropped off your gift.
I could have dropped off your gift if I had known your address.
If he had brought his umbrella, he might not have gotten wet.
He might not have gotten wet if he had brought his umbrella.

third conditional = no possibility
dependent clause: *If + noun + had + past participle + comma*
\+
independent clause: *noun + modal + have + past participle*
OR
independent clause: *noun + modal + have + past participle*
\+
dependent clause: *If + noun + had + past participle*

Mixed Conditionals

Finally, there is a subset of second/third conditionals called mixed conditionals. ***Mixed conditionals*** are so named because they combine the unreal past and unreal present, mixing the components of second and third conditionals to create more dynamic unreal statements.

Some mixed conditionals combine an unreal past situation in the *if* clause (as in a third conditional) with an unreal result in the present (as in a second conditional).

If I hadn't eaten that old yogurt, I wouldn't be so sick right now.

We know that the speaker of this sentence did eat the old yogurt in the past, and that she is sick right now. She states how changing the past could have changed the present situation.

Other mixed conditionals reverse this temporarily and consider an unreal present state of things in the *if* clause (as in a second conditional) with an unreal past event (as in a third conditional).

If he were a nicer person, he might not have gotten divorced.

The first clause makes a general statement about the present (the person we are discussing is not a nice person), and the second clause shows how a past event could have been altered if that truth were different.

Additional Contexts for Use

This section provides examples of contexts where conditional statements are commonly used. The job board at the beginning of this section contained examples of zero, first, second, and third conditionals in one real-world context. Following are some additional real-world contexts in which these statements are commonly found.

Scientific Texts

Zero conditionals are used to show concepts that are true in science.

When you drop a rock, it falls because of gravity.

Scientific Hypotheses

First conditionals are used to formulate hypotheses in scientific experiments.

If I add fertilizer to this plant, it will grow faster.

Job Interviews

Questions containing the second conditional are commonly used in job interviews to test what candidates would do in hypothetical situations.

What would you do if your supervisor asked you to work overtime on a weekend?

Future Plans

We can use first conditionals to discuss possible future plans.

What will you do this weekend if it is nice outside?
What will you do if it rains or snows?

We can use second conditionals to discuss imaginary plans.

What would you do this weekend if you were a billionaire?
Where would you go if you had a time machine?

Lamenting Past Decisions

Third and mixed conditional statements are used to express regret about our decisions or actions in the past.

> **If I hadn't dropped out of college, I would have gotten a better paying job. I might even be rich!**

Conclusion

This concludes not only our section on conditionals but also our unit on additional grammar points. No doubt, there will be grammar points you encounter or are asked to teach that we have not covered in this unit. However, we have included the most common additional grammar points found in curricula and textbooks. As with all the sections of this book, we recommend that you take the quiz on conditionals that can be found in the "Quizzes" section, as well as any other quiz that you have not yet taken.

We hope that you have acquired more knowledge of various parts of speech, sentence and question formation, verb tenses, and other commonly taught grammar points than you had before you began this book. Remember, absolute and immediate recollection of all that you have learned here is not expected of you as a teacher. What will be expected of you is to be knowledgeable enough to know what to look for and to research when you need to answer student questions or prepare for a lesson.

APPENDIX 1
IRREGULAR PLURAL NOUNS

There are some general rules for pluralizing nouns in the "Nouns" section of Unit 1. The following tables show some irregular plural noun patterns and forms.

Nouns that do not have a plural form ending in -s (and follow no other pattern)	
child -> children foot -> feet goose -> geese louse -> lice man -> men	mouse -> mice ox -> oxen person -> people tooth -> teeth woman -> women
Nouns that have the same singular and plural form	
deer -> deer fish -> fish offspring -> offspring species -> species	series -> series sheep -> sheep species -> species
Nouns that follow borrowed plural patterns (based on languages other than English)	
-us -> -i cactus -> cacti focus -> foci fungus -> fungi nucleus -> nuclei octopus -> octopi stimulus -> stimuli syllabus -> syllabi	**-is -> -es** analysis -> analyses basis -> bases crisis -> crises hypothesis -> hypotheses parenthesis -> parentheses synopsis -> synopses thesis -> theses
-um -> -a bacterium -> bacteria curriculum -> curricula datum -> data medium -> media	**-ex/-ix -> -ices** appendix -> appendices index -> indices matrix -> matrices vortex -> vortices
-on -> -a criterion -> criteria phenomenon -> phenomena	

Appendix 2 Irregular Verbs

This table contains many of the most common irregular verbs in English. Note that for some verbs, there are two possibilities for the second and/or third forms. Often, but not always, this is because of geographical differences. For example, when using the past form of the verb *spell*, it is more common in American English to use *spelled*, whereas *spelt* is more common in British English.

Base Verb (V1)	Past Simple (V2)	Past Participle (V3)
arise	arose	arisen
awake	awoke	awoken
be	was, were	been
bear	bore	born/borne
beat	beat	beaten/beat
become	became	become
begin	began	begun
bend	bent	bent
bet	bet	bet
bid	bid	bid
bind	bound	bound
bite	bit	bitten
bleed	bled	bled
blow	blew	blown
break	broke	broken
breed	bred	bred
bring	brought	brought
broadcast	broadcast	broadcast
build	built	built
burn	burned/burnt	burned/burnt
burst	burst	burst
buy	bought	bought
cast	cast	cast
catch	caught	caught
choose	chose	chosen
cling	clung	clung
come	came	come
cost	cost	cost
creep	crept	crept

cut	cut	cut
deal	dealt	dealt
dig	dug	dug
do	did	done
draw	drew	drawn
dream	dreamed/dreamt	dreamed/dreamt
drive	drove	driven
drink	drank	drunk
eat	ate	eaten
fall	fell	fallen
feed	fed	fed
feel	felt	felt
fight	fought	fought
find	found	found
fit	fit/fitted	fit/fitted
flee	fled	fled
fling	flung	flung
fly	flew	flown
forbid	forbade	forbidden
forget	forgot	forgotten
forgive	forgave	forgiven
freeze	froze	frozen
get	got	got/gotten
give	gave	given
go	went	gone
grind	ground	ground
grow	grew	grown
hang	hung	hung
have	had	had
hear	heard	heard
hide	hid	hidden
hit	hit	hit
hold	held	held
hurt	hurt	hurt
keep	kept	kept
kneel	kneeled/knelt	kneeled/knelt
know	knew	known
lay	laid	laid

lead	led	led
leap	leaped/leapt	leaped/leapt
learn	learned/learnt	learned/learnt
leave	left	left
lend	lent	lent
let	let	let
lie	lay	lain
light	lighted/lit	lighted/lit
lose	lost	lost
make	made	made
mean	meant	meant
meet	met	met
mistake	mistook	mistaken
pay	paid	paid
put	put	put
quit	quit	quit
read	read	read
rid	rid	rid
ride	rode	ridden
ring	rang	rung
rise	rose	risen
run	ran	run
say	said	said
see	saw	seen
seek	sought	sought
sell	sold	sold
send	sent	sent
set	set	set
shake	shook	shaken
shed	shed	shed
shine	shined/shone	shined/shone
shoot	shot	shot
show	showed	showed/shown
shrink	shrank	shrunk
shut	shut	shut
sing	sang	sung
sink	sank	sunk
sit	sat	sat

sleep	slept	slept
slide	slid	slid
smell	smelled/smelt	smelled/smelt
speak	spoke	spoken
speed	speeded/sped	speeded/sped
spell	spelled/spelt	spelled/spelt
spend	spent	spent
spill	spilled/spilt	spilled/spilt
spin	spun	spun
spit	spit/spat	spit/spat
split	split	split
spoil	spoiled/spoilt	spoiled/spoilt
spread	spread	spread
spring	sprang	sprung
stand	stood	stood
steal	stole	stolen
stick	stuck	stuck
sting	stung	stung
stink	stank	stunk
strike	struck	struck/stricken
strive	strived/strove	strived/striven
swear	sworn	sworn
sweep	swept	swept
swim	swam	swum
swing	swung	swung
take	took	taken
teach	taught	taught
tear	tore	torn
tell	told	told
think	thought	thought
throw	threw	thrown
thrust	thrust	thrust
understand	understood	understood
upset	upset	upset
wake	woke	woken
wear	wore	worn
weep	wept	wept
win	won	won

wind	wound	wound
withdraw	withdrew	withdrawn
write	wrote	written

Appendix 3
Subordinating Conjunctions

Here is an incomplete list of some the most common subordinating conjunctions.

after
although
as
as if
as soon as
because
before
even though
if
inasmuch
just as
lest
now that
once
provided
rather than
since
supposing
that
though
unless
until
when
whenever
whereas
wherever
whether (or not)
which
while

GLOSSARY

Adjective: Adjectives are descriptive words that modify nouns, and they are used to add detail and specification to those nouns.

Adjective clause: Adjective clauses, also called relative clauses, are dependent clauses that function as adjectives. They closely follow the nouns they are modifying and begin with the relative pronouns *that*, *which*, *who*, *whom*. (e.g., I saw the man <u>who gave me the book</u>.)

Adverb: Adverbs are descriptive words that we use to modify other words in a sentence. Most adverbs modify verbs, but adverbs may also be used to modify adjectives, other adverbs, or an entire clause/sentence. Adverbs that modify verbs are usually formed by adding *–ly* to the end of an adjective (e.g., quick → quickly).

Adverb clause: Adverb clauses are dependent clauses that function as adverbs. They show relationships (time, cause and effect, contrast, condition) between ideas in a sentence and can be inserted before or after the independent clause in a sentence. Adverb clauses begin with subordinating conjunctions. (e.g., <u>When I got to school</u>, I was very tired.)

Article: Articles (sometimes called determiners) are a subcategory of adjectives that modify and give information about nouns. English has two articles: the definite article, *the*, and the indefinite article, *a/an*. There are also instances in which we use no article with a noun, which is sometimes called a zero article.

Aspect: The term aspect refers to the duration of an event, either within or between tenses. Usually when we think about aspect, we think of four basic categories: simple, continuous, perfect, and perfect continuous.

Auxiliary verb: Auxiliary verb are verbs that do not carry their own distinct meaning, but they instead "help" the main verb express the meaning of the sentence. Examples of auxiliary verbs include *be, do, have, will* (all of which can be used as main verbs as well).

Clause: A clause is a group of words containing a subject and a predicate.

Common noun: Common nouns are nouns that are not capitalized and refer to objects in general (as opposed to proper nouns).

Comparative adjective: Comparative adjectives are used to compare two or more different nouns. They are usually formed by adding *–er* to an adjective (e.g., smart → smarter) though there are various spelling rules and irregular forms (e.g., happy → happier, good → better, comfortable → more comfortable).

Comparative adverb: A comparative adverb is used to compare two instances of another word (or words) in a sentence. Comparative adverbs are most often used to modify verbs. To form most comparative adverbs, we leave the adverb unchanged and modify it with the additional adverb *more* (e.g., run more slowly). They can also be formed by adding *–er* to the base adverb (e.g., working harder) or with an irregular form (e.g., feel worse).

Complex sentence: A complex sentence contains a dependent clause attached to an independent clause. (e.g., If you travel abroad, you will see your own culture with new eyes.)

Compound noun: A compound noun is a noun made up of two or more words (e.g., headphones).

Compound sentence: A compound sentence consists of two independent clauses joined by a comma and a coordinating conjunction: *for*, *and*, *nor*, *but*, *or*, *yet*, *so*. (e.g., Hugo ran a mile today, yet he looks well rested.)

Compound/complex sentence: A compound/complex sentence contains at least two independent clauses, as well as at least one dependent clause. (e.g., We're not going to the fireworks display this year because the park gets too crowded, but I will meet you later when I get to the restaurant.)

Conditional statement: Conditional statements are complex sentences that typically contain an *if* clause. (e.g., If I get a day off, I will go on a hike.) Conditional statements can be subcategorized into zero conditionals, first conditionals, second conditional, third conditionals, and mixed conditionals.

Conjunction: Conjunctions connect two or more units of language (words, phrases, or clauses) to form a relationship between those units. This includes common coordinating conjunctions (e.g., *and, but, or, so*) and subordinating conjunctions (e.g., *after, before, when, while, as, by the time, since, until, because, now that, since, if, while*).

Coordinating conjunction: Coordinating conjunctions connect two or more units of language that have equal status in a sentence (and sometimes across sentences). The four main coordinating conjunctions in English are *and, but, or, so*.

Countable noun: Countable nouns are nouns that can be counted and have both singular and plural forms (e.g., apple → apples).
Declarative sentence: A declarative sentence states a fact or an opinion and is punctuated with a period. (e.g., That movie was suspenseful.)

Dependent clause: A dependent clause (also called a subordinate clause) contains a subject and verb. However, a dependent clause does not constitute a complete sentence and cannot stand alone. Dependent clauses often begin with subordinating conjunctions like *since*, *although*, *because*, *while*. (e.g., When we came home, … .)

Dynamic verb: Dynamic verbs (or continuous verbs) are action verbs that can be converted to a present participle and used within the continuous/progressive aspect. These verbs are usually things you can see someone doing (e.g., run, write, read, drive, listen).

Exclamatory sentence: An exclamatory sentence expresses excitement, shock, or surprise and is punctuated with an exclamation mark. (e.g., I can't believe it!)

Gerund: A gerund is a verb ending with *–ing* that functions as a noun. (e.g., I like reading.)

Imperative sentence: A imperative sentence gives a command or suggestion and is punctuated with a period. The subject *you* is dropped but understood. (e.g., Watch your step.)

Independent clause: An independent clause has a subject and predicate and can stand alone as a sentence. (e.g., The mountains are beautiful.)

Interrogative sentence: An interrogative sentence poses a question and is punctuated with a question mark. (e.g., Was the movie suspenseful?)

Intransitive verb: Intransitive verbs are verbs that do not require a direct object. Some common intransitive verbs are *agree*, *arrive*, *live, rain, snow, walk.*

Mixed verb: Mixed verbs are verbs can be either dynamic or stative, depending on their meaning in context (e.g., have, think).

Modal verb: Modal verbs are a subset of the auxiliary verbs of English, and they express a speaker's attitude. Some of the main modal auxiliary verbs in English are *can*, *could*, *had better*, *may*, *might*, *must*, *ought to*, *shall*, *should*, *will*, *would.*

Noun: Nouns are the part of speech, other than pronouns, that denotes a person, a place, or a thing. Nouns act as subjects of complete sentences in English, and they act as the objects of verbs.

Noun clause: A noun clause is a dependent clause that functions as a noun. They begin with keywords such as *that*, *which*, *who*, *whom*, *whose*, *what*, *whatever*, *whichever*, *whoever*, *whomever*, *how*, *if*, *when*, *whenever*, *where*, *wherever*, *whether*, *why*. (e.g., Can you tell me where he went?)

Object: An object is what has been directly affected by a verb in a sentence or clause, identifying the receiver of the action/state. It is usually a noun, noun phrase, or pronoun. (e.g., I need your help.)

Past participle: A past participle is a word ending in *–ed* that functions as a verb within the various perfect tenses (e.g., I have lived here for two years). Some past participles have irregular forms (e.g., She had been there for five hours).

Phrase: A phrase is a group of words that does not contain both a subject and a predicate. Phrases are used as a single part of speech. A phrase cannot stand alone, and it must be used in a clause. (e.g., He walked the long way home.)

Predicate: The predicate of a sentence contains a verb and sometimes an object or other information about the subject. (e.g., I gave the ball to him.)

Preposition: Prepositions show a relationship between words in a sentence. Prepositions of place—such as *on*, *in*, *next to*, *above*, *below*—describe the spatial relationship between two or more objects. Prepositions of time—such as *around*, *at*, *before*, *during*, *on*, *throughout*—describe various temporal relationships.

Present participle: A present participle is a word ending in *–ing* that functions as a verb within the various continuous/progressive tenses (e.g., I am reading).

Pronoun: Pronouns are words that are used to replace nouns that have been previously stated or are already understood. Some of the most common pronouns include: *I, me, you, she, her, he, him, it, we, us, they, them.*

Proper noun: Proper nouns are nouns that refer to particular individuals, places, and things. These are usually official names, and they are always capitalized.

Simple sentence: A simple sentence contains a subject, verb, and sometimes an object. It contains only one independent clause and no dependent clause. (e.g., Bob gave her a gift.)

Stative verb: Stative verbs (or noncontinuous verbs) are verbs that cannot be converted to a present participle; you cannot add an *–ing* ending. These verbs are things you cannot see someone doing, such as emotion or abstract verbs (e.g., l*ike, love, hate, want, need, be*); opinion verbs (e.g., *know, recognize*); possession verbs (e.g., *possess, own, belong*); and sensory verbs (e.g., *taste, smell, see*).

Subject: A subject is the initial element in a clause or sentence. It is usually a noun, noun phrase, or pronoun. It is also sometimes called the agent of a sentence. (e.g., I gave the ball to him.)

Subordinating conjunction: Subordinating conjunctions connect two or more clauses in complex sentences. Subordinating conjunctions show time relationships (e.g., *after, before, when, while, as, by the time, since, until*); cause and effect relationships (e.g., *because, now that, since*); contrasting relationships (*while*); and conditional relationships (e.g., *if, even if, unless*).

Superlative adjective: Superlative adjectives are used to compare three or more nouns. They are usually formed by adding *–est* to an adjective (e.g., hot → hottest) though there are various spelling rules and irregular forms (e.g., easy → easiest, beautiful → most beautiful, bad → worst).

Superlative adverb: A superlative adverb is used to compare three or more instances of another word (or words) in a sentence. Superlative adverbs are most often used to modify verbs. To form most superlative adverbs, we leave the adverb unchanged and modify it with the additional adverb most (e.g., run most slowly). They can also be formed by adding *–est* to the base adverb (e.g., working hardest) or with an irregular form (e.g., feel the worst).

Tense: The term *tense* refers to the point or segment of time when an action occurs. Usually when we think about tenses, we think of three basic categories: the past, the present, and the future.

Transitive verb: Transitive verbs are verbs that must be followed by a direct object. Some common transitive verbs are *cut*, *enjoy*, *send*, *use*, *want*.

Uncountable noun: Uncountable nouns are nouns that cannot be divided into separate elements and do not take a plural form (e.g., water). Some nouns can be both uncountable and countable depending on the context (e.g., I'd like to drink some water OR They sailed the mighty waters).

Voice: Voice is the quality of a verb that indicates whether the subject is the doer or receiver of an action. For sentences in active voice, the subject of the sentence is the agent, or doer, of the action, and the object of the sentence is the receiver of the action (e.g., I developed three different grammar assessments). For sentences in passive voice, the agency is reversed; the subject of the sentence is not the doer of the action, but the receiver of the action, or thing upon which the action is applied (e.g., Three different grammar assessments were developed). Thus passive voice is only possible with transitive verbs.

RECOMMENDED GRAMMAR RESOURCES

There are numerous resources available to you that can help you continue to build your knowledge of English grammar. Here is a small list of excellent materials, and we encourage you to explore them in order to continue your growth as a grammarian and teacher of English.

American English Grammar

- *Understanding and Using English Grammar* (with Answer Key and Audio CDs) by Betty Schrampfer Azar
- *Fundamentals of English Grammar*, 4th Edition by Betty Schrampfer Azar
- *Grammar Sense: Advanced Grammar and Writing* by Susan Kesner Bland
- *Focus on Grammar Level 5* by Jay Maurer

British English Grammar

- *A Practical English Grammar* by Audrey Thomson and Agnes Martinet
- *Teaching Tenses: Ideas for Presenting and Practising Tenses in English (ELT)* by Rosemary Aitken
- *English Grammar in Use* (with Answers and CD-ROM) by Raymond Murphy
- *Practical English Usage* by Michael Swan
- *How to Teach Grammar* by Scott Thornbury

Online Grammar Resources

- All Grammar Concepts: https://owl.english.purdue.edu/owl/section/1/5/
- Tenses: http://www.englishpage.com/verbpage/verbtenseintro.html
- Guide to Grammar and Writing: http://grammar.ccc.commnet.edu/grammar/index2.htm
- Grammar Materials for the Classroom: http://www.azargrammar.com/materials/index.html

Grammar by Proficiency

- ESL/ESOL Standards by Skill: https://www.dllr.state.md.us/gedmd/cs/eslcsskill.pdf
- ESL/ESOL Standards by Level: https://www.dllr.state.md.us/gedmd/cs/eslcslevel.pdf

REFERENCES

Azar, B. (2002). Understanding and using English grammar, third edition. White Plains, NY: Longman.

Bland, S. (2008). *Grammar sense 4: Advanced grammar and writing*. New York, NY: Oxford University Press.

British Council. (2018). Retrieved from https://learnenglish.britishcouncil.org

Cambridge University Press. (2018). *Cambridge dictionary*. Retrieved from http://dictionary.cambridge.org/.

Celce-Murcia, M. & Larsen-Freeman, D. (1999). *The grammar book: An ESL/EFL teacher's course*. Boston, MA: Heinle & Heinle.

ESLgold. (2017). *Wh questions*. Retrieved from http://eslgold.com/grammar/wh_questions/

Englishpage.com. (2018). *Future perfect continuous*. Retrieved from https://www.englishpage.com/verbpage/futureperfectcontinuous.html

Frodesen, J., Eyring, J., & Larsen-Freeman, D. (2000). *Grammar dimensions: Form, meaning, and use*. Heinle & Heinle.

Hacker, D., & Sommers, N. (2011). *A writer's reference*. (7th ed.). Boston: Bedford/St. Martin's.

Mauer, J. (2012). *Focus on grammar* 5. 4th edition. White Plains, NY: Pearson Longman Education.

Siklos, J. & Singer, A. (Eds.). (2016). *English for everyone: English grammar guide*. New York, NY: DK Publishing.

Stilman, A. (2010). *Grammatically correct: The essential guide to spelling, style, usage, grammar, and punctuation*. Cincinnati, OH: F+W Media, Inc.

Tomlin, R. (1986). *Basic word order: Functional principles*. London: Croom Helm.

QUIZZES

The following quizzes will help you assess how much information you have comprehended from this book. Remember, you are not expected to memorize all of this information for your role as an English teacher, but it is important to have a basic understanding of these concepts to easily access the information when needed.

There is one quiz for each section of the book, with the exception of the section on sentence formation, for which there are two quizzes. Each quiz has 8 to 15 multiple-choice questions and is immediately followed by an answer key that contains feedback and an explanation for the correct answers.

The quizzes follow the order of the previous sections of the book:
Quiz 1: Nouns and Pronouns
Quiz 2: Verbs
Quiz 3: Adjectives, Articles, and Adverbs
Quiz 4: Prepositions and Conjunctions
Quiz 5: Sentence Formation I
Quiz 6: Sentence Formation II
Quiz 7: Question Formation
Quiz 8: Present Simple and Present Continuous
Quiz 9: Past Simple and Past Continuous
Quiz 10: Future Simple and Future Continuous
Quiz 11: Present Perfect and Present Perfect Continuous
Quiz 12: Past Perfect and Past Perfect Continuous
Quiz 13: Future Perfect and Future Perfect Continuous
Quiz 14: Active and Passive Voice
Quiz 15: Modal Verbs
Quiz 16: Conditionals

These quizzes are intended to be formative, not summative, meaning that they should be used as part of your acquisition of the material within the book. As such, you should feel free to refer back to the appropriate sections of the book if you feel that you need help while taking the quizzes.

Happy quiz-taking!

Quiz 1: Nouns and Pronouns

Directions: Read each question and choose the best answers. You will find the correct answers and explanations for each question on the page directly following the quiz.

1. Which of the following pairs contain two compound nouns?
   a) people; doorknob
   b) banknotes; fruit fly
   c) money; headphones

2. What type of pronoun is the underlined word?
Caio, I cannot believe that you are going to teach English in Thailand.
   a) subject pronoun
   b) object pronoun
   c) reflexive pronoun

3. What type of pronoun is the underlined word?
Caio is going to teach English in Thailand. He will love it.
   a) object pronoun
   b) reflexive pronoun
   c) subject pronoun

4. Which of the following is not an example of an irregular plural noun?
   a) tooth-> teeth
   b) benefit-> benefits
   c) syllabus-> syllabi
   d) fish-> fish

5. Which type of pronoun is the underlined word?
Ahmed didn't buy a book. The English school may supply him with a textbook.
   a) reflexive pronoun
   b) possessive pronoun
   c) object pronoun

6. Which of the following is not a proper noun?
   a) The Burj Khalifa Tower
   b) French
   c) Seagulls
   d) April

7. Which type of pronoun is the underlined word?
My backpack feels like a bag of rocks.

a) possessive adjective pronoun
b) possessive pronoun
c) reflexive pronoun

8. Which type of pronoun is the underlined word?
Did you know that your book bag looks like mine?

a) possessive adjective
b) possessive pronoun
c) reflexive pronoun

9. Which of the following is an example of a non-count/uncountable noun?

a) mouse
b) rice
c) knife

10. Which of the following underlined words is an example of a reflexive pronoun?
They were expected to help themselves to it.

a) themselves
b) they
c) it

Quiz 1: Nouns and Pronouns Answers and Feedback

1. **The correct answer is b.**
   Explanation: "Banknotes" is a compound noun that includes two nouns combined to create one noun. "Fruit fly" is a compound noun that includes two nouns that form a compound noun, but the words have remained separate.

2. **The correct answer is a.**
   Explanation: This sentence contains a main clause and a noun clause which begins with the word "that." "You" is the subject of the noun clause and it is a subject pronoun.

3. **The correct answer is a.**
   Explanation: "It" is the object pronoun. "It" is the object of the verb "love" and replaces the idea of teaching English in Thailand.

4. **The correct answer is b.**
   Explanation: The noun "benefit" is a common noun with a plural that is formed by adding "–s."

5. **The correct answer is c.**
   Explanation: "Him" is the object pronoun. It is the object of the verb "supply" and it replaces the name, Ahmed.

6. **The correct answer is c.**
   Explanation: "Seagulls" is a common noun. It does not refer to any particular individual, place, or thing.

7. **The correct answer is a.**
   Explanation: "My" is a possessive adjective pronoun. "My" shows ownership of a noun (backpack) and modifies the noun (backpack).

8. **The correct answer is b.**
   Explanation: "Mine" is a possessive pronoun. It shows ownership of the noun (book bag) that was previously referred to.

9. **The correct answer is b.**
   Explanation: "Rice" is a non-count/uncountable noun. It is a noun that cannot be divided into separate elements and as a result cannot be counted numerically. It always stays in the same form and *–s* is not added to make it plural.

10. **The correct answer is a.**

Explanation: "Themselves" is a reflexive pronoun. It is used when the object of a verb or preposition refers back to the subject of the sentence.

Quiz 2: Verbs

Directions: Read each question and choose the best answers. You will find the correct answers and explanations for each question on the page directly following the quiz.

1. Which sentence contains a dynamic verb?
    a) Tomoya walked to the convenience store after class.
    b) Oksana prefers books to movies.
    c) Bella needs her teacher's help after class today.

2. Identify the correct grammatical term for the underlined word.
She is <u>expecting</u> her teacher to grade her assignment fairly.
    a) gerund
    b) infinitive
    c) present participle

3. Which sentence contains an auxiliary verb?
    a) I did my homework already.
    b) He does his homework at 4 p.m. every day.
    c) We will do our homework after our drama club finishes.

4. Which of the following sentences does <u>not</u> include an example of the present participle used in a verb tense?
    a) He is reading a classic novel.
    b) He has been listening to classical music for hours.
    c) Reading is a great past time.

5. Which sentence contains an auxiliary verb?
    a) I did my homework already.
    b) He does his homework at 4 p.m. every day.
    c) We will do our homework after our drama club finishes.

6. The verbs <u>begin</u>, <u>bite</u>, and <u>blow</u> are irregular verbs. Select the answer that shows these three verbs in their past participle form.
    a) begun, bitten, blown
    b) began, bit, blew
    c) beginning, biting, blowing

7. Which of the following is an example of an intransitive verb?
   a) sleep
   b) find
   c) pass

8. Which of the underlined verbs is an example of the infinitive?
The teacher decided to study for a higher level degree so that he could improve his own knowledge and help his students better.
   a) decided
   b) to study
   c) could improve
   d) help

9. Which of the following is not a stative verb?
   a) own
   b) know
   c) recognize
   d) cry

10. Select all of the verbs that are irregular.
   a) drink
   b) grow
   c) walk
   d) hide

Quiz 2: Verbs
Answers and Feedback

1. **The correct answer is a.**
   Explanation: Answer a. contains the dynamic verb "walked" which shows an action that can be seen, and it can be used in the progressive form.

2. **The correct answer is c.**
   Explanation: The verb "expecting" is a present participle within the present progressive verb tense, and it functions as the main verb in the sentence.

3. **The correct answer is c.**
   Explanation: Sentence c. contains the auxiliary verb "will" which assists the main verb (do). It carries future meaning.

4. **The correct answer is c.**
   Explanation: Sentence c. includes the gerund (reading) and it is a noun and the subject of the sentence. Sentence a. and sentence b. include present participles (reading) and (listening) in progressive verb tenses.

5. **The correct answer is c.**
   Explanation: Sentence c. contains the auxiliary verb "will" which assists the main verb (do). It carries future meaning.

6. **The correct answer is a.**
   Explanation: Answer a. shows the past participle form on the three verbs. Answer b. shows the simple past tense of the three verbs. Answer c. shows the present participle form.

7. **The correct answer is a.**
   Explanation: "Sleep" is an intransitive verb because it does not take an object directly after the verb.

8. **The correct answer is b.**
   Explanation: "To study" is the infinitive form because it follows the main verb and it includes "to" + the base form.

9. **The correct answer is d.**
   Explanation: "Cry" is an active or dynamic verb. It is an action that can be seen. It can be used in the progressive (*–ing)* form. The other three verbs are stative verbs and have more

of an abstract meaning that cannot be seen. They cannot be used in the progressive form with the *–ing*.

10. **The correct answers are a, b, and d.**

    Explanation: "Drink" is an irregular verb and includes the following forms: drink, drank, drunk. "Grow" is an irregular verb and includes the following forms: grow, grew, grown. "Hide" is an irregular verb and includes the following forms: hide, hid, hidden.

Quiz 3: Adjectives, Articles, and Adverbs

Directions: Read each question and choose the best answers. You will find the correct answers and explanations for each question on the page directly following the quiz.

1. Which of the following is an example of a comparative adjective?
   a) more comfortable
   b) more quietly
   c) most comfortable

2. Which of the following sentences includes an example of the definite article?
   a) He is reading a magazine.
   b) She has been listening to jazz music for hours.
   c) We are studying the bilingual dictionary that we found.

3. Select <u>all</u> of the answers that show the need for zero articles.
   a) to reference nouns in general: *Cats are quieter than dogs.*
   b) before expressions of quantities and fractions: *He ate a third of the pizza.*
   c) to make generalizations: *Verbs are always challenging.*

4. Which example shows an adverb that modifies the entire sentence?
   a) He meticulously planned the lesson.
   b) The very quiet student was attentive during class.
   c) Fortunately, he wasn't late for class because of the traffic jam.

5. Which of the underlined adjectives is an example of a superlative adjective?
The student earned the <u>highest</u> grade on the exam even though her grade on the <u>last</u> exam was <u>lower</u> than most of her classmates.
   a) highest
   b) last
   c) lower

6. Which of the underlined words is an example of an adverb?
A <u>very</u> <u>small</u> child smiled <u>at</u> me in the <u>checkout</u> line.
   a) small
   b) at
   c) checkout
   d) very

7. Select the situation where an indefinite article should be used.
   a) with nonspecific objects: Does anyone have _ pen I can borrow?
   b) with specific objects: I love _ new house that we bought.
   c) before superlatives: Mrs. Smith was _ best teacher I ever had.

8. Which example shows a comparative adverb?
   a) She studies harder than her classmates.
   b) She studies the hardest.
   c) She hardly studies at all.

9. Which answer shows adverbs of frequency?
   a) quietly, carefully, easily
   b) rarely, never, always
   c) most certainly, the best, the hardest

10. Some adverbs are irregular, which means they change into irregular forms in their comparative and superlative forms. Select <u>all</u> the irregular adverbs.
   a) well
   b) badly
   c) definitely

Quiz 3: Adjectives, Articles, and Adverbs
Answers and Feedback

1. **The correct answer is a.**
   Explanation: "More comfortable" is a comparative adjective. Comparative adjectives are used to compare two or more different nouns. For adjectives that are more than one syllable and do not end in *–y,* we leave the adjective unchanged and modify it with the adverb *more*.

2. **The correct answer is c.**
   Explanation: Sentence c. includes the definite article "the." We use the definite article *the* to modify specific or particular nouns. In this case, there is only one bilingual dictionary, so it is considered a specific or particular noun, and the article "the" is needed.

3. **The correct answers are a and c.**
   Explanation: Answers a. and c. show the need for zero articles. When referencing nouns in general, we do not commonly use articles (often represented with a Ø symbol). Answer b. shows the use of the indefinite and definite articles "a" and "the."

4. **The correct answer is c.**
   Explanation: Answer c. includes the adverb "fortunately" which modifies the entire sentence. Answer a. contains the adverb "meticulously," and it modifies the verb "planned." Answer b. includes the adverb "very" and it modifies the adjective "quiet."

5. **The correct answer is a.**
   Explanation: "Highest" is a superlative adjective. Superlative adjectives are used to compare three or more items. To form a superlative of an adjective that is one syllable in length, we add *–est* to the adjective.

6. **The correct answer is d.**
   Explanation: "Very" is an adverb and it modifies the adjective "small."

7. **The correct answer is a.**
   Explanation: Answer a includes a non–specific object (any pen), so the indefinite article "a" is needed. Answers b. and c. both require the use of the definite article "the."

8. **The correct answer is a.**
   Explanation: Sentence a. uses the comparative adverb "harder." A comparative adverb is used to compare two instances of another word (or words) in a sentence. Comparative

adverbs are most often used to modify verbs. With some comparative adverbs, we add –*er* to the base adverb.

9. **The correct answer is b.**

Explanation: Answer b. shows adverbs of frequency. These adverbs modify verbs and show how frequently an action occurs. Common adverbs of frequency include *always, usually, often, sometimes, seldom, rarely*, and *never*.

10. **The correct answers are a and b.**

Explanation: Answers a. and b. are examples of irregular adverbs. Two common irregular adverbs in their base form are "well" and "badly." They change to "better" and "worse" in their comparative forms and to "best" and "worst" in their superlative forms.

Quiz 4: Prepositions and Conjunctions

Directions: Read each question and choose the best answers. You will find the correct answers and explanations for each question on the page directly following the quiz.

1. Which of the underlined words is a subordinating conjunction?
When I start teaching, this knowledge will be handy, but it is difficult to learn at the moment.
   a) When
   b) but
   c) to
   d) at

2. Which of the following sentences is punctuated correctly?
   a) I want to teach in Spain because, my aunt lives there.
   b) After I finished my TEFL course, I moved to the United Arab Emirates.
   c) Although I can't speak French I can read it quite well.

3. Which answer shows prepositions of place?
   a) at, before, during, around
   b) on, in, above, below
   c) different from, plan on, asked for

4. Select all of the sentences that contain common verb and preposition collocations.
   a) Ireland differs from Scotland in several ways.
   b) I plan on being a vegetarian while teaching overseas.
   c) He is enthusiastic about teaching EFL overseas.
   d) Her daughter is interested in gymnastics.

5. Which of the coordinating conjunctions combines two clauses together to show a result?
   a) and
   b) or
   c) so
   d) but

6. Select the best answer to complete the following definition:
_______________________ connect two or more clauses into a new sentence to form a *complex sentence*.
   a) Prepositions
   b) Subordinating conjunctions
   c) Prepositional phrases

7. Choose the best term to identify the underlined portion of the sentence.
If you want to learn more grammar, there are many great resources available.

a) independent clause
b) noun phrase
c) dependent clause

8. What is the function of the coordinating conjunction "but"?

a) combines two clauses together to show contrast
b) combines two clauses to show added information
c) combines two clauses together to show a result

9. Which sentence shows the use of "before" as a preposition?

a) She couldn't explain the different verb tenses before she studied these grammar modules.
b) Before she studied these grammar modules, she couldn't explain the different verb tenses.
c) She couldn't explain the different verb tenses before these grammar modules.

10. What type of prepositions are the following: around, at, before, during, throughout?

a) prepositions of place
b) prepositions of time
c) prepositional phrases

Quiz 4: Prepositions and Conjunctions Answers and Feedback

1. **The correct answer is a.**
   Explanation: "When" is a subordinating conjunction and it begins the dependent clause, "When I start teaching…."

2. **The correct answer is b.**
   Explanation: Sentence b. contains a dependent clause starting with the subordinating conjunction "after" and the dependent clause is at the beginning of the sentence. If the dependent clause comes first, a comma is needed. Sentence a. should have no comma, and sentence c. should have a comma after "French."

3. **The correct answer is b.**
   Explanation: Prepositions of place, such as *on, in, next to, above*, and *below*, describe the spatial relationship between two or more objects.

4. **The correct answers are a and b.**
   Explanation: Sentences a. and b. contain common verb and preposition collocations. Sentence a. contains the verb "differs" and the preposition "from." Sentence b. contains the verb "plan" and the preposition "on." Sentences c. and d. contain collocations of adjective and preposition.

5. **The correct answer is c.**
   Explanation: "So" is a coordinating conjunction that is used to combine two clauses together to show a result with the clause containing "so" showing the result of the other clause such as in the example: *We were all very tired, so everyone went home.* "So" helps indicate the result of everyone being tired.

6. **The correct answer is b.**
   Explanation: Subordinating conjunctions connect two or more clauses into a new sentence called a complex sentence. Complex sentences have at least one independent clause and one or more dependent (or subordinate) clauses.

7. **The correct answer is c.**
   Explanation: The first part of the sentence is a dependent clause that starts with the subordinating conjunction "if" and it cannot stand alone. It must be connected or subordinated to a main clause.

8. **The correct answer is a.**

   Explanation: The coordinating conjunction "but" is used to combine two clauses together to show a contrast such as in the following sentence: *She wanted to see a movie, but I wanted to eat.* The coordinating conjunction helps show a contrast between what the two people wanted to do.

9. **The correct answer is c.**

   Explanation: Sentence c. uses the word "before" as a preposition. It is specifically a preposition of time that shows a temporal relationship between two things in the sentence. In sentences a. and b., "before" is a subordinating conjunction.

10. **The correct answer is b.**

    Explanation: Prepositions of time, such as *around, at, before, during, on*, and *throughout,* describe various temporal relationships.

Quiz 5: Sentence Formation 1

Directions: Read each question and choose the best answers. You will find the correct answers and explanations for each question on the page directly following the quiz.

1. Read the sentence and identify the sentence type.
Fasten your seatbelt.
   a) Interrogative
   b) Imperative
   c) Declarative
   d) Exclamatory

2. Read the sentence and identify the sentence type.
I'm so happy to be home!
   a) Interrogative
   b) Imperative
   c) Declarative
   d) Exclamatory

3. Read the sentence and identify the sentence type.
Where is the post office?
   a) Interrogative
   b) Imperative
   c) Declarative
   d) Exclamatory

4. Read the sentence and identify the sentence type.
Don't use your cellphone in class.
   a) Interrogative
   b) Imperative
   c) Declarative
   d) Exclamatory

5. Read the sentence and identify the sentence type.
He walked home yesterday.
   a) Interrogative
   b) Imperative
   c) Declarative
   d) Exclamatory

6. What is the basic word order in English for most sentences?
   a) Verb + Object
   b) Object + Verb + Subject
   c) Verb + Subject + Object
   d) Subject + Verb + Object

7. Which sentence type omits one aspect of basic English word order?
   a) Interrogative
   b) Imperative
   c) Declarative
   d) Exclamatory

8. Is the following an independent or dependent clause?
Whenever it rains…
   a) Independent
   b) Dependent

9. True or False: A clause contains a subject, but not a predicate.
   a) True
   b) False

10. Is the following an independent or dependent clause?
The baby cried…
a. Independent
b. Dependent

Quiz 5: Sentence Formation 1
Answers and Feedback

1. **The correct answer is b.**
   Explanation: This is an imperative sentence because it is giving a command, and the subject (you) is dropped but understood.

2. **The correct answer is d.**
   Explanation: This is an exclamatory sentence because it expresses excitement and ends with an exclamation point.

3. **The correct answer is a.**
   Explanation: This is an interrogative sentence because it poses a question and ends with a question mark.

4. **The correct answer is b.**
   Explanation: This is an imperative sentence because it is giving a command, and the subject (you) is dropped but understood.

5. **The correct answer is c.**
   Explanation: This is a declarative sentence because it states a fact.

6. **The correct answer is d.**
   Explanation: Subject + Verb + Object is the basic English word order. Some exceptions to this rule are interrogative and imperative sentences, and sentences using passive voice.

7. **The correct answer is b.**
   Explanation: Imperative sentences do not contain a subject. They are lacking the "subject" part of the basic English word order: Subject + Verb + Object.

8. **The correct answer is b.**
   Explanation: This is a dependent clause. It has a subject (it) and a predicate (rains), but the addition of the subordinating conjunction (whenever) means that this clause cannot stand on its own as a complete sentence.

9. **The correct answer is b.**
   Explanation: A clause must contain a subject and a predicate.

10. **The correct answer is a.**

Explanation: This is an independent clause because it has a subject (the baby) and a predicate (cried), and it can stand on its own as a complete sentence.

Quiz 6: Sentence Formation 2

Directions: Read each question and choose the best answers. You will find the correct answers and explanations for each question on the page directly following the quiz.

1. Read the following sentence and identify its structure.
The computer is running slowly today.
   a) Simple
   b) Compound
   c) Complex
   d) Compound/Complex

2. Read the following sentence and identify its structure.
We will go to the park when it gets warmer.
   a) Simple
   b) Compound
   c) Complex
   d) Compound/Complex

3. Read the following sentence and identify its structure.
The soil is too dry now, but we will plant the flowers after we get more rain.
   a) Simple
   b) Compound
   c) Complex
   d) Compound/Complex

4. Read the following sentence and identify its structure.
Little Billy cries when he's upset.
   a) Simple
   b) Compound
   c) Complex
   d) Compound/Complex

5. Read the following sentence and identify its structure.
My mom, my sister, and I walked quickly through the street in the blustering storm.
   a) Simple
   b) Compound
   c) Complex
   d) Compound/Complex

6. Read the following sentence and identify its structure.
Martin forgot his homework, but he is not too worried because he saved a copy on his USB stick.
   a) Simple
   b) Compound
   c) Complex
   d) Compound/Complex

7. Read the following sentence and identify its structure.
Let's go to the new Italian restaurant, or we could order Chinese.
   a) Simple
   b) Compound
   c) Complex
   d) Compound/Complex

8. Identify the underlined clause in the following complex sentence as a noun, an adjective, or an adverb clause.
The movie that we saw last week was terrible.
   a) Noun clause
   b) Adjective clause
   c) Adverb clause

9. Identify the underlined clause in the following complex sentence as a noun, an adjective, or an adverb clause.
I know when he is coming home.
   a) Noun clause
   b) Adjective clause
   c) Adverb clause

10. Identify the underlined clause in the following complex sentence as a noun, an adjective, or an adverb clause.
The woman who sold our house is on the school board.
   a) Noun clause
   b) Adjective clause
   c) Adverb clause

11. Identify the underlined clause in the following complex sentence as a noun, an adjective, or an adverb clause.
She drank coffee before she biked to work.
   a) Noun clause

b) Adjective clause
c) Adverb clause

12. Identify the underlined clause in the following complex sentence as a noun, an adjective, or an adverb clause.
Since it rained today, we didn't go to the beach.
a) Noun clause
b) Adjective clause
c) Adverb clause

13. Does the following sentence contain correct comma usage for the underlined dependent clause?
The woman, that I met at a neighbor's party, was standing in front of me in line.
a) Yes
b) No

14. Does the following sentence contain correct comma usage for the underlined dependent clause?
While we were waiting, we started chatting.
a) Yes
b) No

15. Does the following sentence contain correct comma usage for the underlined dependent clause?
She told me that Dr. Jones, who is our school's principal, would be retiring soon.
a) Yes
b) No

Quiz 6: Sentence Formation 2
Answers and Feedback

1. **The correct answer is a.**
   Explanation: This is a simple sentence because it contains one independent clause (the computer is running slowly today) and no dependent clauses.

2. **The correct answer is c.**
   Explanation: This is a complex sentence because it contains one independent clause (we will go to the park) and one dependent clause (when it gets warmer).

3. **The correct answer is d.**
   Explanation: This is a compound/complex sentence because it contains two independent clauses (the soil is too dry now) (we will plant the flowers) joined by a coordinating conjunction (but) and one dependent clause (after we get more rain).

4. **The correct answer is c.**
   Explanation: This is a complex sentence because it contains one independent clause (Little Billy cries) and one dependent clause (when he's upset).

5. **The correct answer is a.**
   Explanation: This is a simple sentence because it contains one independent clause. There are many elements in this one independent clause, but there is only one subject (my mom, my sister, and I) and one predicate (walked quickly through the street in the blustering storm), which means there is only one clause.

6. **The correct answer is d.**
   Explanation: This is a compound/complex sentence because it contains two independent clauses (Martin forgot his homework) (he is not too worried) joined by a coordinating conjunction (but) and one dependent clause (because he saved a copy on his USB stick.

7. **The correct answer is b.**
   Explanation: This is a compound sentence because it contains two independent clauses (let's go to the new Italian restaurant) (we could order Chinese) joined by a coordinating conjunction (or).

8. **The correct answer is b.**
   Explanation: The underlined clause is an adjective clause because it is modifying a noun (movie). It directly follows that noun and begins with a relative pronoun (that).

9. **The correct answer is a.**

   Explanation: The underlined clause is a noun clause because it functions as the object of the sentence.

10. **The correct answer is b.**

    Explanation: The underlined clause is an adjective clause because it is modifying a noun (woman). It directly follows that noun and begins with a relative pronoun (who).

11. **The correct answer is c.**

    Explanation: The underlined clause is an adverb clause because it shows a time relationship with the coordinating conjunction (before).

12. **The correct answer is c.**

    Explanation: The underlined clause is an adverb clause because it shows a cause and effect relationship with the coordinating conjunction (since).

13. **The correct answer is b.**

    Explanation: The dependent adjective clause *"that I met at a neighbor's party"* is an example of an essential clause. The subject "*woman*" in the example sentence above is not specific, and the essential adjective clause *"that I met at a neighbor's party"* helps us identify which woman we are talking about. With essential clauses, no commas are used.

14. **The correct answer is a.**

    Explanation: The dependent adverb clause *"While we were waiting"* comes before the independent clause *"we started chatting."* If the dependent adverb clause precedes the independent clause in a sentence, the adverb clause is followed by a comma.

15. **The correct answer is a.**

    Explanation: The dependent adjective clause *"who is our school's principal"* is an example of a nonessential clause. The subject *"Mr. Baker"* in the example sentence above is specific because we know who Mr. Baker is even without the extra information in the adjective clause. With nonessential clauses, commas are used around the adjective clause to indicate that it does not contain essential information.

Quiz 7: Question Formation

Directions: Read each question and choose the best answers. You will find the correct answers and explanations for each question on the page directly following the quiz.

1. Identify which sentence is an example of a **Yes/No** question.
   a) Who is in your class?
   b) Are you interested in learning English?
   c) Where did you go to university?

2. Identify which sentence is an example of a ***Wh*– Predicate** question.
   a) Who is in your class?
   b) Are you interested in learning English?
   c) Where did you go to university?

3. Identify which sentence is an example of a ***Wh*– Subject** question.
   a) Who is in your class?
   b) Are you interested in learning English?
   c) What is your favorite subject?

4. **True or False**: Tag questions are questions we add on to the end of statements.
   a) True
   b) False

5. **True or False**: Both of the following sentences are examples of *Wh*– Predicate questions.
Who made dinner?
What did mom make for dinner?
   a) True
   b) False

6. **True or False**: Both of the following sentences are examples of Yes/No questions.
Did you have fun yesterday?
Have you ever been on a plane?
   a) True
   b) False

7. **True or False**: Both of the following sentences are examples of *Wh*– Subject questions.
Were you at home yesterday?
Who was at home with you?
   a) True

b) False

8. We use tag questions ____________.
   a) To ask for help
   b) To invite someone to do something
   c) To confirm information that we already think is true
   d) All of the above

9. Nonnative speakers sometimes make mistakes with word order when forming questions. Which of the following questions contains **incorrect** word order?
   a) Where are you from?
   b) When did you arrive in our country?
   c) Where you did teach before?
   d) How long will you stay here?

10. Nonnative speakers sometimes make mistakes with tag questions. Which of the following tag questions contains **an error**?
   a) You're new here, aren't you?
   b) You couldn't be my new teacher, couldn't you?
   c) You just arrived yesterday, didn't you?
   d) You like teaching English, don't you?

Quiz 7: Question Formation
Answers and Feedback

1. **The correct answer is b.**
   Explanation: This sentence follows the form for Yes/No questions: **Auxiliary Verb (be/do/have) or Modal verb + Subject + Main Verb.** In addition, this question can be answered simple with "yes" or "no."

2. **The correct answer is c.**
   Explanation: This sentence follows the form for *Wh–* Predicate questions: ***Wh–* question Word + Auxiliary Verb (be/do/have) or Modal verb (will/might/etc.) + Subject + Main Verb.** In addition, the answer can be found in the predicate of the response: "I went to university in <u>Canada</u>."

3. **The correct answer is a.**
   a) Explanation: This sentence follows the form for *Wh–* Subject questions: ***Wh–* question Word + Main Verb.** In addition, the answer can be found in the subject of the response: "<u>Your brother</u> is in my class."

4. **The correct answer is a.**
   Explanation: Tag questions are located at the end of the sentence and communicate a variety of meanings.

5. **The correct answer is b.**
   Explanation: The first question (Who made dinner?) follows the *Wh–* Subject question format (*Wh–* question Word + Main Verb), and the answer can be found in the subject of the response (<u>I</u> made dinner). The second question (What did mom make for dinner?) follows the Wh– Predicate question format (*Wh–* question Word + Auxiliary Verb (be/do/have) or Modal verb (will/might/etc.) + Subject + Main Verb), and the answer can be found in the predicate of the response (Mom made <u>pasta</u> for dinner).

6. **The correct answer is a.**
   Explanation: Both questions follow the Yes/No question format (Auxiliary Verb (be/do/have) or Modal verb + Subject + Main Verb) and both can be answered with a simple "yes" or "no."

7. **The correct answer is b.**
   Explanation: The second question (Who was at home with you?) follows the *Wh–* Subject question format (*Wh–* question Word + Main Verb), and the answer can be found in the subject of the response (<u>My mom</u> was at home with me). The second

question (Were you at home yesterday?) follows the Yes/No question format (Auxiliary Verb (be/do/have) or Modal verb + Subject + Main Verb) and can be answered with a simple "yes" or "no."

8. **The correct answer is d.**
   Explanation: All of the examples above indicate reasons we use tag questions with statements.

9. **The correct answer is c.**
   Explanation: This is a *Wh–* Predicate question, and in forming those types of questions, the subject (you) should come after the auxiliary verb (did).

10. **The correct answer is b.**
   Explanation: This is an example of a negative statement (You couldn't be my new teacher), so when a tag question is used, it should be positive (could you?).

Quiz 8: Present Simple and Present Continuous

Directions: Read each question and choose the best answers. You will find the correct answers and explanations for each question on the page directly following the quiz.

1. Identify which underlined verb tense is an example of the **present simple**:
   a) I've been wanting to go to Saigon for years.
   b) My mother wants me to call her every couple of weeks from Saigon.
   c) I never wanted to take a 9-5 job in the states.
   d) After this job, maybe I will want to try and teach in another country.

2. Identify which underlined verb tense is an example of the **present simple**:
   a) I've never eaten sushi.
   b) I'm going to eat sushi at a Japanese restaurant this evening.
   c) This will be really different for me because I usually eat pasta or pizza for dinner every night.
   d) By the end of the evening, hopefully I will have eaten many different kinds of sushi.

3. Identify which underlined verb tense is an example of the **present continuous**:
   a) My friends are visiting me next week.
   b) They are going to visit some other friends while they are here as well.
   c) While they are here, we will visit many different tourist sites.
   d) Hopefully, we will see some places that I've never visited before.

4. Identify which underlined verb tense is an example of the **present continuous**:
   a) Before I became a TEFL teacher, I had never taught grammar.
   b) Sometimes, I teach verb tenses that I've never really thought much about.
   c) For example, I taught the future perfect for the first time last year.
   d) In fact, I'm teaching that verb tense again right now!

5. Read the sentence and choose which meaning is represented with the underlined verb and the context of the sentence.
   We gather together every year to share a meal and express gratitude.
   a) Habitual actions or truths
   b) Actions happening right now
   c) Scheduled Events

6. Read the sentence and choose which meaning is represented with the underlined verb and the context of the sentence.
   My flight arrives at O'Hare this Saturday!

a) Habitual actions or truths
b) Actions happening right now
c) Scheduled Events

7. Read the sentence and choose which meaning is represented with the underlined verb and the context of the sentence.
She is constantly forgetting to park in the employee section.
a) Actions or events happening right now
b) Near Future Events
c) Repetition or Irritation

8. Read the sentence and choose which meaning is represented with the underlined verb and the context of the sentence.
We are finishing our lunch, and then we'll head straight home.
a) Actions or events happening right now
b) Near Future Events
c) Repetition or Irritation

9. Read the sentence and choose which meaning is represented with the underlined verb and the context of the sentence.
The tickets are going on sale tomorrow morning at 6:00 a.m.
a) Actions or events happening right now
b) Near Future Events
c) Repetition or Irritation

10. Imagine you want to present the present simple in context for a class of EFL students. Choose the real-world context below that will best show the use of the **present simple**.
a) A conversation where two people are narrating events as they happen
b) A description of a family member's characteristics
c) A description of a trip you took last year

11. Imagine you want to present the present continuous in context for a class of EFL students. Choose the real-world context below that will best show the use of the **present continuous**.
a) A conversation where two people are narrating events as they happen
b) A list of your daily rituals
c) A description of a trip you took last year

12. One of the following sentences contains a mistake commonly made by people first learning the simple present tense. Identify which underlined phrase is **incorrect**.

My name is Pablo, and I live in an apartment near school. Every day, I ride my bike to school. Many of my classmates also rides their bikes to school.

13. One of the following sentences contains a mistake commonly made by people first learning the present continuous tense. Identify which underlined phrase is **incorrect**.
I am waiting for the bus, and my friend sitting next to me. We are talking about the test in our English class.

a) I am waiting
b) My friend sitting
c) We are talking

Quiz 8: Present Simple and Present Continuous Answers and Feedback

1. **The correct answer is b.**
   Explanation: In this sentence, the verb "wants" follows the rule of form for the present simple: **Base Verb (+ *–s/–es* in third person singular)**. It is also an example of a habitual action, which is one meaning of the present simple.

2. **The correct answer is c.**
   Explanation: In this sentence, the verb "eat" follows the rule of form for the present simple: **Base Verb (+ *s/es* in third person singular)**. It is also an example of a habitual action, which is one meaning of the present simple.

3. **The correct answer is a.**
   Explanation: In this sentence, the verb "are visiting" follows the rule of form for the present continuous: ***Be* Verb + Present Participle (base form of the verb + ing)**. It is also an example of a near future event, which is one meaning of the present continuous.

4. **The correct answer is d.**
   Explanation: In this sentence, the verb "am teaching" follows the rule of form for the present continuous: ***Be* Verb + Present Participle (base form of the verb + ing)**. It is also an example of an action happening right now, which is one meaning of the present continuous.

5. **The correct answer is a.**
   Explanation: The key words "every year" indicate that the speaker "gathers" habitually year after year. This is one meaning of the present simple.

6. **The correct answer is c.**
   Explanation: "To arrive" is one of the verbs often used to express a future scheduled event, which is further emphasized by the specific time of Saturday. This is one meaning of the present simple.

7. **The correct answer is c.**
   Explanation: The adverb "constantly" emphasizes that the subject of the sentence is repeatedly in the same situation where she is forgetting to park in the correct location. This is one meaning of the present continuous.

8. **The correct answer is a.**

Explanation: The speaker in this sentence implies that he/she is currently eating and finishing their food and makes this even clearer by stating that he/she will go home immediately afterwards. This is one meaning of the present continuous.

9. **The correct answer is b.**

Explanation: The key phrase of "tomorrow morning at 6:00 a.m." highlights the near future time frame that is indicated by underlined verb. This is one meaning of the present continuous.

10. **The correct answer is b.**

Explanation: A description of a family member's characteristics is a great way to show the use of the present simple in context. (e.g., This is my father. He has brown hair, and he wears glasses. He is kind and supportive.)

11. **The correct answer is a.**

Explanation: The present continuous is often used to narrate events as they happen. (e.g., Look! That man is walking in the middle of the street, and the cars aren't stopping.)

12. **The correct answer is d.**

Explanation: In this sentence, the speaker has made a mistake with subject/verb agreement. Instead of "my classmates also rides," the speaker should say "my classmates also ride." The subject is plural, so the verb does not take an "–s."

13. **The correct answer is b.**

Explanation: In this sentence, the speaker has forgotten to include the conjugated form of the "be" verb for the present continuous tense. This should say "my friend is sitting."

Quiz 9: Past Simple and Past Continuous

Directions: Read each question and choose the best answers. You will find the correct answers and explanations for each question on the page directly following the quiz.

1. Identify which underlined verb tense is an example of the **past simple**:
   a) I've never eaten sashimi.
   b) I ate sushi for the first time last week, but I'm not sure I'll like sashimi.
   c) I've been eating new foods every week for the past few months.
   d) Before I ate sushi, I had never eaten Japanese food.

2. Identify which underlined verb tense is an example of the **past simple**:
   a) I am studying Spanish with my colleague later on today.
   b) I study on my own every day, but it's nice to get together and study with someone else sometimes.
   c) We will be studying different verb tenses.
   d) I studied Spanish every summer as a child, but it's nice to be able to review things now.

3. Identify which underlined verb tense is an example of the **past continuous**:
   a) I visited my friends in China last year.
   b) I had never visited any place outside of my home country before this trip.
   c) I celebrated my birthday on this trip, so I was visiting many famous places on my special day.
   d) I'm sure I am going to visit even more amazing places on future birthdays.

4. Identify which underlined verb tense is an example of the **past continuous**:
   a) My little brother complains all of the time.
   b) If there is something little wrong with his order at a restaurant, he will complain about it.
   c) Once, he complained that he didn't have a separate salad fork! I told him that he really only needed one fork.
   d) Even when we were young, he was always complaining about something!

5. Read the sentence and choose which meaning is represented with the underlined verb and the context of the sentence.
The first time I saw a sloth, I was so surprised!
   a) Past habit that is generally no longer true
   b) Specific moment completed in the past
   c) An ongoing action interrupted by another action in the past

d) Ongoing annoying habit or action in the past

6. Read the sentence and choose which meaning is represented with the underlined verb and the context of the sentence.
The vendor who was passing through town that morning stopped to sell them some jewelry.
a) Past habit that is generally no longer true
b) Specific moment completed in the past
c) An ongoing action interrupted by another action in the past
d) Ongoing annoying habit or action in the past

7. Read the sentence and choose which meaning is represented with the underlined verb and the context of the sentence.
On the bus, my seatmate was talking on the phone very loudly, and I couldn't sleep.
a) Past habit that is generally no longer true
b) Specific moment completed in the past
c) An ongoing action interrupted by another action in the past
d) Ongoing annoying habit or action in the past

8. Read the sentence and choose which meaning is represented with the underlined verb and the context of the sentence.
I took swim lessons every summer when I was a kid.
a) Past habit that is generally no longer true
b) Specific moment completed in the past
c) An ongoing action interrupted by another action in the past
d) Ongoing annoying habit or action in the past

9. Imagine you want to present the past simple in context for a class of EFL students. Choose the real-world context below that will best show the use of the **past simple**.
a) An example cover letter that highlights past experiences
b) A description of your everyday habitual actions
c) A plan for a future trip

10. One of the following sentences contains a mistake commonly made by people first learning the **past simple** and **past continuous** tenses. Identify which underlined phrase is **incorrect**.
I lived in Mexico last summer. I studied Spanish while I was there. I was walking to my school every day when I lived there.
a) lived
b) studied
c) was walking

Quiz 9: Past Simple and Past Continuous Answers and Feedback

1. **The correct answer is b.**
   Explanation: In this sentence, the verb "ate" is the irregular form of "eat" in the past simple. It is also an example describing a past event, which is one meaning of the past simple.

2. **The correct answer is d.**
   Explanation: In this sentence, the verb "studied" follows the rule of form for the regular past simple: **VERB + *–ed*.** It is also an example of a past habit, which is one meaning of the past simple.

3. **The correct answer is c.**
   Explanation: In this sentence, the verb "was visiting" follows the rule of form for the past continuous: **Past Tense *Be* Verb + Present Participle (base form of the verb + ing)**. It is also an example of an action in progress at a past time, which is one meaning of the past continuous.

4. **The correct answer is d.**
   Explanation: In this sentence, the verb "was complaining" follows the rule of form for the past continuous: **Past Tense *Be* Verb + Present Participle (base form of the verb + ing)**. It is also an example of the emphasis of an annoying ongoing habit in the past, which is one meaning of the past continuous.

5. **The correct answer is b.**
   Explanation: The verb "saw" refers to one very specific moment, which is framed by the key phrase: *the first time.* This is one meaning of the past simple.

6. **The correct answer is c.**
   Explanation: In the context of the sentence, the vendor was in the process of passing through the town, which is noted by the past continuous, "was passing," and then interrupted by the moment that they "stopped," which is expressed in the past simple. This is one meaning of the past continuous.

7. **The correct answer is d.**
   Explanation: The speaker is annoyed by the ongoing action of the seatmate loudly talking on the phone. This is one meaning of the past continuous.

8. **The correct answer is a.**

Explanation: The verb "took" refers to a past habit that is indicated by the key words "every summer," and we assume that this person no longer takes swim lessons. This is one meaning of the past simple.

9. **The correct answer is a.**

Explanation: The past simple is often used in cover letters to highlight past experience (e.g., When I was in university, I had the opportunity to volunteer in Mexico. I taught English to children at a summer camp.)

10. **The correct answer is c.**

Explanation: In this sentence, the speaker is talking about a past habit. When we talk about past habits, we use the past simple, "walked," and not the past continuous, "was walking."

Quiz 10: Future Simple and Future Continuous

Directions: Read each question and choose the best answers. You will find the correct answers and explanations for each question on the page directly following the quiz.

1. Identify which underlined verb tense is an example of the **future simple**:
   a) I will eat pizza for dinner tonight.
   b) I've been eating pizza every Friday night for a couple of years now.
   c) Because next Thursday is my birthday, I'm eating pizza then, too.
   d) This time next week, I will be eating pizza again!

2. Identify which underlined verb tense is an example of the **future simple**:
   a) I am studying Spanish with my colleague later on today.
   b) I study on my own every day, but it's nice to get together and study with someone else sometimes.
   c) We are going to study different verb tenses.
   d) I studied Spanish every summer as a child, but it's nice to be able to review things now.

3. Identify which underlined verb tense is an example of the **future continuous**:
   a) I will be living in Thailand next year.
   b) I'm going to live in a small town.
   c) Recently, I've been living and teaching in China.
   d) Before I moved here, I had never lived outside of my home country.

4. Identify which underlined verb tense is an example of the **future continuous**:
   a) I'm cooking my son's favorite meal.
   b) Every year, I cook his favorite meal for this birthday.
   c) I've been cooking for two hours now.
   d) Hopefully, I'm not going to be cooking when he gets home!

5. Read the sentence and choose which meaning is represented with the underlined verb and the context of the sentence.
I am going to meet my professor at 10 a.m. tomorrow to discuss my essay.
   a) A prediction
   b) An action in progress in the future interrupted by another action
   c) An expression of a prior intended plan

6. Read the sentence and choose which meaning is represented with the underlined verb and the context of the sentence.

They will already be eating when I arrive.

a) A prediction
b) An action in progress in the future interrupted by another action
c) An expression of a prior intended plan

7. Read the sentence and choose which meaning is represented with the underlined verb and the context of the sentence.
I will help you with your homework when I see you tomorrow.

a) A prediction
b) An action in progress in the future interrupted by another action
c) An expression of a prior intended plan

8. Read the sentence and choose which meaning is represented with the underlined verb and the context of the sentence.
It will snow tomorrow.

a) A prediction
b) An action in progress in the future interrupted by another action
c) An expression of a prior intended plan

9. Imagine you want to present the future simple in context for a class of EFL students. Choose the real-world context below that will best show the use of the **future simple**.

a) A weather forecast
b) The description of weather on a vacation you took last year
c) The current weather conditions

10. One of the following sentences contains a mistake commonly made by people first learning future tenses. Identify which underlined phrase is **incorrect**.
I'm going to visit my grandmother tomorrow. She will be cooking when I will arrive. We're going to bake banana bread together.

a) I'm going to visit
b) She will be cooking
c) I will arrive
d) We're going to bake

Quiz 10: Future Simple and Future Continuous Answers and Feedback

1. **The correct answer is a.**

   Explanation: In this sentence, the verb "will eat" follows the rule of form for the "will" future simple: **Will + Base Form of Verb**. It is also an example of a future plan, which is one meaning of the future simple.

2. **The correct answer is c.**

   Explanation: In this sentence, the verb "are going to study" follows the rule of form for the "be going to" future simple: **Be Going To + Base Form of Verb**. It is also an example of expressing a prior plan, which is one meaning of the future simple.

3. **The correct answer is a.**

   Explanation: In this sentence, the verb "will be living" follows the rule of form for the "will" form of the future continuous: **Will + Be + Present Participle (base form of the verb + ing)**. It is also an example of an ongoing action in the future, which is one meaning of the future continuous.

4. **The correct answer is d.**

   Explanation: In this sentence, the verb "am not going to be cooking" follows the rule of form for the "be going to" form of the future continuous: **Be Verb + Going to Be + Present Participle (base form of the verb + ing)**. This example also contains the word "not" to indicate the negative form. It is also an example of an ongoing action in the future, which is one meaning of the future continuous.

5. **The correct answer is c.**

   Explanation: The verb "am going to meet" and the context of the sentence show an expression of a prior plan, which is scheduled for 10 a.m. the next day. This is one meaning of the future simple.

6. **The correct answer is b.**

   Explanation: The action "will be eating" will already be in progress in the future when another action or event, "arrive," happens. The key word "already" enhances the meaning of an action already in progress. This is one meaning of the future progressive.

7. **The correct answer is c.**
   Explanation: The verb "will help" and the context of the sentence show an expression of a prior plan, which will happen the following day. This is one meaning of the future simple.

8. **The correct answer is a.**
   Explanation: The verb "will snow" refers to a prediction about the weather. This is one meaning of the future simple.

9. **The correct answer is a.**
   Explanation: The future simple is often used in weather forecasting.

10. **The correct answer is c.**
   Explanation: In this sentence, the simple present (I arrive), not the future simple (I will arrive), should be used in the dependent time clause.

Quiz 11: Present Perfect and Present Perfect Continuous

Directions: Read each question and choose the best answers. You will find the correct answers and explanations for each question on the page directly following the quiz.

1. Read the sentence and choose which meaning is represented with the underlined verb and the context of the sentence.
My mom has been in the same house since 1982.
   a) Duration of past action until now (stative verb)
   b) Duration of past action until now (dynamic verb)
   c) Repetitive past action likely to be repeated
   d) An action that did or did not happen at an unspecified time in the past

2. Read the sentence and choose which meaning is represented with the underlined verb and the context of the sentence.
He has eaten at the same restaurant five times recently!
   a) Duration of past action until now (stative verb)
   b) Duration of past action until now (dynamic verb)
   c) Repetitive past action likely to be repeated
   d) An action that did or did not happen at an unspecified time in the past

3. Identify which underlined verb tense is an example of the **present perfect continuous**:
   a) I will be living in Thailand next year.
   b) I'm going to live in a small town.
   c) Recently, I've been living and teaching in China.
   d) Before I moved here, I had never lived outside of my home country.

4. Read the sentence and choose which meaning is represented with the underlined verb and the context of the sentence.
They have been running for three hours!
   a) Duration of past action until now (stative verb)
   b) Duration of past action until now (dynamic verb)
   c) Repetitive past action likely to be repeated
   d) An action that did or did not happen at an unspecified time in the past

5. Imagine you want to present the present perfect in context for a class of EFL students. Choose the real-world context below that will best show the use of the **present perfect**.
   a) A weather prediction segment on the local news
   b) The description of weather on a vacation you took last year
   c) A news report about recent weather trends

6. One of the following sentences contains a mistake commonly made by people first learning the present perfect and present perfect continuous tenses. Identify which underlined phrase is **incorrect**.

I have visited my childhood friend many times recently. We have had a lot of great experiences together. I have been knowing him for 30 years.

a) have visited
b) have had
c) have been knowing

7. Identify which underlined verb tense is an example of the **present perfect**:

a) Who will you study with later today?
b) What will you be studying?
c) What have you studied so far?
d) Where did you study yesterday?

8. Read the sentence and choose which meaning is represented with the underlined verb and the context of the sentence.

She has never lived overseas.

a) Duration of past action until now (stative verb)
b) Duration of past action until now (dynamic verb)
c) Repetitive past action likely to be repeated
d) An action that did or did not happen at an unspecified time in the past

9. Read the sentence and choose which meaning is represented with the underlined verb and the context of the sentence.

I've been studying at the school for a few days now.

a) Duration of past action until now (stative verb)
b) Duration of past action until now (dynamic verb)
c) Repetitive past action likely to be repeated
d) An action that did or did not happen at an unspecified time in the past

10. Identify which underlined verb tense is an example of the **present perfect**:

a) My friends are visiting me next week.
b) They are going to visit some other friends while they are here as well.
c) Hopefully, we will see some places that I have never visited before.
d) By the end of the trip, all of us will have seen many new things!

Quiz 11: Present Perfect and Present Perfect Continuous Answers and Feedback

1. **The correct answer is a.**
   Explanation: The verb "has been" and the key words, "since 1982," show the duration of a past action until the present moment with a stative verb. This is one meaning of the present perfect.

2. **The correct answer is c.**
   Explanation: The verb "has eaten" and the key words, "five times recently," show a repetitive past action that is likely to be repeated. This is one meaning of the present perfect.

3. **The correct answer is c.**
   Explanation: In this sentence, the verb "have been living" follows the rule of form for the present perfect continuous: **Have/Has + Been + Present Participle**. It is also an example of a duration of an action until the present time, which is one meaning of the present perfect continuous.

4. **The correct answer is b.**
   Explanation: The verb "have been running" and the key words, "for three hours," show the duration of a past action until the present moment with a dynamic verb. This is one meaning of the present perfect continuous.

5. **The correct answer is c.**
   Explanation: The present perfect is often used when reporting about news stories that happened recently. Recent weather trends would most likely be described using the present perfect. (e.g., "Recently, it <u>has been</u> very windy on the eastern side of the state.")

6. **The correct answer is c.**
   Explanation: In this sentence, the present perfect (have known), not the present perfect continuous (have been knowing), should be used because "know" is a stative verb, and the present perfect continuous is not used with stative verbs. The present perfect can be used to show ongoing actions with stative verbs.

7. **The correct answer is c.**
   Explanation: In this sentence, the verb "have studied" follows the rule of form for the present perfect: **Have/Has + Past Participle**. It is also an example of a repetitive past action, which is one meaning of the present perfect.

8. **The correct answer is d.**

   Explanation: The verb "have lived" and the key word, "never," show an action that did not happen at an unspecified time in the past. This is one meaning of the present perfect.

9. **The correct answer is b.**

   Explanation: The verb "have been studying" and the key words, "for a few days now," show the duration of a past action until the present moment with a dynamic verb. This is one meaning of the present perfect continuous.

10. **The correct answer is c.**

    Explanation: In this sentence, the verb "have visited" follows the rule of form for the present perfect: **Have/Has + Past Participle**. It is also an example of an action that did or did not happen at an unspecified time in the past, which is one meaning of the present perfect.

Quiz 12: Past Perfect and Past Perfect Continuous

Directions: Read each question and choose the best answers. You will find the correct answers and explanations for each question on the page directly following the quiz.

1. Identify which underlined verb tense is an example of the **past perfect**:
   a) I have lived in Mexico for 3 years, and so many friends have visited me.
   b) My very close friends visited last week.
   c) We visited many tourist attractions.
   d) We saw so many places that I had never visited before.

2. Identify which underlined verb tense is an example of the **past perfect**:
   a) Who will you study with later today?
   b) What will you be studying?
   c) What have you studied so far?
   d) Where had you studied before you started this class?

3. Identify which underlined verb tense is an example of the **past perfect continuous**:
   a) I have been living in Thailand for 2 months.
   b) Before I moved here, I had been living in South Korea.
   c) I am living in a small town here in Thailand.
   d) Hopefully in the future, I will be living in another interesting country!

4. Identify which underlined verb tense is an example of the **past perfect continuous**:
   a) I waited at the doctor's office for such a long time yesterday!
   b) I usually don't wait very long to see my doctor.
   c) By the time the nurse called my name, I had been waiting for an hour.
   d) I hope I won't be waiting that long the next time I see my doctor.

5. Read the sentence and choose which meaning is represented with the underlined verb and the context of the sentence.
I had been studying for five hours when the library closed.
   a) Duration of past action until another point in the past (stative verb)
   b) Duration of past action until another point in the past (dynamic verb)
   c) Action completed (or not completed) before another action or time in the past

6. Read the sentence and choose which meaning is represented with the underlined verb and the context of the sentence.
They had been outside the store for 10 minutes before it opened.
   a) Duration of past action until another point in the past (stative verb)

b) Duration of past action until another point in the past (dynamic verb)
c) Action completed (or not completed) before another action or time in the past

7. Read the sentence and choose which meaning is represented with the underlined verb and the context of the sentence.
She <u>had</u> never <u>lived</u> overseas before she taught English in Chile.
a) Duration of past action until another point in the past (stative verb)
b) Duration of past action until another point in the past (dynamic verb)
c) Action completed (or not completed) before another action or time in the past

8. Read the sentence and choose which meaning is represented with the underlined verb and the context of the sentence.
How long <u>had</u> she <u>been cooking</u> before you got home?
a) Duration of past action until another point in the past (stative verb)
b) Duration of past action until another point in the past (dynamic verb)
c) Action completed (or not completed) before another action or time in the past

9. Imagine you want to present the past perfect in context for a class of EFL students. Choose the real-world context below that will best show the use of the **past perfect**.
a) An account of the previous day's weather
b) A fictional short story
c) A resume

10. One of the following sentences contains a mistake commonly made by people first learning the past perfect tense. Identify which underlined phrase is **incorrect**.
Last night, we <u>saw</u> an opera. We <u>had never saw</u> an opera before. My friend <u>had listened</u> to a lot of opera music, but she <u>had never been</u> to one.
a) saw
b) had never saw
c) had listened
d) had never been

Quiz 12: Past Perfect and Past Perfect Continuous Answers and Feedback

1. **The correct answer is d.**
   Explanation: In this sentence, the verb "had visited" follows the rule of form for the past perfect: **Had + Past Participle**. It is also an example of an action that did or did not happen (visited) before another time or action (saw) in the past, which is one meaning of the past perfect.

2. **The correct answer is d.**
   Explanation: In this sentence, the verb "had studied" follows the rule of form for the past perfect: **Had + Past Participle**. It is also an example of an action that did or did not happen (studied) before another time or action (started) in the past, which is one meaning of the past perfect.

3. **The correct answer is b.**
   Explanation: In this sentence, the verb "had been living" follows the rule of form for the past perfect continuous: **Had + Been + Present Participle**. It is also an example of an action that started in the past (living) and continued to another point in the past (moved), which is one meaning of the past perfect continuous.

4. **The correct answer is c.**
   Explanation: In this sentence, the verb "had been waiting" follows the rule of form for the past perfect continuous: **Had + Been + Present Participle**. It is also an example of an action that started in the past (waiting) and continued to another point in the past (called), which is one meaning of the past perfect continuous.

5. **The correct answer is b.**
   Explanation: The verb "had been studying" and the key words, "for five hours," show the duration of a past action (studying) until another point in the past (library closed) with a dynamic verb (study). This is one meaning of the past perfect continuous.

6. **The correct answer is a.**
   Explanation: The verb "had been" and the key words, "for 10 minutes," show the duration of a past action (been) until another point in the past (opened) with a stative verb (be). This is one meaning of the past perfect.

7. **The correct answer is c.**
   Explanation: The verb "had lived" and the key word, "never," show an action that did not happen (lived) before another time in the past (taught). This is one meaning of the past perfect.

8. **The correct answer is b.**
   Explanation: The verb "had been cooking" and the key words, "how long," show the duration of a past action (cooking) until another point in the past (got home) with a dynamic verb (cook). This is one meaning of the past perfect continuous.

9. **The correct answer is b.**
   Explanation: The past perfect is often used in fictional writing when comparing older past events with more recent past events (e.g., "He walked slowly into the house. He <u>had never been</u> here before, and he wasn't sure if he would be welcome.")

10. **The correct answer is b.**
    Explanation: In this sentence, the past participle is incorrect. It should be "seen" and not "saw." Many nonnative speakers make mistakes with irregular past participles.

Quiz 13: Future Perfect and Future Perfect Continuous

Directions: Read each question and choose the best answers. You will find the correct answers and explanations for each question on the page directly following the quiz.

1. Read the sentence and choose which meaning is represented with the underlined verb and the context of the sentence.
I <u>will have been</u> in my job for 30 years by the time I retire.
   a) Duration of action until a point in the future (stative verb)
   b) Duration of action until a point in the future (dynamic verb)
   c) Action completed (or not completed) before an action or time in the future

2. Identify which underlined verb tense is an example of the **future perfect**:
   a) I <u>will eat</u> pizza for dinner tonight.
   b) By the end of the evening, I <u>will have eaten</u> many different types of pizza.
   c) Because next Thursday is my birthday, I<u>'m going to eat</u> pizza then, too.
   d) This time next week, I <u>will be eating</u> pizza again!

3. Identify which underlined verb tense is an example of the **future perfect continuous**:
   a) I <u>will be riding</u> the train to the airport.
   b) By the time I get to the airport, I <u>will have been riding</u> on the train for 3 hours.
   c) I <u>haven't ridden</u> the train many times before.
   d) I <u>hope to be riding</u> the train more often in the future because it's more convenient than driving.

4. Identify which underlined verb tense is an example of the **future perfect continuous**:
   a) I <u>have been living</u> in Thailand for 2 months.
   b) I <u>am living</u> in a small town here in Thailand.
   c) When I move, I <u>will have been living</u> here for a full year.
   d) Hopefully in the future, I <u>will be living</u> in another interesting country!

5. Imagine you want to present the future perfect in context for a class of EFL students. Choose the real-world context below that will best show the use of the **future perfect**.
   a) A letter home describing a typical day at one's university
   b) A letter home describing accomplishments made so far in university
   c) A letter describing one's goals and intentions for the future

6. Identify which underlined verb tense is an example of the **future perfect**:
   a) I have lived in Mexico for 3 years, and so many friends <u>have visited</u> me.
   b) My very close friends <u>are visiting</u> me now.

c) We will be visiting some tourist attractions in my city tomorrow.
d) By the end of the trip, they will have visited many new places in my city.

7. One of the following sentences contains a mistake commonly made by people first learning the future perfect tense. Identify which underlined phrase is **incorrect**.
She has a test tomorrow, so she is going to study a lot. By the time the library will have closed, she will have been studying for 5 or 6 hours.
a) has
b) is going to study
c) will have closed
d) will have been studying

8. Read the sentence and choose which meaning is represented with the underlined verb and the context of the sentence.
How long will you have been driving by the time you get home?
a) Duration of action until a point in the future (stative verb)
b) Duration of action until a point in the future (dynamic verb)
c) Action completed (or not completed) before an action or time in the future

9. Read the sentence and choose which meaning is represented with the underlined verb and the context of the sentence.
I will have been studying for five hours by the time the library closes.
a) Duration of action until a point in the future (stative verb)
b) Duration of action until a point in the future (dynamic verb)
c) Action completed (or not completed) before an action or time in the future

10. Read the sentence and choose which meaning is represented with the underlined verb and the context of the sentence.
She will have lived in five different countries by the time she gets her TEFL certificate.
a) Duration of action until a point in the future (stative verb)
b) Duration of action until a point in the future (dynamic verb)
c) Action completed (or not completed) before an action or time in the future

Quiz 13: Future Perfect and Future Perfect Continuous Answers and Feedback

1. **The correct answer is a.**
   Explanation: The verb "will have been" and the key words, "for 30 years," show the duration of an action (been) until a point in the future (retire) with a stative verb (be). This is one meaning of the future perfect.

2. **The correct answer is b.**
   Explanation: In this sentence, the verb "will have eaten" follows the rule of form for the future perfect: **Will + Have + Past Participle**. It is also an example of a completed future action (eaten) before a future action or event (end of the evening), which is one meaning of the future perfect.

3. **The correct answer is b.**
   Explanation: In this sentence, the verb "will have been riding" follows the rule of form for the future perfect continuous: **Will + Have + Been + Present Participle**. It is also an example of an ongoing action (riding) before an action or event in the future (get), which is one meaning of the future perfect continuous.

4. **The correct answer is c.**
   Explanation: In this sentence, the verb "will have been living" follows the rule of form for the future perfect continuous: **Will + Have + Been + Present Participle**. It is also an example of an ongoing action (living) before an action or event in the future (move), which is one meaning of the future perfect continuous.

5. **The correct answer is c.**
   Explanation: The future perfect is often used to describe goals and intentions for the future (e.g., "By the time he is 30 years old, he <u>will have completed</u> his Master's degree.")

6. **The correct answer is d.**
   Explanation: In this sentence, the verb "will have visited" follows the rule of form for the future perfect: **Will + Have + Past Participle**. It is also an example of a completed action (visited) before a future action or event (end of the trip), which is one meaning of the future perfect.

7. **The correct answer is c.**
   Explanation: In this sentence, the future perfect should not be used in both the dependent time clause and the independent clause. In the time clause that begins with

"by the time," the simple present (closes) should be used. The independent clause in the sentence contains the future perfect construction (will have been studying).

8. **The correct answer is b.**
   Explanation: The verb "will have been driving" and the key words, "how long" and "by the time," show the duration of an action (driving) until a point in the future (got home) with a dynamic verb (drive). This is one meaning of the future perfect continuous.

9. **The correct answer is b.**
   Explanation: The verb "will have been studying" and the key words, "for five hours," show the duration of an action (studying) until a point in the future (library closes) with a dynamic verb (study). This is one meaning of the future perfect continuous.

10. **The correct answer is c.**
   Explanation: The verb "will have lived" and the key words (by the time), show an action that will happen (lived) before another time in the future (gets). This is one meaning of the future perfect.

Quiz 14: Active and Passive Voice

Directions: Read each question and choose the best answers. You will find the correct answers and explanations for each question on the page directly following the quiz.

1. Identify which sentence contains an example of the **passive voice**:
   a) The teacher decided to postpone the test.
   b) The test results will decide whether you progress.
   c) The result of the election had been decided beforehand.
   d) Everyone has decided what to order for dinner.

2. Identify which sentence contains an example of the **passive voice**:
   a) We learned a lot in class last week.
   b) This week, we have been learning a lot as well.
   c) We will learn even more next week.
   d) A lot has been learned in our class.

3. Identify which question contains an example of the **passive voice**:
   a) How have you been?
   b) What have you been doing?
   c) Have you been teaching English long?
   d) Have you been trained to teach English?

4. Identify which sentence contains an example of the **active voice**:
   a) My window was broken last week!
   b) All of my money was stolen!
   c) I was broke!
   d) Luckily, I was given a loan for my rent.

5. Read the sentence and choose which meaning is *most likely* represented with the underlined passive voice verb and the context of the sentence.
   The test scores <u>have been posted</u> in the hallway by our teacher.
   a) Unknown/unimportant agent
   b) Focus on receiver of action
   c) Avoidance of mentioning agent

6. Read the sentence and choose which meaning is *most likely* represented with the underlined passive voice verb and the context of the sentence.
   Stuff happens, and mistakes <u>are made</u>, but we will always be a team.
   a) Unknown/unimportant agent

b) Focus on receiver of action
c) Avoidance of mentioning agent

7. Read the sentence and choose which meaning is *most likely* represented with the underlined passive voice verb and the context of the sentence.
The back door was left open last night! Somebody needs to pay more attention.
a) Unknown/unimportant agent
b) Focus on receiver of action
c) Avoidance of mentioning agent

8. Read the question and choose which meaning is *most likely* represented with the underlined passive voice verb and the context of the question.
Has the new employee been properly trained on how to use this equipment?
a) Unknown/unimportant agent
b) Focus on receiver of action
c) Avoidance of mentioning agent

9. Imagine you want to present passive voice in context for a class of EFL students. Choose the real-world context below that will best show the use of the **passive voice**.
a) An account of the previous day's activities
b) A weather report for the coming weekend
c) A description of the manufacturing processes of a product

10. One of the following sentences contains a mistake commonly made by people first learning the passive voice. Identify which underlined verb or verb phrase is **incorrect**.
My friend was arrested last night! He was involved in a nasty fight. Luckily, he was released in the morning. He was arrived home at 8 a.m.
a) was arrested
b) was involved
c) was released
d) was arrived

Quiz 14: Active and Passive Voice Answers and Feedback

1. **The correct answer is c.**
   Explanation: In this sentence, the verb phrase "had been decided" follows the rule of form for the passive voice in the past perfect tense: **Had + Been + Past Participle**. It is possible that the agent/decider is unknown, which is one meaning of the passive voice.

2. **The correct answer is d.**
   Explanation: In this sentence, the verb phrase "has been learned" follows the rule of form for the passive voice in the present perfect tense: **Has + Been + Past Participle**. The sentence focuses not on the agent (or learners), but rather on what has been learned ("A lot") by making it the subject of the sentence.

3. **The correct answer is d.**
   Explanation: In this sentence, the verb phrase "have...been trained" follows the rule of form for the passive voice in the present perfect tense: **Have + Been + Past Participle**. The question focuses not on the agent (or trainer), but rather the person who has (or has not) been trained ("you") by making it the subject of the question.

4. **The correct answer is c.**
   Explanation: In sentence c, the verb "was" follows the rule of form for active voice in the past simple, and "broke" is a past participle used as an adjective. Sentences a, b, and d all follow the rule of form for the passive voice in the past simple tense: **Was/Were + Past Participle**. Sentences a and b are examples in which the agent/thief is unknown, which is one meaning of the passive voice. Sentence d focuses not on the agent (or giver of the loan), but rather on who the loan was given to ("I") by making it the subject of the sentence.

5. **The correct answer is b.**
   Explanation: It is most likely that the passive was used because the speaker wanted to focus on the test scores (the receiver of the action), not the person who posted the scores (our teacher).

6. **The correct answer is c.**
   Explanation: It is most likely that the speaker of this sentence did not want to attach an agent to the mistakes that the team members make, so they used passive voice.

7. **The correct answer is a.**

Explanation: It is most likely that the speaker of this sentence used passive because the agent (the person who left the door open) was unknown.

8. **The correct answer is b.**
   Explanation: While it is possible that the agent (the trainer) is unknown/unimportant, it is more likely that the passive was used because the speaker wanted to focus on the new employee, not the (possible) trainer.

9. **The correct answer is c.**
   Explanation: Passive voice is often used in describing processes because the focus is placed on the item, not the agents/processors (e.g., "The coffee I am drinking was grown in Colombia. First, the coffee plants were planted, watered, and given plenty of sun. Then, after the beans were harvested, they were roasted and...").

10. **The correct answer is d.**
    Explanation: The verb "arrive" is intransitive, and the passive voice cannot be used with intransitive verbs. It should be "arrived," not "was arrived."

Quiz 15: Modal Verbs

Directions: Read each question and choose the best answers. You will find the correct answers and explanations for each question on the page directly following the quiz.

1. Identify which sentence contains a **modal verb**:
   a) My test is in about an hour.
   b) I might be late for the test.
   c) I'm on the bus, but it is running late.
   d) I hope I don't miss the test!

2. Identify which sentence contains a **modal of certainty**:
   a) I am in my classroom.
   b) But, nobody else is here.
   c) I must be in the wrong room.
   d) I need to check the room list again.

3. Identify which sentence contains a **modal of necessity**:
   a) Would you pass the salt?
   b) I should add more flavor to my food.
   c) I have gotten some negative feedback about it lately.
   d) Hopefully, it will be better tonight.

4. To express an idea of 100% obligation with **modals of necessity**, which underlined modal would be used?
   a) I am supposed to pass the test.
   b) I should pass the test.
   c) I could pass the test.
   d) I must pass the test.

5. Which sentence contains the modal that expresses the most **certainty**?
   a) She could be the teacher.
   b) She must be the teacher.
   c) She may be the teacher.

6. True or False: Both of the underlined phrases have about the same degree of certainty.
She could have been there.
She couldn't have been there.
   a) True
   b) False

7. True or False: Both of the underlined phrases have about the same degree of certainty.
The party <u>might start</u> on time.
The party <u>may start</u> on time.

a) True
b) False

8. True or False: Both of the underlined phrases have about the same degree of necessity.
I <u>have to finish</u> my work before dinner.
I <u>must finish</u> my work before dinner.

a) True
b) False

9. True or False: Both of the underlined phrases have about the same degree of necessity or obligation.
You <u>don't have to work</u> tomorrow.
You <u>must not work</u> tomorrow.

a) True
b) False

10. One of the following sentences contains a mistake commonly made by people first learning to use modals in English. Identify which underlined phrase is **incorrect**.
I am leaving for my trip to Chile tomorrow. I <u>might to take</u> the bus to the airport, but I'm not sure. I <u>may take</u> a taxi instead. The taxi <u>could be</u> too expensive, though. Also, I <u>might not be considering</u> all of the possible ways for me to get to the airport.

a) might to take
b) may take
c) could be
d) might not be considering

Quiz 15: Modal Verbs
Answers and Feedback

1. **The correct answer is b.**
   Explanation: In this sentence, the phrase "might be late" contains the modal "might."

2. **The correct answer is c.**
   Explanation: In this sentence, the phrase "must be" contains the modal of certainty "must." Sentence D also contains a modal, but "need to" is a modal of necessity in this sentence.

3. **The correct answer is b.**
   Explanation: In this sentence, the phrase "should add" contains the modal of necessity "should." Sentence A also contains a modal, but the modal "Would" is used to make a polite request in this sentence.

4. **The correct answer is d.**
   Explanation: The modals "must" and "have got to" express the most obligation with modals of necessity. The modals in the other example sentences express less necessity decreasing in this order: "should," "be supposed to," and "could," with "could" being the modal that expresses the least amount of necessity.

5. **The correct answer is b.**
   Explanation: The modal "must" indicates the most certainty. The modals "could" and "may" express a lesser amount of certainty.

6. **The correct answer is b.**
   Explanation: The phrase in the first sentence "could have been" shows about 50% certainty about something in the past. When changed to the negative form "couldn't have been" in the second sentence, the degree of certainty is raised to about 90%.

7. **The correct answer is a.**
   Explanation: The phrases "might start" and "may start" have about the same degree of certainty, which is about 50%.

8. **The correct answer is a.**
   Explanation: The phrases "have to finish" and "must finish" have about the same degree of necessity, which is about 100%.

9. **The correct answer is b.**

Explanation: The modals "have to" and "must" have about the same meaning except when in negative forms. In these sentences, "don't have to work" shows no obligation to work the next day, and "must not work" shows a very strong obligation not to work the next day.

10. **The correct answer is a.**

Explanation: In this sentence, the modal should be followed by the base verb "take" and not the infinitive "to take." This is one mistake commonly made by nonnative speakers.

Quiz 16: Conditionals

Directions: Read each question and choose the best answers. You will find the correct answers and explanations for each question on the page directly following the quiz.

1. Read the following sentence and determine the sentence type.
If I had taken the subway to work, I wouldn't have been late.
   a) Zero Conditional
   b) First Conditional
   c) Second Conditional
   d) Third Conditional
   e) Mixed Conditional

2. Read the following sentence and determine the sentence type.
When you heat ice, it melts.
   a) Zero Conditional
   b) First Conditional
   c) Second Conditional
   d) Third Conditional
   e) Mixed Conditional

3. Read the following sentence and determine the sentence type.
I would be a poor teacher if I hadn't gotten the TEFL certificate.
   a) Zero Conditional
   b) First Conditional
   c) Second Conditional
   d) Third Conditional
   e) Mixed Conditional

4. Read the following sentence and determine the sentence type.
She would have finished her homework if she hadn't procrastinated.
   a) Zero Conditional
   b) First Conditional
   c) Second Conditional
   d) Third Conditional
   e) Mixed Conditional

5. Read the following sentence and determine the sentence type.
I would exercise regularly if I had more free time.
   a) Zero Conditional

b) First Conditional
c) Second Conditional
d) Third Conditional
e) Mixed Conditional

6. Read the following sentence and determine the sentence type.
If he graduates this May, he will start looking for a job.
a) Zero Conditional
b) First Conditional
c) Second Conditional
d) Third Conditional
e) Mixed Conditional

7. Read the following sentence and determine the sentence type.
If I spoke Spanish, I wouldn't have had so much trouble at the border.
a) Zero Conditional
b) First Conditional
c) Second Conditional
d) Third Conditional
e) Mixed Conditional

8. Read the following sentence and determine the sentence type.
The grass gets wet when it rains.
a) Zero Conditional
b) First Conditional
c) Second Conditional
d) Third Conditional
e) Mixed Conditional

Quiz 16: Conditionals
Answers and Feedback

1. **The correct answer is d.**
   Explanation: This is the third conditional because it talks about an unreal situation in the past and contains had plus a past participle (had taken) in the dependent clause and a modal plus have plus a past participle (wouldn't have been) in the independent clause.

2. **The correct answer is a.**
   Explanation: This is the zero conditional because it talks about a general truth and contains simple present verbs (*heat* and *melts*) in both clauses.

3. **The correct answer is e.**
   Explanation: This is a mixed conditional because it mixes present and past hypotheticals; it talks about an unreal situation in the present (*I would be a poor teacher* [now]) in the independent clause and an unreal situation in the past with *had* plus a past participle (*hadn't gotten the TEFL certificate* [in the past]) in the dependent clause.

4. **The correct answer is d.**
   Explanation: This is the third conditional because it talks about an unreal situation in the past and contains *had* plus a past participle (*hadn't procrastinated*) in the dependent clause and a modal plus *have* plus a past participle (*would have finished*) in the independent clause.

5. **The correct answer is c.**
   Explanation: This is the second conditional because it talks about an unreal possibility in the present or future and contains a simple past verb (had) in the dependent clause and a modal followed by a verb in its base form (would exercise) in the independent clause.

6. **The correct answer is b.**
   Explanation: This is the first conditional because it talks about a real possibility in the future and contains a simple present verb (graduates) in the dependent clause and a simple future verb (will start) in the independent clause.

7. **The correct answer is e.**
   Explanation: This is a mixed conditional because it mixes present and past hypotheticals; it talks about an unreal situation in the present and uses the past simple

(*spoke Spanish* [now/in general]) in the dependent clause and an unreal situation in the past with a modal plus *have* plus a past participle (*wouldn't have had* [in the past]) in the independent clause.

8. **The correct answer is a.**
   Explanation: This is the zero conditional because it talks about a general truth and contains simple present verbs (*gets* and *rains*) in both clauses.

INDEX

Made in the USA
Middletown, DE
18 November 2023

43037711R00161